Globalization and War

GLOBALIZATION

Series Editors
Manfred B. Steger
*Illinois State University, University of Hawai'i—Manoa,
and Royal Melbourne Institute of Technology*
and
Terrell Carver
University of Bristol

"Globalization" has become *the* buzzword of our time. But what does it mean? Rather than forcing a complicated social phenomenon into a single analytical framework, this series seeks to present globalization as a multidimensional process constituted by complex, often contradictory interactions of global, regional, and local aspects of social life. Since conventional disciplinary borders and lines of demarcation are losing their old rationales in a globalizing world, authors in this series apply an interdisciplinary framework to the study of globalization. In short, the main purpose and objective of this series is to support subject-specific inquiries into the dynamics and effects of contemporary globalization and its varying impacts across, between, and within societies.

Globalization and Culture
Jan Nederveen Pieterse

Rethinking Globalism
Edited by
Manfred B. Steger

Globalization and Terrorism
Jamal R. Nassar

Globalism, Second Edition
Manfred B. Steger

Globaloney
Michael Veseth

Globalization and War
Tarak Barkawi

Forthcoming in the Series

Globalization and American Empire
Kiichi Fujiwara

Globalization and Law
Adam Gearey

Globalization and Feminist Activism
Mary Hawkesworth

Globalization and International Political Economy
Mark Rupert and M. Scott Solomon

Globalization and Labor
Dimitris Stevis and Terry Boswell

 Supported by the Globalization Research Center at the University of Hawai'i, Manoa

GLOBALIZATION AND WAR

TARAK BARKAWI

ROWMAN & LITTLEFIELD PUBLISHERS, INC.
Lanham • Boulder • New York • Toronto • Oxford

ROWMAN & LITTLEFIELD PUBLISHERS, INC.

Published in the United States of America
by Rowman & Littlefield Publishers, Inc.
A wholly owned subsidiary of The Rowman & Littlefield Publishing Group, Inc.
4501 Forbes Boulevard, Suite 200, Lanham, Maryland 20706
www.rowmanlittlefield.com

P.O. Box 317, Oxford OX2 9RU, UK

British Library Cataloguing in Publication Information Available

Library of Congress Cataloging-in-Publication Data

Barkawi, Tarak.
    Globalization and war / Tarak Barkawi.
       p.   cm.— (Globalization)
    Includes bibliographical references and index.
    ISBN 0-7425-3700-5 (cloth : alk. paper)—
    ISBN 0-7425-3701-3 (pbk. : alk. paper)
       1. Globalization.   2. War.   3. International relations.   I. Title.
    II. Series: Globalization (Lanham, Md.) JZ1318.B364   2005
    303.6'6—dc22   2005001950

Printed in the United States of America

♾ ™ The paper used in this publication meets the minimum requirements of
American National Standard for Information Sciences—Permanence of Paper
for Printed Library Materials, ANSI/NISO Z39.48-1992.

for Paul

CONTENTS

Preface   ix

Acknowledgments   xvii

1   The False Dawn of "Globalization"   1

2   Behind "Globalization": Nation-States, Empires,
        and Democracies at War   27

3   Globalization and War: Britain, India, and
        the Indian Army   59

4   War and Culture in Global Context   91

5   "Terror" and the Politics of Global War   127

Afterword   167
Notes   173
References   181
Index   191
About the Author   199

PREFACE

In 1943, an Indian soldier serving in the veteran British Fourth Indian Division wrote home from Tunisia with news of his "exciting and adventurous life," exclaiming, "I think the recruitment slogan 'Join the Army and See the World' is quite right."[1] The Fourth Indian had fought in Egypt and across Libya and Tunisia. Later, it would battle its way up the Italian Peninsula. For the peasant sons of the Punjab, many of whom had never seen the sea or heard of Germany and Italy before the war, service in the Mediterranean theater was indeed exotic and exciting, as well as dangerous and unsettling. Aside from the perils of combat service shared with soldiers of all nationalities, the Indians were introduced to Western culture of the noncolonial variety, serving alongside British and Commonwealth troops in North Africa and later among Italian civilians. British intelligence officers, with an eye to maintaining British rule over India after the war, became worried that Indian soldiers were "absorbing ideas about democracy and freedom," perhaps from some of the British soldiers who would help vote in a Labour government at Winston Churchill's expense in the general election of July 1945.[2] In letters home, Indian soldiers argued India should be reconstructed along Western lines, with a strong emphasis on greater education for all. Some of the cleverer ones, exposed for the first time to different social and cultural arrangements, became aware of how the British had maintained and reinforced caste divisions as a way of exerting control through "divide and rule," both in the Indian army and in Indian colonial society more generally. They called for modifications in the caste system as part of a more general modernization of India.[3]

More will be said later of how an Indian colonial army came to fight for the British in a war ostensibly about freedom and democracy, but for now the vignette serves to make two introductory points about globalization and war. The first is that war involves many aspects that, in contemporary discussions, fall under the rubric of globalization. At root, globalization is about the circulation of people, goods, and ideas around the planet, all of which are evident in shipping out an Indian army to the West. In traveling abroad, soldiers reformulated their ideas about home and how it might be changed, reaching toward a critique of colonialism. Writing of today's world, with its well-integrated communications and globe-trotting elites, some scholars argue that the ties between culture and place are weakening, that identity is increasingly not reducible to a single homeland. For Indian soldiers fighting British wars, or African soldiers in French service (Echenberg 1991), such cultural hybridity and complexity were already commonplace. Skeptics of globalization often argue that all of this circulation is mainly limited to a minority of wealthy elites, businesspeople, and Western tourists. They forget that soldiers have been traveling the world for millennia. Alexander the Great marched his army to India and back in the fourth century BC; Napoleon took his to Moscow; and many American soldiers saw Europe and numerous other places before and after jet air travel and the modern tourist industry were born.

It would seem, then, that the military and war have much to teach us about globalization, and vice versa. But, and this is the second point, those who have written about globalization have had very little to say about war and the military. Indeed, "globalization"—the scare quotes refer to the various ways in which globalization has been understood or thought about in different times and places— "globalization" has had very curious relations with war. "Globalization" initially came to prominence in the wake of the Cold War. It was the peace built on worldwide free trade and democracy that followed the collapse of the Soviet bloc in 1989. War was seen as part of the bad old world of competing ideologies and nation-states. History, as Francis Fukuyama told us at the time, was coming to an end, humanity having finally discovered that liberal democracy and capitalism were the best ways of organizing its affairs (1992). Where it still existed, war was interpreted as stemming from even older atavisms of tribe and ethnicity, as in Africa and the Balkans. The prescribed cure was democratic elections and free trade, administered by well-meaning nongovernmental organizations (NGOs) and the International Monetary Fund (IMF). War was a sign of the past, but "globalization," set to the strains of "world music," of the now.

Toward the end of the 1990s, this neoliberal and pacific view of globalization was subject to trenchant critique along several lines. Nation-states were not passing out of history. The so-called global economy was mainly limited to Europe, North America, and parts of Asia (Hirst and Thompson 1999). More to the point, some scholars identified various ways in which economic globalization *caused* wars, distinctive kinds of wars in places like Africa (e.g., Reno 1998). These might involve tacit alliances between various international business interests and "warlords," who had gained control of certain particularly resource-rich pieces of territory, whether timber, diamonds, or some precious mineral. Others pointed out how the neoliberal response to the collapse of the communist states in eastern and southern Europe, which emphasized "shock therapy" and radical free market reforms in the absence of a social safety net, was an important cause of the rise of ethnic nationalism and the wars in the former Yugoslavia (Woodward 1995). A global arms trade and a global war economy sustained the fighting in Yugoslavia, Africa, and elsewhere (Kaldor 1999, chap. 5). Here was a very different construction of the relations between war and globalization than that initially imagined by the "first wave" theorists. Far from making the world safer, "globalization" entailed its own dangers. The Clinton administration framed its last national security strategy, released in December 2000, in terms of the security threats inherent in an interdependent "global age," highlighting the diffusion of technology, the problems caused by open borders, terrorism, organized crime, and proliferation of weapons.

With the strikes of September 11, 2001, and the wars that followed, this darker view of globalization as a threat, as a cause and context of war and other political violence, became dominant.

"Western globalization" stoked the fears of many Muslims that their societies were being transformed in profane ways. Meanwhile, in the West, other aspects of globalization seemed newly threatening. Islamic militants made use of their Western technical training and cultural knowledge to mount attacks. Governments sought to clamp down on the circulation of people, particularly if they were Arab or Muslim. A variety of "nonstate" threats were imagined by those tasked to defend and secure Western societies, ranging from cyber attacks to chemical, biological, and nuclear weapons. Previously, only states had had access to the resources necessary to cause mass destruction. But now the knowledge and materials necessary for such ventures were loose in the world, uncontrolled by any state, circulating in the form of illicit commodities, electronic data, mercenary weapons scientists, and well-traveled and culturally *au fait* militants who could "pass" in secular, Western society without drawing attention to themselves.

There is much to be said for the argument that neoliberal economic policies were an important source of political violence and war around the world after the Cold War. It is an important corrective to the "false dawn" of 1989 (Gray 2002). But the view that globalization causes war still does not get us to the heart of the matter or to the thesis of this book, for "war" remains in this construction something separate from "globalization." Globalization is about circulation, and through circulation peoples and places become interconnected with one another, such that, for example, the price of coffee on the Chicago commodity exchanges determines the fates of coffee growers in El Salvador or that Malaysian and French teenagers can hum the same Michael Jackson tune. Is war not precisely about the breakdown of such circulation and connection? War involves the drawing, and defending, of boundaries, not the crossing of them, except by force; it elevates one's own nation and state above others; and it leads not to cultural hybridity but to national chauvinism. War does involve these things and others, but it does so, this book argues, because war is itself a form of *interconnection*, and a historically pervasive and significant one at that. War in this sense is a *globalizing force*, and it has been for a long time.

To make this case will involve critiquing and reformulating our understandings of both globalization and war, which is the burden of the chapters to come. How India was in part transformed through its participation in the world wars, in ways more important than the opening vignette indicates, is one example of interconnections occasioned by war, interconnections that reshaped societies and politics. The wars that followed 9/11 offer other examples, as American, Afghani, and Iraqi politics became bound up with one another through invasion, occupation, and resistance. More generally, elements of the West and of Islam are now locked in an embrace that is transforming and radicalizing both sides through the medium of armed conflict. A renewed and virulent American nationalism feeds on a modernist Islamic fundamentalism, and vice versa in a violent spiral. In and through war, people on both sides come to intensified awareness of one another, reconstruct images of self and other, initiate and react to each other's moves. To be at war is to be interconnected with the enemy. Such connections involve social processes and transformations that should be understood under the rubric of globalization.

Chapter 1 begins with "globalization" as found in the wake of the Cold War, when it was conceived as the opposite of war. If war was about the state, globalization was about the end of it; if war was part of the past, the future was a pacific vision of a fully globalized world. The chapter argues that in fact states and state power were agents, not victims, of globalization and that globalization is a much older and more multifaceted phenomenon than we typically think. The chapter concludes with a discussion of some of the long-term and systematic connections between the spread of free trade and war. Such connections suggest that the hopes of many liberals and enthusiasts that global laissez-faire produces peace are misplaced.

Chapter 2 takes up war, the modern story of which is mostly told in terms of the wars of nation-states. Introducing a "war and society" approach, the chapter will touch on the many ways wars transform the societies involved—as, for example, in how total war leads to a mobilization of the home front. However, few areas of inquiry are as pervasively Eurocentric as military history, which is concerned almost entirely with wars between and among the great powers. A discussion of the military dimensions of empire and imperialism will illuminate some of the rich, if generally neglected, connections between war and the basic themes of globalization studies. The chapter closes with an argument that the "war and society" approach needs to be globalized to address the ways in which war shapes and transforms world politics more generally, as well as how war impacts on North-South relations.

Chapter 3 draws together the themes of the first two chapters to develop a perspective on globalization and war. It explores two levels of analysis. The first concerns the "bilateral" relations between countries at war, how war interconnects places and reshapes them. The second looks at the ways in which developments in particular locales, as well as wider transformations in the nature and utility of military force, shape transregional and worldwide contexts, contexts that in turn determine what is and is not possible in many different places. These levels of analysis are explored through an extended discussion of the relations between and among India, the British empire, and the Indian army. The history of the Indian independence struggle can be understood only through global contexts, while the relations between India and Britain shaped one another as well as the wider world in profound ways.

Chapter 4 explores the cultural dimensions of war and globalization. Nationalism is sometimes assumed to be the opposite of cultural globalization, which is about cosmopolitanism and hybridity. However, nations and nationalists require other nations against which to define themselves. That is, even imagining your part of the world as separate and different from other parts of the world is a form of interconnection with others. The chapter explores various geographic imaginaries that play a role in world politics, such as the distinction between a modern and advanced West and a backward and barbarian Orient, or that of a wealthy global North and an impoverished global South. It then identifies the roles that war and the military play in sustaining and transforming these visions of the world, looking particularly at the cultural consequences for Western powers of military defeat in the non-European world.

Chapter 5 applies the themes developed throughout the book to the developing War on Terror, focusing in particular on the politics of this global struggle. It considers the geopolitical and geocultural constructions of the conflict as a clash of civilizations and as a war for civilization against terrorism. It looks also at the interconnections between the Israeli-Palestinian conflict and the War on Terror as well as the growing affinity between American and Israeli visions of the Islamic enemy.

A brief afterword summarizes the main theme of the text: that in and through the interconnections it occasions, war is transformative of world politics and of the peoples and places it reaches out and touches.

ACKNOWLEDGMENTS

Scholarship is a collective enterprise, and it is always a pleasure to recognize this fact. This book has its origins in a conversation with Terrell Carver at a reception at Birkbeck College, University of London. Having just taken up a temporary lectureship there in "global politics," I noted the relative lack of attention to war in the globalization literature. Terrell offered me the opportunity to help rectify this situation. Whether I have done so is for readers to judge, but thanks are due to Terrell and his coeditor Manfred Steger for their support in making this volume possible.

More or less unknowingly, many colleagues and friends have contributed to this book. Its basic approach grows out of my intellectual collaboration and friendship with Mark Laffey, which began in graduate school at the University of Minnesota and continues today in the United Kingdom. Mark read and commented on the text several times at various stages. His suggestions were invaluable, and his criticisms saved me from more than one embarrassment. Many of the ideas developed here were influenced by conversations over delicious pints of London Pride in the Queen's Larder with Shane Brighton, John Game, and Julian Reid. Also, for suggestions and assistance with various aspects of the text, thanks are due to Geoffrey Aronson, Susan Carruthers, Tina Chen, Stefan Elbe, Rosemary Hollis, Christopher Swift and Naveed Sheikh. Mention must be made of my colleagues at the Centre for International Studies, University of Cambridge, who provide a congenial and supportive environment for research. For their patience and help in preparing the manuscript thanks also to Pelham Boyer, Jennifer Knerr, Renee Legatt, and Alden Perkins at Rowman & Littlefield. I am responsible for the faults and errors of judgment that remain in the text.

Parts of the text draw on my previously published work. Chapters 1 and 2 are elaborations of arguments first made in "Connection and Constitution: Locating War and Culture in Globalization Studies," *Globalizations* 1, no. 2 (December 2004). The discussion of the "Democratic Peace" and war in imperial context in chapter 2 is derived in part from my coedited and coauthored work with Mark Laffey, in particular our edited volume *Democracy, Liberalism and War: Rethinking the Democratic Peace Debates* (2001) and our article "The Imperial Peace: Democracy, Force and Globalization," *European Journal of International Relations* 5, no. 4 (December 1999). The discussion of Janice Thomson's work in chapter 2 appeared in "Democratic States and Societies at War: The Global Context," a review essay of Margaret Levi's *Consent, Dissent and Patriotism* in *Comparative Social Research*, vol. 20 (2002). Parts of chapter 4 were developed from "Globalization, Culture and War: On the Popular Mediation of 'Small Wars,'" *Cultural Critique*, no. 58 (Fall 2004). Finally, some of the ideas in chapter 5 were first formulated in "On the Pedagogy of 'Small Wars,'" *International Affairs* 80, no. 1 (January 2004).

This book is dedicated to Professor Paul Hirst, who died suddenly in June 2003. I owe many debts of gratitude to Paul, as mentor, colleague, friend, and especially for his invaluable support during a very difficult time in my career. Paul was a model of the politically engaged scholar and teacher, but he always insisted on beginning with the world as we find it rather than as we wish it to be. I will struggle to emulate his example all my days.

THE FALSE DAWN OF "GLOBALIZATION"

Ideas have histories, and they also participate in making history. In thinking about an idea like globalization, which rocketed to prominence in the wake of the Cold War, it is important to begin with how people have understood it. What content has been given to "globalization" by different groups in different social locations? What political work has this idea done? What realities has it obscured or elided? Through critical analysis of "globalization" as an ideology that was very influential in the 1990s, we can begin to work out a more rigorous account of what we mean by globalization as a category of historical and social processes. Only then will we be prepared to consider the relations between globalization and war—past, present, and future.

In the period between 1989 and the strikes of September 11, 2001, "globalization" was largely understood to refer to a set of ostensibly inevitable processes occurring in the world economy. The basic claim was that the intensification of international trade and investment had reached a point at which national economies were

1

dissolving into a "global economy determined by world market forces" (Hirst and Thompson 1999, xii). Consequently, the only viable public policy, it was argued, was one that continued to deregulate trade, investment, and capital movements while dismantling the social welfare state. This conception of "globalization" was hugely influential, especially in the United States and the United Kingdom, as well as in international economic institutions such as the IMF, the World Bank, and the World Trade Organization (WTO), where it was referred to as the "Washington Consensus."

"Globalization" developed out of an economic doctrine known as "neoliberalism." "Globalization" was in many ways simply neoliberalism globalized, an ideology Manfred Steger terms "globalism" (2002). The basic neoliberal idea is that state regulation and interference in the economy should be reduced to a minimum so that an unrestricted free market can stimulate economic growth and efficiently allocate resources. Globalizing this idea entails two things. First, all national economies should be organized along the same free market lines. Second, all barriers to international trade and capital movements should be progressively removed. The outcome of such policies would be a single global economy in which market forces were unimpeded and nation-states ceased to be significant centers of power.

Underlying neoliberal thinking were some basic assumptions about society, politics, and economy. Humans are essentially instrumentally rational agents who will act in line with their economic self-interest. The market is a "natural" mechanism for regulating the competition of economically rational agents for resources and profits and the most efficient way of generating wealth. Any interference in the market, whatever its other effects, will reduce the overall size of the economic pie. The goal of politics, therefore, should be simply to "allow" the market to operate freely—hence the phrase *laissez-faire*, to leave alone, used to describe such policies. The result of a free market approach, according to this strand of economic theory, will be steady economic growth, which will address poverty and inequality far more effectively than a welfare state can.

Globalizing this ideology involved a further assumption as well, that the free market was a *universal* solution to the problem of the right ordering of politics, society, and economy (e.g., Fukuyama

1992; Mandelbaum 2002). Despite the fact that free market thinking was rooted in Anglo-American historical experience (and was never fully applied in either the United States or the United Kingdom), the globalists argued that this was a "one size fits all" solution for the entire planet. Many in the global South were quick to point out that the United States had industrialized behind a towering wall of protectionist tariffs and only adopted free trade policies, to the degree it did, when its economic dominance—and hence success in the free market—was assured. Britain's initial rise to industrial power had involved a similar reliance on protected markets. But critics in the global South or elsewhere did not have the power to put their ideas into practice. The globalists did. They occupied commanding positions of power in government, the media, the academy, and among opinion leaders in the United States, the United Kingdom, and to a lesser extent in other Western countries. Throughout the 1990s, neoliberal policies were imposed with great energy on the debt-laden economies of Africa and Latin America. In East Asia, with some significant exceptions, more powerful states were able to protect their successful state-led development policies. In the former communist countries in eastern and southeastern Europe, an accelerated form of neoliberalism known as "shock therapy" was applied (see e.g., Hoogvelt 2001, chaps. 8 and 11).

An immediate paradox presents itself. Neoliberals and globalists argue in strenuous terms that the state should "get out" of the economy. State intervention in the economy is "artificial" and "distorting," while the free market is in accord with basic principles of human nature. Yet constructing a free market in one country, much less globally, is a *political* project of the first order (John Gray 2002, 23). It requires tearing down a whole set of intermediary institutions that typically have stood between individuals and the unrestrained operations of the market. These include the entire range of welfare protections, wage and price controls, trade unions, environmental regulations, local governments, community organizations, and so on. In order to bring down such institutions, many of which have long histories and deep roots, such as trade unions in the United Kingdom, neoliberals had to rely on, and increase the power of, the central state. Yet further reliance on the central state, and in particular its powers of coercion, would be necessary to deal with the social and economic disruption caused by neoliberal policies. Margaret Thatcher, the great proponent of the minimalist "night watchman" state, had to rely on and expand her police forces in order to crush the trades union movement and confront the mass resistance to the "poll tax," a flat-rate local services tax her government attempted to introduce. She also appropriated to the central government powers that had long been in the hands of democratically elected local authorities.

Globally, this paradox took a similar form. The neoliberals argued that "globalization" was inevitable, that it could not be resisted, and that states should deregulate their economies, reduce welfare provision, and apply other aspects of neoliberal doctrine, such as allowing unrestricted capital movements, in order to grow their economies. Any other course of action was counterproductive, it was claimed. Yet here too the project of globalism required frequent and extensive resort to state power—a "neo-liberal statecraft," as John Gray puts it (2002, 43). Old policies and programs had to be brought to an end and new policies put in place, the entire economy, and with it society, restructured. The financial and legal apparatus for foreign direct investment and other capital movements had to be erected and governed. As in Thatcher's Britain, the social dislocation caused by neoliberal policies often led to an increased role for the police and prisons. In general, central state power was used to overcome the resistance of local, often democratic, associations to the introduction of neoliberal policies.

A crucial aspect of the role of state power in global neoliberalism is that it was often *international* in nature. Not only did the major international financial institutions play important roles, but so too did the United States, with its legions of advisors and officially sponsored NGOs dedicated to helping economies "transition" to the free market (see e.g., Robinson 1996, chap 2). Yet another role for the United States and the IMF was the periodic need for massive bailouts when neoliberal policies went wrong. When the Mexican peso was devalued in December 1994 after years of neoliberal policies, the United States and IMF organized a bailout to the tune of $58 billion. This effectively transferred the market risks institutional U.S. investors had taken in Mexico to U.S. and Mexican taxpayers, while for the mass of Mexicans only further austerity was on offer.

4

Evidently, a great deal of state power is necessary to build a globalist world.

To investigate the role of the state in neoliberal globalization further, we will look in more detail at one of the central claims of the globalists in the 1990s—that the era of the nation-state was coming to an end. Focusing on the state is important for our purposes, because the state is the primary war-making institution. Then we will turn to another core aspect of how "globalization" is popularly understood—that it is new, a historically recent process driven in large measure by developments in communications technologies. This is crucial, because this book will take a much longer-term view of what globalization is about in world politics, a view that in some respects stretches back to the ancient world. We will then be in a position to consider critically what the globalists, and "globalization," have to say about matters of war and peace.

The End of the Nation-State?

In a time in which the state has taken renewed importance in our lives, it is difficult to imagine that little over a decade ago it was widely argued that the era of the nation-state was coming to an end. The purported grave digger of the state consisted of developments in the world economy, coupled with new communications technologies. Released from the "artificial" geopolitical borders of the Cold War, the newly "interlinked economy" was subsuming the old national economies. One of the most consistent proponents of this point of view was the international business guru Kenichi Ohmae, who developed his arguments in two widely read books published in several editions—*The Borderless World* and *The End of the Nation State*. "The modern nation-state itself," he argued in 1995, "has begun to crumble" (Ohmae 1995, 7).

The interlinked economy was based around the triad of the United States, Western Europe, and Japan, supplemented by Taiwan, Hong Kong, and Singapore. This new global economy was "becoming so powerful that it has swallowed most consumers and corporations, made traditional national borders almost disappear, and pushed bureaucrats, politicians, and the military toward the status of declining industries" (Ohmae 1994, xi). Ohmae's basic premise was that both production and consumption had "gone global." Corporations were now able to organize production largely without regard to national boundaries, locating facilities wherever business conditions were best. Similarly, consumers, drawing on new global sources of information, purchased the best-value products without regard for national sentiments. For Ohmae, the globalization of production and consumption was leading to a new global consumer culture in which tastes and lifestyles were chosen without regard to the old local ways of doing things. In a passage rather revealing of the social circles in which Ohmae himself moved, he asked, "Do you write with a Waterman or a Mt. Blanc pen or travel with a Vuitton suitcase out of nationalist sentiments? Probably not. You buy these things because they represent the kind of value that you're looking for" (Ohmae 1994, 3).

For Ohmae and others, often called "hyperglobalizers," these developments meant that the world was becoming "borderless" and was in the process of liberating itself from the "awkward and uncomfortable truth" that the "cartographic illusion" of a world divided into nation-states "no longer works" (Ohmae 1995, 20; on "hyperglobalism," see Held et al. 1999, 3–5). It would seem, however, that the world is not becoming borderless in the way Ohmae predicted. One of the consequences of 9/11 is a reinvigoration of state efforts to control movements of people and goods across borders. For example, the United States is implementing a new biometric policy for foreign travelers. This will require that passports and visas store body-identifying data. When visitors arrive in the United States, they will put their hands on scanners and stand in front of facial-recognition cameras in order to see if the sensor data matches that stored on the computer chip in their passport or visa.[1] Massive efforts are under way around the world to regulate containerized cargo on ships, a campaign initiated by U.S. legislation that any containers arriving in the United States be screened in the port of origin and complete manifests be sent to U.S. Customs officials. The fear is that cargo containers will be used for terrorist attack. Even free trade is subject to setbacks. In March 2002, President G. W. Bush imposed on steel imports to the United States new tariffs ranging from 3 to 8 percent, in order to protect domestic steel producers, withdrawing them only after losing a case before the WTO and being threatened with EU retaliation. Meanwhile, massive U.S. and European farm subsidies continue to devastate agricultural economies in Africa and elsewhere. Countries like Mali have been forced to liberalize their economies, but their agricultural exports are unable to compete with their heavily subsidized Western counterparts. European dairy farmers, in fact, dump their subsidized powdered milk on Mali, driving Malian farmers out of their own domestic markets.[2] The World Trade Organization ministerial conference at Cancun, Mexico, in September 2003 collapsed in part because of these issues, although more recently there has been some progress.

States, borders, and political intervention in the economy seem alive and well in today's world. But was Ohmae entirely misguided in forecasting the end of the nation-state? Across Europe, states are sacrificing important dimensions of their sovereignty to the European Union. In Africa and elsewhere, many speak of "collapsing" and "failed" states. There is an increase in the authority and reach of international entities, such as the WTO and United Nations (UN), which can exercise, especially in the global South, powers we associate with states. Moreover, in what is known as "extra-territorial legislation," the United States often issues regulations and passes laws that require *other* states and their corporations to enforce particular policies. For example, the Helms-Burton Act and the Iran and Libya Sanctions Act penalized any companies, whether or not they were U.S.-owned, that did business with Cuba, Iran, or Libya. Security concerns about container cargo in the United States are forcing ports around the world to conform to U.S. practice. Something does seem to be happening to the state, if not its demise. To understand where Ohmae went wrong and to recover the kernel of truth in his approach, we must return briefly to a critique of the neoliberalism that informed his worldview.

Markets, as places where goods and services are exchanged, have always been around in one form or another. They are typically shaped by a whole variety of cultural, social, and political factors that regulate their functioning in different times and places. In precapitalist Europe, for example, religious beliefs, clan loyalties, and feudal norms influenced economic exchange. In England, peasants and commoners had rights and access to large common lands ostensibly owned by feudal lords. Peasant communities also had a variety of mechanisms, not least the extended family, for caring for those who could not earn a living. Craftsmen's guilds retained authority over the production and sale of their products. In order to transform this medieval and early-modern context into a capitalist free market, in order to "disembed" the market from its social constraints, central state power was required (Polanyi 1944). The free market as we know it is not "natural" but *made* through political action.

The classic example is the series of Enclosure Acts through which the English Parliament turned common lands—overlaid by a variety of rights of access and use—into the sole, exclusive, private property of landlords. Through an act of state that awards a title to the land, "property" in land was created where it had not existed before in the same way. A market in land, the "naked" buying and selling of it, became possible, replacing the feudal clutter of hereditary claims, rights to access, and so on. The Enclosure Acts had the additional consequence of clearing the peasants off the land, concentrating many of them in urban locations, where their labor was now subject to the market; they had to sell it to earn a living. Deprived of the traditional means of sustaining their existence, these landless peasants formed the nascent industrial working class.

Like all ideology, neoliberalism is bad history. It fails to understand the social, political, and historical origins of the free market it celebrates. Even something as basic to the free market and capitalism as property does not exist in nature but is fundamentally dependent upon a legal and political order that constitutes certain goods—land, commodities, labor—as private property that can be bought and sold. That order is, of course, provided by the state, especially its ability to legislate and enforce its laws, in the last instance through police and other forms of coercive power. The state is an essential source of the power of capitalism and capitalists, because through its laws it guarantees the "control of the major means of production, distribution, communication, and exchange by private, inherently undemocratic banks and corporations" (Panitch 1996, 108). The public power of the state is necessary if the free market is to function. Contemporary calls for the state "to get out of the economy" are in fact calls for it to limit its role in the economy to that of providing the essential legal and political framework for the capitalist market. Similarly, as in England in the early-modern period, arguments that Third World countries should adopt free market policies are in fact calls for them to use state power to transform society and economy in particular kinds of directions.

We now have some tools with which to return to the question of the end of the nation-state. Creating a free market in a territory ruled by one state does not address the problem of how to enable and regulate trade with and investment in other countries. For modern economies to trade with and invest in one another, the legal and political framework that allowed the free market to function in one country had to be to a degree *internationalized*. Currencies had to be exchangeable, rights to property respected in different countries, agreed transparent mechanisms put in place for the shipment of goods and the levying of customs duties, and so forth. There are essentially two general ways in which this framework can be internationalized, both of which are evident in the contemporary international economy. The first is for different states to adopt identical or compatible laws. So for example, to attract foreign capital investment the formerly communist countries of Eastern Europe had to adopt legal codes that enabled foreigners to own property, manage economic enterprises, and repatriate profits. The second way is to create an international regulatory apparatus, to fashion entities that fulfilled statelike functions at the international level. The most obvious examples are the regulatory and enforcement functions of the EU, the WTO and the North American Free Trade Agreement (NAFTA) tribunals, all of which *override* local state authority in certain areas. Less visible are the welter of international agencies that regulate everything from fishing to air travel, such as the Universal Postal Union and the International Maritime Organization.

Quite clearly, from 1945 there has been a vast and sustained expansion in this second form of regulating the international economy. In the economic sphere, there has been a partial *internationalization of the public power,* such that we can speak of a nascent "international state" (e.g., Shaw 2000). We will return to the idea of an international state later, but for now it can be seen that Ohmae was both wrong and right in his exaggerated claim about the end of the nation-state. He is fundamentally wrong in implying that a global capitalist economy could function without, much less subsume, state authority. All manner of state regulation is necessary for markets to function and for individuals and companies to own and sell property, invest, and produce goods. The kernel of truth in his claim, however, is that much of this regulation increasingly takes place at an international level or is driven by powerful states, most particularly the United States, which have international reach. Nation-states are not becoming extinct, but many of them have seen their power and authority reduced substantially in a variety of spheres. This power and authority has not "evaporated," however, but has been transferred to other, often international, entities. Certainly some states can be seen as relatively powerless in the face of "markets" (Strange 1996), but the point here is that those markets are not functioning in the absence of *any* state regulation, even if a particular local state is subject to, say, capital flight if it tries to overly regulate or tax foreign investment.

This critique of hyperglobalist claims about the end of the nation-state, such as Ohmae's, enables us to correct a widespread and pervasive misunderstanding about contemporary economic globalization. Globalization is almost always seen as operating *against* the state; the more globalization there is, the less control states have of flows across their borders, in a zero-sum tradeoff. This idea is one of the chief sources of the notion that nothing can be done about globalization, that states simply have to adapt to the realities of a free market–driven global economy. But as should be evident from the discussion above, states are not victims of economic globalization so much as they are *agents* of it. Contemporary economic globalization is in part the result of the uses of state power to pursue the political project of a global free market. "Capitalist globalization . . . takes place in, through, and under the aegis of states; it is encoded by them and in important respects even authored by them; and it involves a shift in power relations within states that often means the centralization and concentration of state powers as the necessary condition of and accompaniment to global market discipline" (Panitch 1996, 86).

To take a small but revealing example, in the 1990s the provincial government of Ontario, Canada, run by the New Democratic Party, wanted to replace private auto insurance with a government-run, provincewide scheme that reduced auto insurance costs for all citizens by 25 percent. Under NAFTA provisions, U.S. auto insurance companies challenged the Ontario scheme as a nontariff barrier to trade that prevented them from doing business in Canada's most populous province. The central government of Canada agreed that the widely popular scheme would be counter to its treaty commitments under NAFTA and informed the Ontario provincial government that if it put the auto insurance scheme in place—a major plank of the platform on which the NDP had been elected—it would have to reimburse U.S. auto insurance companies for millions of dollars in lost business. Ontario backed down, its citizens' democratic will was thwarted, and exorbitant auto insurance rates were left in place. As can be seen, the question at issue here is not "state" versus "free market" but of *how* state power to regulate economic activity was to be utilized. A local, democratically elected provincial government was overridden by a combination of the central Canadian state and an international regulatory apparatus. As Leo Panitch puts it, NAFTA's various provisions "have the effect of redesigning the Mexican and Canadian states' relation to capital to fit the mold made in the United States" (Panitch 1996, 97).

The reasons for recovering the place of the state and the role of politics in economic globalization will become clearer below. Briefly, by seeing economic globalization as a political project it becomes possible to better conceptualize the nature of *resistance* to globalization, as stemming from alternative political projects, and of the role of force in both enforcing globalization and fighting it. War and the use of force can then be located within and against processes of economic globalization. But for now, we must turn to another popular understanding of what "globalization" is all about, the idea that it is a relatively recent historical process enabled in large measure by developments in communications technologies, such as satellite TV and the Internet.

Technology, History, and Globalization

For government and business elites, and those sectors of the academy and media most closely related to them, "globalization" in the 1990s meant the spread of free markets and the rise of a global economy. But there was another, more general meaning of "globalization" at work in the academy and in popular understandings of the term. This was the idea that localities were increasingly affected by events in faraway places, that the local and the global had become linked in large measure through the intensive development of communications technologies in the latter half of the twentieth century. Here, globalization is a kind of interconnection across borders, "a *stretching* of social, political and economic activities across frontiers such that events, decisions and activities in one region of the world can come to have significance for individuals and communities in distant regions of the globe" (Held et al. 1999, 15).

This more general meaning of "globalization" suggested that globalization might consist of something more than simply the spread of free markets, that other processes were involved. For example, in *No Logo,* Naomi Klein offered an analysis of the culture and economics of "branding," the corporate use of such distinctive brand names and symbols as Nike's swoosh or McDonald's golden arches (2000). In many ways, Klein's analysis, while critical, accepted that something like neoliberal globalization was occurring. Shoe and clothing companies took advantage of the increased freedom for capital, locating more manufacturing in low-wage Third World countries, often in special "export processing zones" (EPZs) that offered tax breaks and other incentives, such as prohibitions on union organizing. Similarly, the whole idea of a global brand depends on Ohmae's view that consumption patterns were increasingly homogenized, such that young people in many different countries wanted to wear Nike trainers and valued the swoosh as a mark of being cool and hip.

Klein was, however, attentive to other, less felicitous processes set in train by the global economics of branding. Activists in Europe and America made consumers aware that their stylish clothing directly linked them with the hard fates of EPZ workers. For example, a living wage in China in the late 1990s was approximately U.S.$0.87 an hour, but a "1998 study of brand-name manufacturing in the Chinese special economic zones found that Wal-Mart, Ralph Lauren, Ann Taylor, Esprit, Liz Claiborne, Kmart, Nike, Adidas, J. C. Penny [*sic*] and the Limited were only paying a fraction of that miserable 87 cents—some were paying as little as 13 cents an hour" (Klein 2000, 212). The high price of a branded product like Nike shoes went to cover the huge costs of marketing a brand, as well as for corporate profits. Those making Nike shoes in the Third World were not only paid little but worked in conditions long outlawed in Western Europe and North America: "The workday is long. . . . The management is military-style, the supervisors often abusive, the wages below subsistence and the work low-skill and tedious" (Klein 2000, 205). Organizing under slogans like "Justice. Do it, Nike," activists in different locations sought to link the Nike brand to sweatshop labor. On October 18, 1997, activists in eighty-five cities in thirteen countries participated in the International Nike Day of Action. Often in creative ways, activists sought to discomfit shoppers at Foot Locker and Nike Town stores with the realities of where their shoes came from (Klein 2000, 366–67).

Klein and others draw our attention to global processes and global-local linkages that differ from, and are a backlash against, the neoliberal narrative of the global economy. Klein develops a critique of neoliberalism, arguing that EPZs will not lead to the more general development of economies in the global South. But of more immediate interest are the ways in which activists, consumers, corporations, and sweatshop labor in widely divergent locations become connected with one another. Nike's global brand generates a global resistance campaign. That resistance campaign, part of a broader anti-globalization movement, is itself dependent on the new linkages made possible by cheap air travel and the possibilities for organizing offered by the Internet. The anti-WTO demonstrations in Seattle in December 1999, as well as in other cities, provided an example of how activists and protestors could respond to global free trade with global protest (Steger 2002, chap. 5). The "global" was a frame of reference for thought and action in a new kind of way (Robertson 1992). One does not have to exaggerate the importance of such protests to see that they represent a kind of globalization not accounted for in the dominant, neoliberal narrative.

However, an important issue needs to be raised. There is a widespread assumption that these forms of global interconnection are of relatively recent origin. The reason is that they are said to be dependent upon the ways in which modern technology has compressed time and space, making it possible to transmit data and images instantaneously around the globe and for people to travel at the speed of jet aircraft. It is, on this account, the relatively recent intensification of the circulation of people, goods, and ideas made possible by time-space compression that has produced "globalization." This view entails the assumption that globalization is something that happened to a world previously composed of relatively discrete, separate places that were not connected in the ways that new communications technologies made possible.

There is a great deal at stake here. Much writing, both academic and in the media, takes a "presentist" stance toward globalization. Claims are made to the effect that the world has been recently interconnected in wholly new ways, such as the "near real time" transmission of financial data that links events in the world's stock exchanges together. However, it was in the second half of the *nineteenth*, not the twentieth, century that the world's markets were first linked by "near real time" communications, with the laying of submarine intercontinental telegraph cables:

> The idea that the contemporary era of communications technology is unprecedented again needs to be challenged. The coming of the electronic telegraph system after 1870 in effect established more or less instantaneous information communications between all the major international financial and business centres. . . . Compared to reliance on the sailing ship (and even steam propulsion), the telegraph marked a real qualitative leap in communications technology, in many ways more important than the shift into computer technology and telematics after 1970 (Hirst and Thompson 1999, 37–38).

This is a useful corrective to the presentism of much writing on globalization. Many aspects of the modern world are not as new as they seem to us. While the Internet makes possible a far denser network, with many more nodes, the telegraph linked distant places together and was widely used to transmit news as well as facilitate business, government, and military communications. It was even possible in the late nineteenth and early twentieth centuries to organize an international human rights campaign against the Belgian king Leopold's depredations in the Congo, in particular the use of slave labor in extracting commodities for export to Europe, a campaign that made extensive use of news media in over a dozen countries (Hochschild 2002).

Expanding our historical horizon, however, does not resolve the conceptual issues at stake. Is globalization dependent upon the ways in which modern communications technologies have compressed time and space? Or are the dynamics of "interconnection" between localities in principle separable from modern communications? Usually, these two questions get mixed up together. For example, John Tomlinson writes: "Globalization [is] an empirical condition of the modern world: what I shall call *complex connectivity*. By this I mean that globalization refers to the rapidly developing and ever-densening network of interconnections and interdependencies that characterize modern social life" (1999, 1–2). Interconnection is articulated, via "developing" and "ever-densening," to modern communications technologies.

There is an additional and equally important matter at stake as well. To say that two places are connected to one another, even complexly, is to assume that places—and the societies, cultures, economies, and governments located there—were in significant measure *separate* from one another, independent, discrete, *until* joined in some way by "globalization." The implicit image of world history here is of countries developing independently of one another until the era of "complex connectivity" begins.

This image is manifestly false, and the tale of sugar in the early modern world suggests why (Drayton 2002; Mintz 1985). The human palate has a bias for sweetness, an evolutionary development designed to direct us toward fruits and vegetables. Sugar cane was originally found in New Guinea and was then cultivated extensively in India and the Arab world, where it and the complicated process of extracting sucrose were discovered by the Crusaders. Growing cane and producing sugar was both labor intensive and highly profitable. For these reasons, the Portuguese and Spanish transplanted sugar to the New World, where vast sugar plantations worked by slaves shipped from Africa were developed. The profits were immense and contributed crucially to the growth of the great financial centers of Europe, which were tied in to trade in wheat from Eastern Europe and luxury goods and spices from the Orient. "Polish serfs worked seven days a week, and slaves in Martinique and Jamaica six, in order that Swedes and Prussians might drink sugared coffee in Chinese porcelain, and gentlemen in Hamburg, Bordeaux and London might add credits to their ledgers" (Drayton

2002, 102–103). This "slave-powered globalization" declined from the early years of the nineteenth century, but not before drawing together Europe, Africa, and the Far East in a complex chain of interconnections: "What we now call Europe, Africa, the Americas and Asia were constructed together in the midst of a relationship, at once economic and cultural, military and political" (Drayton 2002, 103, 110). Links between the local and the global, which seem to us so much a feature of the contemporary world, are in fact common features of world history. Our world is in many ways the result of such links and their histories.

What the tale of sugar suggests is that it has more or less *always* been wrong to think about places as having separate histories. To help think about this further, consider the Haitian Revolution, which began as a slave revolt in 1791 and ended with the establishment of the independent state of Haiti in 1803 on half of the island of San Domingo. San Domingo was a French colony, the largest single slave market in the Atlantic slave trade and responsible for two-thirds of France's overseas trade. The slaves were inspired by the French Revolution in 1789; C. L. R. James entitled his classic study of the Haitian Revolution *The Black Jacobins* (1994 [1938]), a title that emphasized the crossover between events in France and Haiti. Paris first heard of the uprising in San Domingo from the British ambassador, who got the information from Jamaica via a London newspaper. From then on, the "colonial question"—whether the Rights of Man applied to blacks—became a major issue in the shifting struggles of the French revolutionaries. The more radical revolutionaries were in favor of the abolition of slavery and the granting of citizenship to the colonized. As one agent of the French colonists in San Domingo wrote worriedly from revolutionary Paris, "One spirit alone reigns here, it is horror of slavery and enthusiasm for liberty. It is a frenzy that wins all heads and grows every day" (quoted in James 1994 [1938], 120). News of the uprising in San Domingo would later inspire the masses in Paris, encouraging them to press for more radical measures.

Meanwhile, Toussaint L'Ouverture, the leader of the Haitian revolt, rallied slaves to his cause with the words of the French revolutionaries: "I want Liberty and Equality to reign in San Domingo. I work to bring them into existence. Unite yourselves to us, brothers, and fight with us for the same cause" (quoted in James 1994 [1938], 125). Events in the two revolutions had become caught up with one another in complex ways, and they involved as well Spain and Britain, which also had possessions in the Caribbean. "The slaves in San Domingo by their insurrection had shown revolutionary France that they could fight and die for freedom; and the logical development of the revolution in France had brought to the front of the stage masses who, when they said abolition, meant it in theory and in practice" (James 1994 [1938], 120). Later, of course, such "logical developments" would usher in Napoleon Bonaparte, who reversed course and sent an expedition to suppress the Haitian revolt, but this expedition was defeated in 1803.

Two important points can be made through this example. The first is that the interconnections between the French and Haitian revolutions did not require satellite TV, the Internet, or even the telegraph, but only the sailing ship, albeit in the well-developed form of late eighteenth-century European transoceanic maritime power. The fact that the news received via Jamaica was several weeks out of date by the time it arrived did not lessen its impact. Interconnections of this kind are not dependent upon electronic communications, although of course electronic communications intensify and shape such interconnections in our own day in fundamental ways. This observation allows a more fine-grained sense of just what is and is not new about contemporary globalization. The second point is in many ways the more important one: It is not possible to understand "France" and "Haiti" as two separate, discrete places, each with its own independent history of development. "Events in both locations affected each other, shaped what happened and defined what was possible" (Hall 2002, 9). The interconnections between Haiti and France transformed each location and worked to *constitute* each as a particular kind of entity. They did so, it is important to point out, amidst a massive imbalance in power between France and Haiti.

At the most general level, then, globalization is about processes of *interconnection* and *mutual constitution* ("making together") in world politics. When we put it this way, we are able to compare historical globalizing processes with contemporary ones and appreciate the broad similarities as well as important differences. It also enables

17

us to see that neoliberal understandings of "globalization" are an instance of a larger category of historical processes.

There is an important caveat to this way of conceiving globalization: It is not global in a literal sense. This does not necessarily make it different from other understandings of "globalization." Ohmae's "global" economy was based primarily on North America, Western Europe, and Japan, for example. Nonetheless, he was drawing attention to a series of economic linkages between places that, he argued, cannot be understood using, say, a conventional model of the international economy based on separate, discrete national economies. Similarly, showing how French and Haitian history became intertwined draws attention to the ways in which separate "national" histories—as most history is written—are not adequate to understanding how "Haiti" and "France" were in part produced through processes of mutual constitution.[3] Globalization, it is being argued here, is the general category for investigating interconnections of this kind.

The price of using the term in this way is that it risks leaving empty the category of "global" itself. There is a difference between interconnectedness that is transregional in scope and that which is genuinely global in some sense. In particular, it is arguable that a genuinely global image of the world came about as a result of European exploration, imperial expansion, and associated cartography between the fifteenth and eighteenth centuries. It became possible to imagine the world as a single place in new ways, even if there was not a single world culture. As Roland Robertson argues, the "global" increasingly became the reference point for human thought and action in new ways (1992). We will return to this argument later, and in chapter 4 we will look at its interrelations with war.

War and Free Trade

In this final section of the chapter, the two previous sections are drawn together in a discussion of the relationship between free trade and war in historical context. Neoliberal conceptions of "globalization" in the 1990s, such as Ohmae's, focused almost exclusively on the utilitarian calculus of increased wealth promised by the spread of free markets and free trade. Liberal thought, however, often emphasized that in addition to wealth, free markets and free trade promoted democracy and peace. The period after the Cold War saw the reinvigoration of these strands of liberal thinking as well.

For classical liberals, free trade abroad as well as liberal governance at home boded well for a potentially greater benefit than wealth—peace. Adam Smith argued that the rise of commerce and manufacturing in a country would lead to order and good government, creating the conditions for liberty and security "among the inhabitants of the country, who had before lived almost in a continual state of war with their neighbours" (1993 [1776], 260). Agitating for an end to the Corn Laws in 1843, Richard Cobden held that bringing down barriers to trade also brought down barriers between nations, "those barriers behind which nestle the feelings of pride, revenge, hatred and jealousy . . . feelings which nourish the poison of war and conquest" (quoted in Howard 1987, 43).

A variety of mechanisms were proposed through which liberalism would end war. Ever since Smith's critique of mercantilism, it has been hoped the prospects of increased profit through free trade would overcome the desire for outright conquest. In *On Perpetual Peace*, Immanuel Kant argued that peace would come about through the territorial spread of republican governance and rule of law (1992). One of his central arguments was that the ordinary citizens of a country bore the costs of war, while the elites were more likely to benefit. Hence, the more say citizens had in matters of war and peace, the less likely was war. In these and other ways, liberals articulated a vision of a "modernity without violence" (Joas 2003, 29–42). In this frame, the possibility of armed conflict stemmed from the existence of nonliberal powers in the world system; with their demise or transformation into liberal states, a new, peaceful and prosperous world order came within reach. War, for liberals, was associated with atavism, with premodern social and political forms such as those purportedly found outside the West.

The end of the Cold War saw a renewed emphasis on the pacific qualities of liberalism. In Francis Fukuyama's view, capitalism and liberal democracy together met both the material and ideal needs of humans (1992). For him, the collapse of communism was the end of the last serious ideological competitor to the Western vision of capitalism and liberal democracy. As a result, this way of organizing politics and economy would become the "final form of human government," and its spread around the world was inevitable (Fukuyama quoted in Steger 2002, 3). History would end, according to Fukuyama, in the sense that the great ideological struggles and the wars they produced would be finished. Even after the spate of anti-globalization protests around the turn of the century and the strikes of September 11, 2001, liberal thinkers such as Michael Mandelbaum maintained that "the market-centered international order of the twenty-first century commanded almost universal allegiance" (2002, 4). In his *The Ideas That Conquered the World,* Mandelbaum reiterated the essential elements of the liberal vision of a pacific modernity, arguing that democracies tended to have peaceful foreign policies and that free markets, over time, promoted democracy (2002, 11).

Shortly after the world's leading liberal democratic power led the invasion and conquest of Iraq in 2003, President Bush echoed these same themes in a speech calling for a U.S.–Middle East free trade zone. Free trade would "drain" the "bitterness" from the region and increase U.S. security. "Over time, the expansion of liberty throughout the world is the best guarantee of security throughout the world. Freedom is the way to peace."[4] Iraq had first to be invaded and occupied before the United States could attempt to transform it into a liberal power. But for classical liberals, wars were not caused by liberalism; they were "the relics of a dying age that had not yet been illuminated by the dawn of the Enlightenment" (Joas 2003, 30). As "Reform" and "Progress" overcame despots and the warrior castes of the aristocracy, and free trade fueled prosperity, wars civil and foreign would pass into history. President Bush's policy of promoting liberalism through war suggests that the classical liberals may have overlooked something—the role of war and armed force in *making liberal* the illiberal. Such a policy, it turns out, long predates President Bush's government. If one looks at free trade and war in historical perspective, some specifically liberal tendencies to war come to light, as well as other sources of war and political violence in a world being made liberal and modern in diverse and important ways. Some discussion of relations between Europe, Britain, and China in the nineteenth century illuminates these points.

Wealthy Europeans had long coveted luxury goods from the Orient. The discovery of gold and silver in the New World provided Europeans with sufficient wealth to purchase tea and spices from China. Massive amounts of gold bullion flowed from Europe to China to finance the trade. However, the Chinese were not importing many goods from Europe in return, leading in the early decades of the nineteenth century to concern about the imbalance in trade. The British East India Company faced a similar problem. It had created a virtuous circle whereby raw cotton was exported to Britain and manufactured textiles were imported to India from the Manchester mills. But like Europe, India was increasingly unable to afford imported manufactured cloth, its main income being from cheap, raw cotton exports and other commodities.

The potential solution to both problems lay in opening Chinese markets. India had long been producing opium for export to China, where it was outlawed but was nonetheless imported in large quantities. As with illegal drugs in our day, the very fact that opium was illegal increased its profitability. By the 1820s, one-seventh of the East India Company's revenues were derived from opium (Hernon 2002, 300). Were China to import larger amounts of opium, India would increasingly be able to afford manufactured goods from Europe. Moreover, by opening Chinese markets to other European manufactured goods, not only could the tea and spice trade be balanced but yet further profits beckoned from a China market long fabled for its potential size. The problem was that since 1757 the Chinese had allowed trade with Europeans through only one port, Canton. The opium trade, while profitable, was limited by its illicit nature, which made it a difficult and risky business involving bribing Chinese officials.

Matters came to a head as the Chinese imperial government became increasingly concerned about the social effects of widespread opium addiction, particularly among soldiers. It has been suggested that between ten and twelve million Chinese were addicted by the mid-1830s (Hernon 2002, 304). A crackdown on the use of opium was launched. A zealous Chinese official surrounded European traders near Canton and held them hostage until they surrendered nearly three million pounds of raw opium, which was subsequently destroyed. News of this affair reached London in September 1839. Interested British businessmen launched a well-funded campaign in pamphlets and newspapers to advocate their cause to the public and government. "The public . . . were told that Englishmen were in danger in a foreign country and that they were being harshly treated and recklessly imprisoned," whereas in fact the European traders had suffered little and had all been released once they surrendered their illegal goods (Hernon 2002, 308). Heavily influenced by the wealthy merchant William Jardine, Prime Minister Palmerston and his cabinet declared war on China, sending an expeditionary force and demanding that China reimburse the opium traders, pay the costs of Britain's military expedition, open four new treaty ports to allow European goods access to the China market, and hand over Hong Kong island to the British. Thus began the Opium War of 1839–42.

The historians P. J. Cain and A. G. Hopkins have referred to Britain's China policy in particular and Victorian imperialism in general as a "peculiar mixture of compulsion and liberalism" (2002, 362). The Opium War itself was mostly a lopsided affair. Chinese junks and soldiers, many armed only with bladed weapons, were no match for British naval power, including steamers, and the well-drilled troops of the British army and the East India Company's sepoy regiments. Many engagements resulted in heavy Chinese casualties and comparatively light losses for the British, as at Ningpo in 1842, where anywhere from four to nine hundred Chinese soldiers died as against British losses of three dead and twenty wounded (Hernon 2002, 327). The Chinese finally capitulated when a British force threatened defenseless Nanking. The Treaty of Nanking, signed aboard a British warship, opened up four new treaty ports, placing British consuls at each of them; imposed reparations on the Chinese for both the lost opium and the costs of the war; ceded Hong Kong island to the British; and imposed uniform tariffs on imports and exports, among other trade-related demands.

The Opium War and a similar war fought twelve years later that opened more ports were not wars of territorial conquest by Britain, which sought only the island of Hong Kong and later Kowloon for direct rule. Their main goal was to open up the China market to British and other foreign trade. After the fighting, Britain sought to support the ailing imperial government in Peking in order to guarantee political stability and orderly commerce (Cain and Hopkins

2002, 363). The Anglo-Chinese wars were thus wars for free trade. Britain came to dominate the China trade for some time, and India's opium exports increased, although the wilder hopes of a huge China market remained unfulfilled. However, the wars also led to the beginnings of what one Chinese revolutionary would later call "invisible financial control by foreign powers" (quoted in Cain and Hopkins 2002, 375). The City of London organized loans to the Chinese government that could be secured against customs revenues from trade controlled by European officials in the treaty ports. This enabled large-scale lending to China, which became a very profitable business, with little fear that China would default.

As emphasized above, the creation of free markets and free trade is a *political policy,* and war is one instrument of such a policy, as exemplified by Britain's relations with China and elsewhere in the nineteenth century. However, another important connection between war and free trade is revealed by the China example. Many British liberals sincerely believed that through political stability and commerce, progress and reform would take root and that China and other parts of the British Empire would become liberal. As one put it, "Our interests are so manifestly connected with the advancement and improvement of the native states, that it is obvious we can have no views which are not equally to their advantage" (quoted in Drayton 2002, 110). But the presence in China of Europeans, their manufactured goods, and the increased opium trade had rather different effects. They contributed to a series of uprisings, rebellions, and revolutions that plagued China for over a hundred years after the Opium War. Chinese rebels resented the role of foreigners in their land and saw the imperial government as a pawn of foreign powers. Britain and other European powers, as well as European and American soldiers of fortune, assisted the Chinese imperial government in putting down such resistance. The Taiping Rebellion, for example, which lasted from 1850 to 1864, was "the longest, fiercest and most destructive war of the nineteenth-century world" and left an area as large as France and Germany combined devastated and depopulated (Jack Gray 2002, 75). Civilian and military deaths caused by the war reached some twenty million.

For China, liberalism in the nineteenth and twentieth centuries resulted not in peace and progress but in war and revolution.

Broadly speaking, European penetration of China initiated modernization processes that were generative of social and political tensions that frequently issued in violence. This is a rather different outcome of free trade than that expected by Adam Smith and Richard Cobden. The Anglo-Chinese wars suggest that not only is war sometimes necessary to initiate free trade but that free trade and free markets can be *productive* of war and other political violence. War is repositioned here as an inherent aspect of economic globalization rather than something that will disappear from history because of it.

This brief critique suggests that the classical liberal vision of a pacific modernity is seriously askew. Neoliberal promises of a link between peace, free markets, and democracy may be as illusory in the twenty-first century as they were in the nineteenth. That is a matter we will take up later. There is, however, a final point to be made about this look at relations between China and the West, about their shared and intertwined history. Above it was suggested that at base, globalization is about interconnection and mutual constitution in world politics. Some of the violent consequences for China of this intertwining in the nineteenth century have been described. What has not been mentioned is that this history continued to be generative of violent conflict for *both* China and the West. The various rebellions and revolutions in China would finally bring Mao Zedong to power. The People's Republic of China played a major role in the Asian land wars of the Cold War, confronting U.S. and UN forces directly in Korea and supporting communist revolutionary movements elsewhere, most prominently in Indochina. All of these events were major moments in *American* Cold War history. The "loss of China" to communism in 1949 was a significant contributing factor to the McCarthyite Red Scare, while China's military role helped embroil the United States in two costly and indecisive land wars—the second of which, in Vietnam, was a watershed moment in U.S. history, with consequences that are still very much with us. Through the medium of war, as well as other kinds of interconnection, Chinese, European, and American histories in part constituted one another, with effects that ranged widely in time and space.

Before exploring some of these consequences, and the expansive interrelations between war and globalization that this chapter has sought to open up, we must first subject "war" to the same treatment given to "globalization" above. For war is quintessentially a topic associated not with globalization but with nation-states and their borders.

BEHIND "GLOBALIZATION": NATION-STATES, EMPIRES, AND DEMOCRACIES AT WAR

The discussion of some of the links between war and free trade at the end of the last chapter suggests that hopes that global laissez-faire will lead to peace are misplaced. It suggests also that there are systematic, if often neglected, connections between war and the basic themes of first wave "globalization" theorists. War was necessary to initiate free trade, and it was the outcome of processes set in train by the expansion of free trade. There is another and ultimately more significant point to be drawn here. War is often seen as something separate from normal politics. Many approaches to understanding politics and society, as with first-wave "globalization," were developed in isolation from consideration of war. At the same time, the analysis of war is often reduced to purely military matters—the course of campaigns, narratives of battles, and accounts of soldiers' exploits. Modern strategic studies are too often narrowly focused on the properties of particular weapon systems and their use rather than on the broader and more important political and social context of the use of force. The discussion of war and free trade demon-

27

strated that war is intimately interrelated to other social and historical processes, to economy, society, culture, and politics. War is both shaped by these processes and, in turn, exercises its own influence on them. War is always already part of "normal" social existence. Before the connections between war and globalization can be addressed directly in the following chapter, war must first be placed in its broader social and political context; that is the task of this chapter.

The place to begin is with the basic insight of the "war and society" approach (e.g., Bond 1998; Howard 1962, 1976; Shaw 1988). War shapes society, and society shapes war. Industrial societies fight industrial war. In turn, war encourages industrialization as well as other transformations in society, such as furthering scientific and technological development along warlike lines, turning large numbers of young men into soldiers who, as veterans, influence postwar politics, and so on. This is a simple enough idea. Its significance becomes apparent when one reflects on the fact that many of the basic approaches to social science were developed in absence of serious consideration of war, despite the fact that it is one of the oldest and most pervasive features of human history. The classical sociological tradition, with the exception of Max Weber, developed theories about the rise of industrial society and capitalism without much reference to war. Indeed, in Enlightenment thinking generally, the view was that modernity and modern reason contributed to peace. "The theory of the peaceful nature of industrial society was constitutive for sociology" (Joas 2003, 132). War does not figure centrally either in Karl Marx's account of the origins of capitalism or his prognosis for its demise. Yet, to cite just one of many connections, industrialization in Britain was crucially boosted by military spending during the Napoleonic Wars (McNeill 1982, 210–11). Even today, in the social sciences and humanities, "the major theories that are the subject of general discussion . . . contain hardly any mention of war and peace" (Joas 2003, 126).

Specialists in war and the military pay insufficient attention to society, politics, and culture, while sociologists, cultural theorists and to a lesser degree political scientists are not sufficiently attentive to the importance of war for their subject matters. The corrective, as Martin Shaw argues, is that "war must be seen as a social activity related to the whole complex of social life and organisation." Equally, "war must be seen as a very unique social activity, with its own character and logic that cannot be reduced to any ordinary social dynamic" (Shaw 1988, 11). War and society stand in a dynamic interrelationship with one another. Changes in warfare affect society, while changes in society affect warfare. The first section below provides some background on the changing relations between war and society in the Western world, and on the preeminent theorist of war between modern states, Carl von Clausewitz. As will be seen, changes in the medieval military order in Europe led to the rise of the modern states, while the French revolution unleashed political forces—primarily the "nation"—that transformed the face of warfare.

Most analysts of war and the military, including those who take a war and society approach, focus on Europe and the West more generally. As such, the history of modern warfare is very often told as the history of warring nation-states, which in the first half of the twentieth century took the form of total war between competing national ideologies. Voltaire quipped that God is always on the side with the big battalions. So too, it turns out, are military historians, as few areas of inquiry are as pervasively Eurocentric as military history. The vast majority of both popular and scholarly texts on military matters concern war between the great powers, which have been mostly located in Europe and the West. This is perhaps to be expected, but the result is that conceptions of warfare and its relation to politics are heavily based on experience in the West. In particular, war and the military are often seen as the special property of the sovereign and territorial nation-state, despite the widespread incidence of imperial war in modern times. The fact that almost all popular writing on war and the military in the United Kingdom and the United States concerns their national armed forces only furthers this perception, and it is one indication of the extraordinarily close relation between war and national identity—a topic for chapter 4.

The close association between war and the nation-state, derived from a particular view of European warfare, not only distorts analysis more generally but also contributes to the perception that "globalization"—supposedly about the corrosion of the nation-state—stands in opposition to war. Recall that Ohmae said the military would become a declining industry because the nation-state was passing from history, as if armed conflict were only as old as the nation-state or only caused by nation-states. To overcome this Eurocentricity, the second section of the chapter looks at some of the imperial dimensions of war and military power. In the colonies, relations between war and society took considerably different form. Moreover, these relations were of direct significance for the European balance of power, for European nation-states were also imperial states.

Attention to some of the "North-South" dimensions of warfare also serves another purpose. Once a war and society approach is adopted, it is easy to see how war can affect what happens inside a state, and vice versa. But a more general or global perspective would attend to the ways in which changes in modes of warfare are related to the entire organization of world politics, and vice versa. That is, the war and society approach needs to be globalized. Forms of organizing violence, and prevailing ideas regarding its use, shape and condition world politics as a whole in far-reaching ways. For example, during the Cold War the nuclear balance between the United States and the Soviet Union made a direct conflict along the inter-German border unlikely, while simultaneously increasing the likelihood of war by proxy in the Third World, where the risk of nuclear escalation was much less. Globalizing a war and society perspective will primarily be the burden of the next chapter, but discussion of imperial war here clears some ground.

In the final section of this chapter, the various themes will be drawn together to critique some of the ways in which liberalism influences the study of war (see, e.g., Howard 1978). This is important because "globalization" is in many ways a profoundly liberal discourse, as seen in chapter 1. It relies on an account of the pacific nature of liberal democratic states and societies, and conversely on the implicit or explicit view that the origins of war are to be found in the existence of nonliberal states and societies in world politics. Only in this way could one come to the view that the global spread of democracy and free markets would end war and bring peace. This section will show how the combination of liberal politics and assumptions about the sovereign state have obscured some of the pervasive and important connections between war, the military, and the basic themes of globalization studies.

War, State, and Society in the Western World

To illustrate the nature and significance of the war and society approach, as well as provide essential background, this section addresses some episodes in the rise of the modern state out of medieval Europe and the subsequent development of Western warfare. Its aim is to demonstrate the dynamic interrelations between war and political and social developments.

In medieval Europe, armored knights on horseback constituted the dominant offensive weapons system. The ancients had evolved techniques by which disciplined infantry armed with pikes could resist heavy cavalry, but this knowledge and the means to act on it had fallen into disuse. The military dominance of aristocratic cavalry versus that of infantry in various societies had historically reflected different kinds of political and social structures. Where highly skilled warriors on horseback were dominant, it was very difficult for the central authorities to collect taxes or other goods from their domains, as knights could offer effective resistance. This resulted in forms of feudalism and political fragmentation. By contrast, where a central authority could raise an effective infantry army, it became possible to exercise sovereign control over a large domain (McNeill 1982, chap. 1).

These relations between military organization and politics were evident in medieval Europe. Knights were expensive to maintain and equip, and only men of means could afford armor for themselves and their war band, but there was little that could resist a charge by such a force. On the defense, generally only prolonged siege could bring down a well-stocked and well-fortified castle. These military realities were expressed in the parcelization of political authority in medieval Europe, where encastellated nobles could exercise domination over local peasants and the surrounding areas, retreating behind castle walls when bandits or other hostile raiders appeared (Drake 2001, chap. 6). Nobles were in various relations of vassalage to their kings and other feudal superiors, but they also had their own power bases. Only a large, well-funded expedition could besiege a noble's castle, whereas kings were dependent upon their nobles to supply military forces.

In different combinations in different areas, a set of new developments began to shift this relative balance of power between sovereigns and nobles in favor of the former (Tilly 1992). Smaller castles and fortifications became vulnerable to the new cannon. The crossbow, like the English longbow, could penetrate armor, but unlike the latter, it did not require specialist knowledge and long years of training to use effectively. This helped to end the battlefield dominance of noble knights, who began a transformation into a class of more or less professional officers commanding other troops in the king's service. This process was accelerated by the increasing sophistication and usability of firearms. There was a rediscovery of ancient, and especially Roman, military art, which led to a reinvigoration of infantry techniques. The Swiss had revived the pike and demonstrated the defensive and offensive power of a dense formation of determined and disciplined pikemen. These and other developments led to the reappearance in Europe of "regular infantry" —trained, disciplined, drilled, organized into units that could be combined into larger formations or broken down into subunits, and officered by men who made war their profession. Taken together, these military developments facilitated the centralization of political power from the sixteenth century, as sovereigns could effectively challenge recalcitrant nobles by raising armies composed of infantry, artillery, and cavalry (Parker 1988; Roberts 1956).

However, such armies cost money. Centralizing states required regular sources of funds to maintain their military establishments. It became possible to establish a virtuous circle between merchant capital and the new military forces. By using force to expand the territory directly under their control, sovereigns could tax economic activity and charge customs duties for goods traversing their domains. Rather than having to pay off the local notable in every valley they crossed or risk having their merchandise appropriated by armed men, merchants might now pay a uniform fee to the central authority. Trade and other economic activity were to a degree liberated from the exactions of feudal lords, encouraging growth. Sovereigns could use their new treasuries to raise further forces, in order to bring more territory under their control, and hire more tax collectors and other officials to administer it. In simplified and abstract terms, these relations between military force, capital, and sovereigns led to the development of recognizably modern territorial states in Europe by the turn of the seventeenth century (Tilly 1992). An important aspect of the military power of sovereigns was the resulting internal pacification of their territories, both bandits and feudal nobles being largely deprived of significant armed force.

The relatively small regular armies of Europe's sovereigns in the eighteenth century consisted of well-drilled infantry armed with musket and bayonet, as well as cavalry and cannon. As the stakes for which wars were fought rarely involved the potential loss of political independence, commanders were reluctant to risk their expensive forces in pitched battle. Campaigns often involved a great deal of maneuver, resulting in less than decisive battles, if nonetheless involving a great deal of bloodshed for those involved. William McNeill reminds us "how amazing it was for men to form themselves into opposing ranks a few score yards apart and fire muskets at one another, keeping it up while comrades were falling dead or wounded all around. Instinct and reason alike make such behavior unaccountable. Yet European armies of the eighteenth century did it as a matter of course" (McNeill 1982, 133). It is even more amazing when one considers the fact that such armies were composed of the very lowest social classes; the dregs of society ended up in the rank and file of Europe's regiments of the line. Those who did the fighting had the least to gain from victories or from the social and political order they defended.

Military life served to create powerful bonds of solidarity between soldiers, to make them obedient to the commands of their officers, and to take pride in the martial qualities of their formations. Military discipline was therefore fully compatible with very sharp class divisions in civil society. Despite the fact that they came from the ranks of the poor, trained soldiers were capable of enforcing their sovereign's writ against peasants' and workers' rebellions; equally, they followed orders when asked to fight against recalcitrant nobles and foreign enemies. "Overwhelming force came to reside in the hands of soldiers obedient to the king's own bureaucratically appointed officers. Neither aristocratic challenges to royal power nor lower-class protests against perceived injustice had the slightest chance of success as long as well-drilled troops were available to defend royal prerogatives" (McNeill 1982, 139). The new militaries were able to secure domestic order while also defending the realm from external attack. Sovereign borders began to acquire a "hard" character, and states in Europe increasingly took on the form of "bordered power containers" (Giddens 1985).

However briefly, it is important to provide this background on the changing interrelationships between war, politics, and society that brought about the modern state in Europe. One reason for this is that nearly the entirety of analyses of armed conflict assume, implicitly or explicitly, a world composed of sovereign and national states. That is, the social and political context in which militaries operate and war is fought is taken for granted. A European model derived from a particular time and place is considered globally applicable. Military force is seen as an instrument of policy in a historically given system of international politics composed of sovereign states. Most inquiry into the use of force in world politics, whether in international relations, strategic studies, or military history, simply assumes this model. Organized violence is monopolized by the state domestically and projected outward to secure national interests.

Analyses indebted to this "nation-state ontology" of world politics—that is, seeing the world as composed mainly of nation-states—are particularly bad at addressing how such a world came about. Equally, analyses that assume a system of sovereign states are largely blind to the social forces and reconfigurations of political and military power that may undermine or transform it. More importantly, as will become clear in the next section on empire, a nation-state ontology *never* applied to more than a limited domain of world politics, primarily in Europe, for the major nation-states were also imperial states. But for now we want to look at the thinker whose philosophy of war best expresses what war was all about in a European system of sovereign and national states, and to continue our brief and episodic encounter with the development of Western warfare.

From Clausewitz to Total War

A Prussian officer, Carl von Clausewitz's career spanned the period of the French revolution, the Napoleonic Wars, and their aftermath.[1]

He was no mere theorist of war, having first come under fire at the age of thirteen, campaigning against the First French Republic. A patriot, he fought the French until Prussia was conquered by them in 1807. When his defeated king signed an alliance with Napoleon, Clausewitz was among a group of officers who offered their service to the Russians in order to carry on the fight. He was at the great battle of Borodino outside Moscow in 1812 and saw Napoleon's shattered army cross the Beresina River after its failed invasion of Russia. When Prussia again turned against the French, he returned to help raise new forces and later served in the Waterloo campaign. After the Napoleonic Wars, he was appointed to the directorship of Prussia's war college, where he delivered the lectures that would make up his great work, *On War*. Tasked to stop a cholera epidemic spreading from the East in 1831, he contracted the disease and died. His wife collected the lectures, which he had been in the process of redrafting, and had them published.

War, for Clausewitz, was "a continuation of political intercourse, carried on with other means" (Clausewitz 1976, 87). Much followed from this definition. Relations between political entities, such as nation-states, involve a variety of different instruments, or means by which each seeks to fulfill its objectives. These include diplomacy, trade, sanctions, financial inducements, espionage, threats and displays of force, alliance-building, propaganda, and so on. The actual *use* of military force was simply another such means, which could be "mixed" with others to achieve goals. Clausewitz wished in particular to draw attention to the idea of the goal itself, or the political purpose for using force. A state goes to war to achieve some end; military operations should be directed toward this end; and once it is achieved, operations cease. Clausewitz was encouraging heads of state and their commanders to think rationally, or strategically. What end was being sought, and why? How could military force, among other means, achieve this end? How would the opponent *and his forces* and other instruments of policy be countered?

Underlying these issues was a more worrying one. Leaders desire to use force to achieve particular goals, but *war itself* might drive events in other directions. In his experience in the Napoleonic Wars, Clausewitz had observed that war had a tendency to generate more war, to become ever more intense, drawing in more and more people and resources. It had the potential to exceed the rational objectives sought by heads of state. In saying, then, that war was a continuation of politics, Clausewitz can be read as both defining war and pleading with commanders to struggle to limit and contain war's tendency to spiral out of control and serve itself rather than politics.

Clausewitz was aware of this problem because the French Revolution had added a new dimension to warfare—the energies of a mobilized, national people. Sovereigns of the eighteenth century, with their small professional armies, had been able to wage the kind of limited war for limited ends that Clausewitz envisaged. But once "the nation" arrived on the field of battle, things began to look rather different. "The people became a participant in war; instead of governments and armies as heretofore, the full weight of the nation was thrown into the balance" (Clausewitz 1976, 592). The revolution in France mobilized the masses and involved them in politics in new ways, enabling the Republic and later Napoleon to raise very large armies, the popular character of which gave them a certain *élan*. "Under these conditions the war was waged with a very different degree of vigor" (Clausewitz 1976, 592). Again we see the complex interrelationship between war and other social and political factors. The changes in France meant that other states had to adapt if they were to compete successfully; Austria, Prussia, Russia, and Britain all had to expand their armies through conscription and other means, thus involving "the people" in war. "Since Bonaparte, then, war, first among the French and subsequently among their enemies, again became the concern of the people as a whole.[2] . . . War, untrammeled by any conventional restraints, had broken loose in all its elemental fury" (Clausewitz 1976, 592–93).

Clausewitz was keenly aware of these changes in warfare wrought by the French revolution, because he had entered an *ancien regime* army only to fight in the new national wars. His life ended in a period of reaction, when Europe's sovereigns were again trying to put the genie back into the bottle. To varying degrees, European powers after the Napoleonic Wars reverted to small professional armies and established a Concert of Europe pledged to crush antimonarchical rebellion across the continent. In response to the history he had lived through, Clausewitz drew a distinction between two kinds of war, limited and absolute (or total). In a limited war, states fought for what Clausewitz called favorable terms of peace—

that is, some goal that involved less than the complete conquest of one or another of the combatants. Limited war might be fought to acquire a province or a colony, or some lesser object. Absolute war, on the other hand, was fought when the independence or very existence of one or more of the combatants was at stake. This was the kind of war Napoleon had waged. Total war, for total stakes, logically implied the total mobilization of a society's resources. The problem was that once the passions of a mobilized and aroused nation were involved in war, it would become ever more difficult to control those passions and limit the war. Hence the significance of Clausewitz's central problematic, the tension between the intrinsic nature of war—which was to become ever more total or absolute—and those forces that limited war's violence, such as political control or the various factors he grouped under the notion of "friction." Friction was essentially a kind of military Murphy's Law; it referred to all the human and other factors that limited war's violence, such as fatigue, mistakes, or bad weather. Further difficulties arose from the fact that it takes two to keep a war limited. The side that fought total war for total stakes would always have an advantage against a side that fought for limited objectives with limited resources, as the United States was to discover in Vietnam.

In Clausewitz's day, even the most total efforts at mobilizing society for war were limited. Muskets, uniforms, and other necessities were still largely produced by artisanal methods. Populations were relatively small, and large numbers had to work in agriculture to produce sufficient food. Even in the mid-nineteenth century, these factors constrained what was possible. In 1840, the Prussians introduced a new rifle that was loaded at the breech rather than the muzzle. The workshops that produced the new "needle guns," which fired a modern cartridge, could only manage ten thousand a year. That meant that equipping the 320,000-strong Prussian army and its reserves would take over thirty years (McNeill 1982, 235–36). All of this began to change with the introduction of mass-production techniques, first developed in the United States, and the ability to fabricate the component parts of firearms in identical, prescribed shapes, which then could be used interchangeably. By 1863, with the new techniques in place, the Enfield arsenal in Britain was able to produce over a hundred thousand rifles a year. For the first time in modern history the notion of the "armed people" ceased to be simply metaphorical, as it became possible to arm a large percentage of adult males if desired. Other technological innovations and economic developments, particularly railways and steamships as well as in the control of disease, meant that the new mass armies of conscripts could be fed, clothed, transported, and otherwise maintained in the field. Clausewitz's notion of "total war" became less and less merely an idea pushed to its logical extremes and more and more of a historical possibility, one that was tragically to be realized in the first half of the twentieth century—twice.

Over the latter half of the nineteenth century, changes in weapons technology and relative stasis in tactics and doctrine created the conditions for the killing fields of the First World War. For a variety of reasons, many of them sound, infantry continued to be organized in close-order formations, shoulder to shoulder, two or three lines deep for defense or in a deeper "column" for the assault. Professional officers were keenly aware of how terrifying battle could be. Ever since the ancients evolved the phalanx formation, soldiers in battle had valued the reassurance of the close physical proximity of comrades. Men were then less inclined to flee, for fear of leaving their comrades in danger or appearing cowardly, or simply because the density of the formation prevented it. The introduction of firearms changed these ancient realities less than might be supposed. Muskets were extremely inaccurate and had an effective range of about two hundred yards. Volley fire from well-drilled, closely packed troops increased the effectiveness of muskets. Even so, an attacking column had to endure defensive fire only so long as it took to cover that distance or the longer range of cannon. Considering that it took time to load muskets from the muzzle, especially when fear and losses disrupted volleys, the odds were not unbearably poor of surviving before contact was made and the weight of the column could break the thinner defensive line—or at least such was the ideal.

However, from the 1840s there was an increase in the accuracy and range of firearms. Rifling barrels increased the effective range out to about a thousand yards. When coupled with the new Minié ball cartridge, which could be loaded far more easily than its predecessors, rifle fire became both accurate and rapid. Artillery could be rifled as well, and the technology of exploding shells was steadily improved. The invention of modern cartridges, which drastically reduced loading times, and of breechloading weapons increased the rate of fire, as did the introduction of primitive machine guns and other repeating, clip-fed, and automatic weapons by the end of the century. However, infantry continued to fight largely in close-order formations. There could only be one outcome—drastically increased casualties.

On the third day of the Battle of Gettysburg in the American Civil War, July 3, 1863, Confederate generals James J. Pettigrew and George E. Pickett lined up their divisions in front of Seminary Ridge for an attack on the Union center on Cemetery Ridge. Over one thousand yards of open ground lay between the two ridges, which the Confederates crossed under heavy, sometimes enfilading (that is, from the flank), rifle and cannon fire. Between twelve and fifteen thousand Confederate troops participated in the attack; of these about ten thousand were killed, wounded, or captured. In Pickett's division, all fifteen regimental commanders became casualties. "Most of the casualties inflicted by rifle fire in the Civil War resulted from long-range accurately aimed defensive fire from behind entrenchments and log breastworks" (Black 1998, 177).

While the Confederates suffered heavily that day, the three days at Gettysburg exemplified what was already an enduring feature of war between first-rate powers. In ancient warfare, the victorious army normally suffered relatively few casualties compared to the defeated, as the insightful French soldier and military thinker Ardant du Picq observed (1921). The bulk of casualties occurred when one side broke and ran; routed soldiers could be run down and killed individually, often by light troops specially equipped for the task. This fact in that era provided veteran soldiers with a strong incentive to maintain formation and keep fighting—paradoxically, for reasons of self-preservation. At Gettysburg, by contrast, the victorious Union army suffered twenty-three thousand killed, missing, and wounded, while the defeated Confederates (for whom numbers are less reliable) suffered between 20,500 and 25,000. These losses represented 27 percent and between 30 and 34 percent of the entire strength of the Union and Confederate armies engaged, respectively. Modern firepower, then, worked to ensure that defeated and victorious alike suffered high casualties. In the fighting around Verdun between February and June 1916, the French and the Germans each lost over two hundred thousand men killed and wounded. In the month of July 1916 alone, in the Somme offensive, the British and French lost over two hundred thousand men, while the Germans suffered 160,000 casualties, having been pushed back a mere three miles. While by the middle of the First World War infantry tactics had become more sophisticated and were reaching toward a modern open-order, fire-and-movement approach, the vast increase in firepower, particularly artillery and the machine gun, more than compensated.

Another important change was the continuous nature of combat operations in modern warfare. Battles were no longer discretely contained within a single or a few days but lasted months. Previously, only siege operations generally had had this character. Coupled with the new firepower, this meant that infantry soldiers on all sides faced a very high likelihood of being killed, wounded, or captured during their service. Of the eleven million men Germany mobilized in the First World War, nearly 65 percent became casualties. Of the nearly eight and a half million the French mobilized, over 76 percent became casualties. These figures are all the more impressive when it is remembered that casualties were overwhelmingly concentrated among the infantry as against the various support services, many of which required significant manpower.[3]

Such numbers begin to give an idea of just how "total" conventional war could become. World War I originated, at least in an immediate sense, from limited objectives sought in the Balkans by Austria-Hungary and Russia. However, once under way, an expensive but largely stalemated war of attrition took hold on the Western Front in particular. This initiated two broad developments characteristic of modern, total war, one concerned with state organization of society and the other with ideology and nationalism. Clothing, feeding, and supplying armies that numbered in the millions required increased mobilization and organization of the human and material resources of the home front. Staggering amounts of ammunition alone had to be manufactured and transported to the fighting front. In 1915, the French army required a hundred thousand shells a day, while the Russians reportedly needed 250 million a month.

By 1916, Britain was producing over forty-five million shells a month. Only the state could organize production on such a vast scale, which required rationing available resources and directing them toward war production and other essential industries. Increasingly, private corporations, government armories, labor unions, and the military coalesced into what amounted to a "single national firm for waging war" (McNeill 1982, 317). Western states acquired the large public bureaucracies and the administrative and economic competence to regulate modern economies and welfare programs in part as a consequence of these organizational developments during the First and Second World Wars. "The experience of wartime direction of economic life was . . . an 'education in state socialism'" (Bond 1998, 116–17).

The second broad development characteristic of modern war concerned ideology and nationalism. When armies were composed of professional regulars, it was possible for the state to expend their lives for limited objectives. However, when nearly one in four of the entire male population, as in England and Scotland during World War I, were mobilized, rather grander reasons had to be offered to the public as to why such sacrifice was necessary. Thus the Germans, in British propaganda, became "the Hun" (from "Germ-hun," implying the Germans were akin to "Asiatic barbarians"), raping, pillaging and murdering their way across Belgium, while to get the Americans involved in the bloodbath in Europe President Wilson promised a war to end all wars (on "Germ-huns" see Fussell 2000, 77). War was becoming total in terms of *ideological* stakes as well as in terms of the mobilization of human and material resources.

At Versailles, despite a harsh peace settlement, the old limited objectives reasserted themselves. While Austria-Hungary was broken up, defeated Germany remained an independent, sovereign state. But the aftermath of World War I created a Europe composed of three sharply differentiated ideologies—communism, fascism, and liberal democracy—associated with and drawing strength from different nationalisms. Each ideology provided a different account of the ultimate meaning of public life, of the right ordering of politics and society, and of the appropriate legitimation of political authority. It was no longer God or the divine right of kings that conferred right but elections, the pronouncements of *der Führer,* or the decisions of the central committee of the party. Ultimate, uncompromising "religious" conceptions of politics had reentered secular, modern Europe through the back door of political ideology. Since each ideology was embodied in one or more nation-states with their national armies and national war myths, representations of soldiers' sacrifice helped further to conjoin and sanctify an emotionally powerful package of nation, territory, and ideology.

A total war of ideas had a strong tendency to intensify the actual war on the ground. Demands for "unconditional surrender" were far more likely in wars framed by competing ideologies. As it became clear that Nazi Germany would lose the Second World War, Hitler remarked to his private circle that he may have lost the war but he had achieved his real political aim—eliminating European Jewry (Bond 1998, 184).[4] Clausewitz's hope that "politics" would limit war's violence, by orienting it toward rational, achievable objectives, was turned on its head. Ideology served the exact opposite purpose, creating "total" objectives that served to justify only more war and other political violence. For Hitler, racial ideology and the Final Solution provided reasons for waging war until he was utterly defeated; he ended his days in a concrete bunker, his writ reduced to a few devastated city blocks of Berlin. Ideology was no longer merely a subtheme or propaganda tool used to mobilize the population, as had been largely the case in World War I. From 1945, it was the *world* and not merely Europe that was to be divided between two diametrically opposed sets of political ideas.

We will have occasion to consider the Cold War below. This section has sought only to provide a rough and ready guide to the historical development of the complex interrelations between armed forces, war, politics, and society in the Western world from the Middle Ages to the world wars. As suggested in the introduction to this chapter, in popular as well as scholarly terms this story is very often understood in national and sovereign-state terms. The imperial dimensions of modern warfare are neglected. These include both the nature of military organization and war in the non-European world, as well as the ways in which empire was centrally implicated in the military competition among great powers. In fact, as much recent scholarship has emphasized, Europe and the colonies developed together, in relations of mutual constitution (Cooper and Stoler 1997;

Hall 2002). European culture, economy, and military power all developed in dynamic interaction with the world outside Europe. As Frantz Fanon remarked, "Europe is literally the creation of the Third World"—and vice versa, it should be added (1967, 81). Such observations suggest strongly that the Eurocentricity and nation-state ontology of analyses of war and the military have obscured significant aspects of the nature of military power in world politics.

States, Empires, and Military Power

Max Weber, the seminal German social and political thinker, drew a close connection between the state as an administrative and legal apparatus, a given territorial area over which it ruled, and the successful upholding of the claim to the monopoly of the legitimate use of armed force in that territory (Weber 1978, 54). Weber was a careful and historically oriented scholar. He intended this definition of "state" to apply only to the European states of his day (the late nineteenth and early twentieth centuries). He was aware that in other times and places, political entities had taken different form and had had multiple and complex relations with territory and armed force. However, his notion of the state as a social-territorial package, with "hard" sovereign borders, became a fundamental, taken-for-granted assumption in much thinking about international relations and war.

The sovereign nation-state came about in Europe as the result of a complex process of historical development, a process that is presumably not irrevocable, as the development of the European Union indicates. But once the ideal of a sovereign state was in place, it became possible to think about international relations in a distinctive, binary manner defined by the "inside" and "outside" of sovereign borders (Walker 1993). "Inside" was the settled peaceful order provided by the modern state. The "outside" was defined by the absence of a common power, such as the state provides domestically, and so was conceived as an "anarchy" in which ultimately power, particularly military power, mattered most (e.g., Waltz 1959, 1979). States were caught in a "self-help" system, where each had to rely on its own resources to ensure its survival and prosperity. This nation-state ontology of the world created a convenient academic division of labor. Scholars in international relations addressed relations between states, while academic disciplines like sociology, comparative politics, and "national" history studied what happened inside sovereign borders. This neat division of the world depended crucially on various assumptions about the nature of armed force, principally that it was "monopolized" by the state behind its borders and projected outward to secure national interests. Is this a historically accurate model of how armed force works in modern world politics?

In *Mercenaries, Pirates and Sovereigns,* Janice Thomson answers this question in the affirmative (1994). Reviewing her work illuminates some of the key issues at stake. She argues that over the course of the late eighteenth and nineteenth centuries states slowly gained a monopoly on the authoritative use of external violence from nonstate actors. In addition to pacifying their sovereign territory, states brought large-scale, organized violence for external, foreign-policy purposes under central control. Pirates, mercenaries, and the armed forces of trading companies had been common features of international politics in early modern Europe. The British East India Company, like similar outfits in other European powers, fielded a navy and considerable ground forces. States launched expeditions against pirates; the great trading companies were deprived of their legal right to raise private armed forces; and laws were passed prohibiting the hiring of mercenaries in national armies, as well as prohibiting citizens from serving as mercenaries in other countries. The long-term and widespread practice of using foreign mercenary companies in the armies of Europe's sovereigns was brought to an end. While there are a few surviving anomalies even today, such as the French Foreign Legion or the Nepalese Gurkha regiments in the British and Indian armies, Thomson argues that "the last instance in which a state raised an army of foreigners was in 1854," when Britain hired some mercenaries for use in the Crimean War (1994, 88).

If we believed the traditional narrative of "globalization," that it is corrosive of the power of nation-states, we would accept Thomson's account for the nineteenth- and twentieth-century heyday of the nation-state but argue that it is increasingly untrue. It is often argued that in the contemporary world, nation-states are gradually losing their grip on organized violence, in the face of the privatization of security and the rise of warlords and other nonstate actors with control of significant armed force. Private military companies, for exam-

44

ple, are back in evidence (Singer 2003). Between 1994 and 2002, the U.S. Department of Defense entered into over three thousand contracts for a total value of around $300 billion with private military companies.[5] "Contractors are training security forces in Iraq, flying gunships in Columbia, training civilian police in Bosnia and Kosovo and protecting Afghanistan's President Hamid Karzai."[6] Executive Outcomes, a South African company, fought in Angola and Sierra Leone, while Military Professional Resources, Inc., helped plan Croatia's offensive against the Bosnian Serbs. Additionally, while it is not a mercenary outfit, al-Qaeda represents another form of the stateless organization and projection of violence.

Such a critique, while important, would leave Thomson's central argument standing for the nineteenth and twentieth centuries, when in fact she conflates two distinct issues. On the one hand there is the question of sovereign or public control of armed force. That is, nonstate actors were increasingly prevented from wielding legitimate force by sovereign states. On the other hand, there is the notion of using foreigners in the armed forces. Britain may have ceased hiring private mercenary companies after the Crimean War, but it fielded many tens of thousands of foreigners before and after 1854. The British Indian army numbered approximately 160,000 in 1900 and was to reach a strength of nearly two million men during the Second World War (Perry 1988, 116). The British Indian army *was* under the sovereign control of the British Government of India, and above it, London. However, it was most definitely *not* composed of British nationals, except as officers, but of colonial subjects. Moreover, the British Indian army was not a small part of Britain's overall military power; the "Indian army was the leading British strategic reserve on land" (Black 1998, 178). It also made Britain an Asian land power for nearly two hundred years. France similarly fielded large forces of West and North Africans in the nineteenth and twentieth centuries, over two hundred thousand of whom would serve on the Western Front in World War I (Clayton 1988, 98).

There are a number of other examples that do not fit into Thomson's neat categorization of private and public, national and foreign. In China in the second half of the nineteenth century, a variety of mercenary forces helped the weak central state put down rebellions. Examples include the mainly Filipino Foreign Rifle Corps, raised by the American adventurer Frederick Townsend Ward; the French-commanded Ever-Triumphant Army; and the British-run Ever-Victorious Army, commanded by "Chinese" Gordon (Black 1988, 182; Carr 1992). While these forces ostensibly served the Chinese emperors, they were also indirect tools of Western policy, which was seeking to prop up a Chinese regime friendly to Western trade and other financial interests. At the turn of the twentieth century, King Leopold II of Belgium was controlling the Congo in brutal fashion with the Force Publique, his own private army of white-officered African mercenaries (Hochschild 2002). Leopold, a constitutional monarch with very limited powers in Belgium itself, ran the Congo as a private fiefdom.

But surely, it might be claimed, Thomson's argument has more validity after decolonization, when all these imperial exceptions evaporated and the new states in the Third World took over their own militaries, becoming sovereign nation-states. The British Indian army, for example, was split into the Indian and Pakistani armies in 1947. Thomson, as a way of showing just how "illegitimate" mercenarism has become in our own day, asks: Is it possible to imagine "a rich state like the United States [forming] an army by recruiting, say, poor, unemployed Mexicans?" (1994, 146) It so happens that there were approximately thirty thousand foreign-born, non-U.S. citizens in the American armed forces as of September 2003, including Mexicans and other Hispanics.[7] The U.S. Army's cyber-recruiting operation holds daily online chat sessions in English and Spanish.[8] In addition to its Gurkhas, today's British army recruits significant numbers of Fijians. There were even calls for the formation of a U.S. foreign legion during the Cold War, composed, it was sometimes suggested, of Eastern Europeans who would earn U.S. citizenship in exchange for their service; there were various other proposals as well to develop forces composed of foreigners (e.g., Wolf and Webb 1987). But there are far more important exceptions to Thomson's argument in the postcolonial era.

Whereas for imperial powers she conflated sovereignty and nationality, subsuming the identity of colonial soldiers under the nationality of the imperial power, for the new states of the Third World she implicitly assumes that their formal, "juridical" (or legal) sovereignty means that they are *actually* sovereign. In this view, Third

World states are just like nation-states in the First World, just less powerful. However, the armed forces of Third World states and other secondary powers were almost always dependent upon superpower patrons during the Cold War, and many became more or less direct instruments of superpower foreign policy. For example, no one would argue that the sovereign armed forces of the Warsaw Pact countries, like East Germany, Poland, and Czechoslovakia, were independent of the Soviet Union. They were trained, supplied, and ultimately controlled by the Soviets. Not entirely dissimilar, during the Cold War the armed forces of the NATO powers were integrated to a significant degree, especially in respect of command and control, and an American general was always the supreme commander. Indeed, the largest NATO military aside from that of the United States, that of the former West Germany, lacked an independent national command structure.

In the Third World, the United States exercised even more direct influence over the armed forces of nominally sovereign states. In the Panama Canal zone, the United States established a "School of the Americas" (moved to Fort Benning, Georgia, when the United States gave up sovereign control of the Canal Zone). This school trained Latin and Central American officers and, along with other U.S. programs of "advice and support," sought to turn Latin militaries into imperfect instruments of U.S. policy, chiefly for repressing indigenous rebellions and leftist political forces. There were many other examples of this phenomenon. Officially speaking, the half-million-strong Army of the Republic of Vietnam (ARVN) was the army of a sovereign state, South Vietnam. In actual fact, it was largely the creation of U.S. power, its soldiers even wearing U.S. helmets and using other equipment too big for their smaller frames. Rather than the progressive nationalization of armed forces as Thomson argues, world politics is marked by different forms of the *transnational* organization of military power.

Very early on in the Cold War, the United States realized that it could not confront what it perceived as the communist threat everywhere in the world with its own, national armed forces. As President Eisenhower said in 1957, "the United States could not maintain old-fashioned forces all around the world," so it sought "to develop within the various areas and regions of the free world indigenous forces for the maintenance of order, the safeguarding of frontiers, and the provision of the bulk of the ground capability." The "kernel of the whole thing," he remarked, was to have indigenous forces— that is, non-Americans—bear the brunt of any future fighting (quoted in Gaddis 1982, 153). Subsequent administrations developed and expanded similar policies. Between 1955 and 1981, nearly four hundred thousand Third World officers were brought to the United States for military training, a figure that does not take account of the large-scale programs for training soldiers abroad (Neuman 1986, 28–29).

There were yet other foreign elements of the U.S. coercive apparatus in the Cold War. During the Indochina conflict, the U.S. Special Forces in Laos mobilized an army of some thirty thousand Hmong, known as L'Armée Clandestine, in addition to making use of a variety of "third country personnel," such as Thais and Filipinos (Castle 1993). More generally, the covert-action arm of the CIA consisted of an exotic cosmopolitan mix (Prados 1996). Nationalist Chinese pilots flew in the CIA-sponsored invasion of Guatemala in 1954. Free Polish and Czech pilots, who had flown for Britain against the Nazis and remained in the United Kingdom after the Soviet takeover of their homelands, were later recruited for CIA missions in Albania, Indonesia, and elsewhere. Two Poles were killed flying CIA missions during the U.S. covert intervention in Indonesia in 1957–58 (Conboy and Morrison 1999, 90; see also Kahin and Kahin 1995).

As can be seen, the model of the sovereign nation-state is a poor guide, in any era, to the organization of military power in world politics. Thomson is right to argue that armed force came to reside overwhelmingly in the hands of states, but she is wrong to suggest that either sovereignty or the nation-state provide adequate conceptual tools to understand this process. While in purely *European* terms it may appear that France, Britain, and Germany were "bordered power containers," mobilizing their national armed forces at home and projecting them outward, the moment a global perspective is taken it is immediately evident that states and their coercive power took very different form outside Europe. Britain's leading strategic reserve came from India, while it also drew heavily on the military power of the Commonwealth states. Moreover, foreign forces were extensively used in European wars as well. Nearly fifty thousand Indian soldiers died in World War I alone. These losses and the 144,000 from Canada, Australia, New Zealand, and South Africa who also died add up to nearly 22 percent of all "British" deaths in the First World War.

The British Empire is perhaps the last word in constituting military power from foreign populations, but the phenomenon is historically pervasive and widespread. The Germans waged their four-year campaign in East Africa in World War I with an army of fourteen thousand Africans and 2,200 Germans; they were opposed largely by South Africans, East Africans, and Indians in British service (Kiernan 1998, 188). In addition to the two hundred thousand West Africans serving France on the Western Front in World War I, there were also over 250,000 North Africans, of whom about fifty thousand were killed (Clayton 1988, 98). There were eighty thousand West Africans in French service at the outbreak of World War II, and they would make up 20 percent of the Free French forces in France in 1944 (Echenberg 1991, 26, 88). There were even more North Africans liberating France in 1944, so many that Gen. Charles de Gaulle instituted a policy of "whitening" Free French forces so that France could be liberated by the French (Echenberg 1991, 98–99). Meanwhile, some 275,000 colonial soldiers were serving the Allies in Italy (Ready 1985, 220). Even after World War II, France maintained an army of nearly forty thousand West Africans, eighteen thousand of whom, in addition to thirty thousand North Africans and two hundred thousand Indochinese, served France in its war in Indochina (Clayton 1988, 160; Echenberg 1991, 26). Despite its racial ideology in World War II, Nazi Germany made extensive use of foreign troops. A half-million served in the Waffen SS alone, with foreigners outnumbering native Germans by the end of the war (Stein 1966, 137–38).

Taken as a whole, these observations about the transnational nature of military forces do considerably more than simply complicate a narrative of "globalization" leading to a decline of the nation-state. The heavily Eurocentric and nationalist bias of military history has occluded the fact that military power has long been organized on a global scale. Attention to the transnational dimensions of armed force opens up a variety of questions for globalization studies. Many of these center around the global spread of a particular form of military organization, that associated with European military institutions. How was it possible to recruit non-Europeans into European-style militaries? What processes of cultural transmission and transformation were involved? That is, there is a strong but neglected military dimension to the processes of worldwide Westernization that have so occupied scholars of both imperialism and contemporary globalization. Another set of questions involves the broader political, economic, and social consequences of adopting European military forms (Ralston 1990). In the formerly colonized countries, the military was frequently the most developed state institution—often a product of the resources colonial powers put into internal security. As such, militaries came to play a large role in post-independence politics, frequently overthrowing civilian authorities. Militaries could also serve as conduits for foreign influence, as in the examples offered above. The transnational organization of military power shaped world politics as a whole, as will be discussed in the next chapter. The war and society approach needs to be globalized.

This list of topics for investigation could be considerably expanded. Two points, however, are important for present purposes. If we take as our guide to the exploration of war and the military a nation-state ontology of world politics, we would hardly be able to pose, let alone analyze, the questions above. The world military order does not fit, and never has fitted, neatly into sovereign state categories. That is the first point. The second is that even in the cursory discussion of transnational military organization provided so far, numerous connections with the basic themes of globalization studies are evident. There is of course the circulation of people, goods, and ideas around the globe involved in constituting military force and using it. Complex identities, traveling cultures, and cultural hybridity—major themes in the analysis of cultural globalization—are very much in evidence in the transnational nature of military power and are discussed in chapter 4.

Perhaps the most important connection to globalization studies, however, is the fact that only by taking a global perspective can we understand the roles played by war and the military in history and in the present. As the anthropologist Eric Wolf observed, we cannot properly understand human societies and cultures until we learn "to visualize them in their mutual interrelationships and interdependencies in space and time," because "human populations construct their cultures in interaction with one another, and not in isolation" (Wolf 1997, x, xv; see also Gupta and Ferguson 1997). What is true of culture is also true of society, economy, and politics, as well as military power. As Wolf observed of Spain after the discovery and exploitation of the New World, "together, Spanish sheep and American silver underwrote large-scale Spanish military operations in Europe and the growth of a royal bureaucracy far beyond the ultimate capabilities of the Spanish economy" (Wolf 1997, 113). We return here to globalization as processes of mutual constitution, but now with a focus on the military and war. So for example, "European" military prowess came in part from Europe's early encounter with others. The impressive range and sailing qualities of European vessels in the age of exploration and fighting sail derived in part from the incorporation of Arab-style lateen rigs with the traditional square rig (Wolf 1997, 235). This technological hybridity was made possible through contacts with the Arabs developed during the Crusades. Other "European" military innovations involved borrowing from the Turks, while yet others came about as a result of having to fight outside Europe (Black 1998, 91–93).

If military power was constituted through transnational processes of these kinds, war itself played out globally. Already in the middle of the eighteenth century, Black observes, there "was a growing interconnectedness of war around the world: conflict in Europe affected North America or India and vice versa" (Black 1998, 111; see also Anderson 2001). In the nineteenth century, as in the Cold War, the great powers could pursue their rivalries more easily in the non-European world, where fewer resources were required and there was less chance of major war erupting. Together, the transnational nature of military power and the global interconnectedness of war form the primary subject matter of "globalization and war." The war and society approach enables us to see how this subject matter interacts with other political, cultural, and economic phenomena and, in turn, how these phenomena shape war and the military.

These topics will be directly addressed in the next chapter. In the concluding section of this chapter, the "democratic peace," one of the most prevalent theories concerning war and peace in the contemporary world, is critiqued. This is the idea that democratic states do not make war on one another, with its more than implicit suggestion that a world composed entirely of liberal democratic states would be a peaceful world. The "democratic peace" represents an effort from within a liberal worldview, based on a nation-state ontology of world politics, to understand global patterns of war and peace. Seeing where and how the "democratic peace" goes wrong provides a good summary of many of the themes of this chapter while introducing the next one.

It also serves another purpose. All scholarship is significantly shaped by the politics of the scholar. In the U.S. and British academies, broadly liberal political values underlie much inquiry. "Globalization," as pointed out in the first chapter, is very much a liberal discourse, one that had distinctive liberal blind spots concerning not only war but also the contradictions of interest between rich and poor in the world economy. Critiquing the democratic peace is a salutary lesson in just how much can be obfuscated by scholars who genuinely believe they are objective and are basing their arguments on facts alone. Characteristically, these liberal scholars also believe that it is liberal democracy that has solved the problem of war, despite the fact that the United States and the United Kingdom are two of the most militarily powerful and warlike states history has ever seen (at least in times past, in the case of the latter).

Democracy, Sovereignty, and Statistics

In his classic *The Twenty Years' Crisis,* E. H. Carr observed that theories of international morality are the product of dominant nations or groups of nations.

> For the past hundred years, and more especially since 1918, the English-speaking peoples have formed the dominant group in the world; and current theories of international morality have been designed to perpetuate their supremacy and expressed in the idiom peculiar to them. . . . Both the view that the English-speaking peoples are monopolists of international morality and the view that they are consummate international hypocrites may be reduced to the plain fact that the cur-

rent canons of international virtue have, by a natural and inevitable process, been mainly created by them (Carr 1946, 79–80).

Advocates of the "democratic peace" would have done well to consider Carr's wise words.

The basic proposition of the "democratic peace" is that democratic states do not wage war on other democratic states (e.g., Doyle 1983; Russett 1993; Weart 1998; cf. Barkawi and Laffey 2001). This proposition is intended as a scientific statement, as if having the force of a physical law. It is based on the intersection of two statistical databases, one that identifies democracies, or liberal states for some authors, and one that identifies interstate wars since 1815. The criteria used for "democracy" are not as straightforward as may seem at first glance, for by contemporary criteria of a universal adult franchise, there were very few democracies before the middle of the twentieth century, making the "democratic peace" not a very impressive or long-lasting observation. As such, some scholars admit as "democratic" states that had a franchise for as few as 10 percent of adult males, while others insist on at least 30 percent (Russett 1993, 15). Given the meaning of the term "rule by the people," it is unclear how a state can be labeled a democracy when none of the women and not all of the men even have the vote.

Identifying interstate war is even more complicated. The "democratic peace" uses a database developed by the Correlates of War project (CoW) at the University of Michigan (Small and Singer 1982). This database makes a fundamental distinction between interstate and intrastate (or civil) wars. The states in question are sovereign states and are defined by juridical criteria, such as legal recognition by other states or membership in the UN or League of Nations. Hence, like Thomson, the CoW database takes sovereignty at face value. A war is deemed to have occurred only when a thousand battle deaths have been suffered. This is an unfortunate mistake, as it defines war with a measure of intensity rather than a substantive conception of what war *is*, as in "organized violence between political entities." The Falklands War, for example, involved only around 970 battle deaths, but that does not make it any less of a war, and CoW includes it in its database despite the shortfall in casualties.

When the databases of "democracies" and of "interstate wars" are compared, the proposition that no democracies have ever fought interstate war with one another appears to be established beyond doubt. As can be seen however, the "democratic peace" is firmly based upon a vision of the world as consisting of sovereign territorial states. CoW has another category of "imperial" and "colonial" wars, which are deemed to have ended when Third World states were granted formal, sovereign recognition. Third World states could be party to civil war or interstate war only after independence. Neocolonial wars or informal empires *within* a sovereign state system are not even considered as possibilities, given the way CoW has defined its databases. That is, CoW's data is *not* neutral with respect to contending approaches to the study of world politics; specific assumptions about war and international relations are built into the data, whereas other possibilities, such as neocolonialism, are excluded. As a result, very obvious features of international relations during, for example, the Cold War, are obfuscated. As Raymond Aron wrote in 1974, "Imperialism in the form of behavior calculated to construct an empire in the classic and political sense has receded from the foreground, while imperialism in the form of a nonegalitarian relationship between states and a great power's will to influence the domestic life and foreign conduct of a small power has, like Descartes's common sense, never been so widespread as it is in our own time" (Aron 1974, 259).

Sometimes this "nonegalitarian" relationship between the United States and Third World states involved "regime change," when a government the United States perceived as communist or leftist came to power or threatened to. Where possible, this regime change was accomplished through covert instrumentalities. For example, the United States wanted to overthrow the democratically elected government of Jacobo Arbenz in Guatemala in 1954. To do so, the CIA raised a mercenary force composed of Guatemalan exiles and Latin and North American soldiers of fortune. This force trained in Nicaragua and invaded Guatemala from Honduras, fighting several actions with the Guatemalan army. The CIA supplemented the invasion force with a small air force of approximately a dozen ground-attack aircraft of World War II vintage piloted by employees of the CIA's proprietary airline, Civil Air Transport (which later became

Air America). These aircraft flew a variety of strike missions that, coupled with the invasion force, finally induced the Guatemalan military, already partly sympathetic to the oligarchy Arbenz had been elected to reform, to overthrow him. A military regime came to power, and opposition forces in Guatemala turned to guerrilla war and away from the ballot box.

The operation in Guatemala was not an abnormal occurrence in the early Cold War, yet it utterly confounds the statistical categories used to produce the "democratic peace." To begin with, although it involved the use of force to achieve political aims and the Guatemalans did fight back, it is not a "war" according to CoW, because only a few hundred were killed. Moreover, and quite bizarrely, some scholars classify the operation as a Nicaraguan and Honduran invasion of Guatemala! (Holsti 1996, 216) This is a reflection of a major confusion. CoW considers a state at war only if its national armed forces participate and suffer casualties, regardless of the degree of clandestine involvement (Small and Singer 1982, 218–19). Accordingly, CoW considers Guatemala 1954 to be a civil war, because "there was no formal American participation in this war, although the CIA armed, trained, and financed the winning rebel force" (Small and Singer 1982, 324). The use of the term "formal" is crucial here, as it refers to legal or official participation in war. But without the "informal" CIA operation—ordered by the legally constituted government of the United States—there would have been no "civil" war. Similarly, Russett writes that the Guatemalan operation was not an interstate war, because it was not "openly fought by military units of the United States" operating in "organized fashion" (1993, 123). Naturally, in a *covert* operation a state does not openly or formally use its official military forces. Rather, CIA operatives hired, trained, supplied, and advised foreign mercenaries. Where necessary, personnel from the U.S. armed forces were seconded to the CIA to operate under cover. In any case, the national identity of the soldiers is not really relevant to determining that this was a *U.S.* operation, which it in fact was. By taking seriously U.S. efforts to conceal its role, advocates of the "democratic peace" are in effect accepting at face value the "plausible deniability" of covert operations in their social scientific analyses, even though everyone is aware that the CIA wholly armed and financed the invasion of Guatemala with the express purpose of overthrowing a democratically elected government. This is just one indication of the machinations necessary to maintain the idea that democracies are peaceful in their relations with one another.

Additional examples could be considered, such as the U.S. covert operations in Iran, Indonesia, Brazil, Chile, and Nicaragua after the elections in 1984. But there is a more important point to be made. The juridical division of the world into the territories of sovereign states makes it very easy to use legal categories to collect and categorize statistics. Very good statistics are available on the "official" deaths of a state's soldiers. The idea of "inside" and "outside" a state makes for a clean distinction between civil and interstate wars. "Democracy," too, is safely relegated behind sovereign borders, conceived merely as elections of heads of government. This is crucial, because an idea like democracy is very subversive. On a world scale, it might imply that the rich and powerful countries—the "Western democracies"—are in fact anti-democratic, benefiting from the horrifying divides of wealth and power that characterize the international economy, for example.

If one accepts a nation-state ontology of world politics, one can collect a variety of statistics and other facts that will validate theories in an apparently "scientific" fashion. However, none of the various definitions and categories of the "democratic peace" get us to the crucial issues. War in the Cold War was fundamentally shaped by nuclear weapons and guerrilla insurgency; these factors ordered war on a worldwide basis. Nuclear weapons not only shunted conflict to the Third World but also placed a premium on the use of clients, allies, and covert operations so that U.S. and Soviet forces never "directly" confronted one another in battle, an event that would have been pregnant with the possibility of nuclear escalation. The real crux of democracy and war was to be found in the numerous "peoples' wars" fought in the formally colonized world as Western powers, and particularly the United States, sought, in many cases, to install authoritarian client regimes friendly to Western interests. Such wars, however, were almost always classified as "civil" by CoW, even though Western and Soviet bloc "advice and support" were often crucial to sustaining both sides. The "democratic peace" addresses none of these relatively obvious and well-known aspects of war and its relation to politics and society around the world during the Cold War. Instead, it helps contribute to the Panglossian view that the Western democracies not only have the best form of government but are also peaceful.

As will be seen in the next chapter, attending to the global and transnational dimensions of war in any given historical period provides a far more reliable guide to understanding than a nation-state ontology of world politics. Said another way, it is necessary to rethink war and the nation-state with the conceptual tools of globalization studies.

GLOBALIZATION AND WAR: BRITAIN, INDIA, AND THE INDIAN ARMY

> That the Indian Expeditionary Force arrived in the nick of
> time, that it helped to save the cause both of the Allies and
> of civilization . . . has been openly acknowledged by the
> highest in the land, from the Sovereign downwards. I recall
> that it was emphatically stated to me by Lord French himself.
>
> —Lord Curzon

Thinking globalization and war together involves combining the central ideas from the first two chapters. Globalization is about interconnection and mutual constitution between different locales and the peoples found there, the "making together" of world politics. War involves interconnections between parties to conflict, interconnections that transform society and politics. To study globalization and war is to attend to interconnections in world politics occasioned by war. This is a massive domain of analysis, but it is delimited somewhat by emphasizing the specific terms previously offered. Globalization draws attention to the intersection of the local and the global, to those points of contact and forms of circulation through which international forces remake the local and, conversely, to how local developments influence the global. A "war and society" perspective leads not to attention to all aspects of war and armed forces but to those interactive aspects that generate social and political change, and to the ways in which social and political context shapes war and armed forces.

The last chapter remarked that the war and society perspective needs to be globalized. Typically, war and society analyses are based on the image of nation-states at war—how was Germany affected by World War I? How did the Napoleonic Wars boost the industrial revolution in Britain? How did the Second World War increase the capacities of the U.S. state? Certainly these are important questions for analysis. But the discussion of globalization in chapter 1 suggested that such questions do not go quite far enough. It was argued that we cannot rely on histories that implicitly assume that places— such as nation-states—developed separately until connected by "globalization." Rather, places develop together through interactive dynamics, cultural, social, political, and economic. These dynamics— and the social processes and structures that set them in train—form a larger "field" of relations or context within which particular territories and populations are situated, and in and through which they develop in distinctive ways. Globalizing the war and society perspective, then, involves attention not only to social transformations occasioned by war in particular countries but also to transregional and worldwide military orders and to historical transformations in the organization and use of force that make possible certain societies, politics, and cultures in different times and places.

For example, the states-system in Europe developed through interactive, continent-wide social, political, and military processes that transformed the feudal order. States arose together, not individually, forming a "multi-power-actor civilization," in Michael Mann's term (1986, 1993). Once particular military and political leaders in early modern Europe discovered how to counteract the dominance of knightly cavalry and build a central state apparatus, it was only a matter of time before others emulated them. A wide-ranging transformation was set in train across Europe, out of which the separate states of France, Britain, and Spain, etc. were eventually formed and consolidated. As suggested in the last chapter, key elements of the developing European financial strength and military prowess relied on the wider world: American gold financed the new armies; Arab sailing innovations helped European ships in unfavorable winds; African and other slaves worked in mines and on plantations; and indigenous armed men protected European colonies and trading stations.

This attention to worldwide or transregional context is a key dimension of a globalized war and society perspective. Broadly speaking, there are two levels of analysis at work. First are the ways in which localities become interconnected with other localities in and through war, shaping and conditioning one another. Iraqi and U.S. history have become bound up with one another in new and important ways since Iraq invaded Kuwait in August of 1990, and even more so since the U.S. conquest of Iraq in the spring of 2003. The actions of Iraqis and others resisting the American-led occupation were centrally implicated in the 2004 U.S. presidential campaign, while the course and outcome of American involvement will have profound consequences for the future of Iraq. Similarly, Spanish participation in the coalition occupying Iraq was in part behind the bombings of public transport in Madrid in March 2004 by Islamic terrorists. The bombings changed the predicted outcome of national elections that occurred a week later. Rather than the incumbent conservative People's Party, which had committed Spain to supporting U.S. policy in Iraq, the Socialists won; shortly after the new government took office, it announced the withdrawal of Spanish troops from Iraq. Events and developments in widely disparate places—Iraq, Spain, the United States—shape and inform one another through relations of war, making them *different* kinds of places.

The second level of analysis concerns not relations between localities directly but between localities and the larger context in which they are situated. Interactions between localities form a larger field of relations, which shapes and conditions peoples and territories on a transregional or even global scale. Here too, relations are mutually constitutive. Developments in particular localities shape the transregional or global context, while that context shapes localities. An example that this chapter focuses on is provided by the colonial British Indian army. The British had at their disposal a "fire brigade" of reliable troops who could meet challenges to British interests from China to the Persian Gulf and beyond, without having heavy recourse to the British army proper and the domestic political and financial difficulties that that might entail. The first level of analysis points to the ways in which India and Britain were shaping one another, and to the "bilateral" connections between India and wherever the Indian army traveled, such as Afghanistan, Iraq, or

China. This second level of analysis, however, draws attention to the reliable "fire brigade" as a crucial piece of the wider British imperial order itself. The Indian army was part of the transregional context within which other localities were situated, and which fundamentally shaped those localities. Resistance to British rule anywhere could be met by Indian or other "outside" troops. This helped determine what was and was not possible in widely disparate places. Philip Mason offers a partial list of expeditionary campaigns launched from India in the last half of the nineteenth century alone:

> There was the Abyssinian expedition of 1868. . . . There were three expeditions to China. Then there was the Third Burmese War, a swift campaign followed by three years of a "subaltern's war" in which small bodies . . . of British or Indian troops pursued in thick jungle Burmese parties whom they regarded as dacoits, or armed robbers, but who might also be looked on as the remnants of patriotic resistance. There was the Second Afghan War and several larger-scale [Northwest] Frontier campaigns, of which the most serious, the Malakand affair, kept the equivalent of four divisions busy for a year; there were expeditions to Aden and to Somaliland, several to the Persian Gulf, to the Lushai Hills, to Sikkim and Tibet (1974, 373–74).

The Indian army was kept very busy maintaining British imperial power over a wide area.

Further examples of this second, global level of analysis are found in the Cold War and after. The United States and the USSR become involved in conflicts in many Third World countries, with all of the "bilateral" war and society relations that implies, as between the United States and Vietnam or the USSR and Afghanistan. However, the second level of analysis points toward the worldwide Cold War order, in which two superpowers vied for allies and influence in the Third World. This meant that Third World leaders could "play off" one superpower against the other to some degree in order to gain aid and other support. A particular kind of politics became possible in many different countries, those of Cold War patron-client relations, which played out differently in particular cases. When the Cold War was superseded by a period of U.S. unilateral military hegemony, the old game of playing off superpowers against one another was over, and American aid levels and interest in Third World countries declined. A different global field was created, in which different kinds of politics became dominant. During the Cold War, the United States sustained authoritarian, corrupt, and economically inefficient Third World regimes for strategic reasons; from the mid 1980s, it was more willing to allow such regimes to be subjected to International Monetary Fund structural adjustment policies and democratic transformation. This new, wider context shaped developments in many countries; it was part of the global field shaping and determining events.

The two levels of analysis bleed into one another in practice but are conceptually distinct. A final example is offered by the new transnational terrorism of the post-9/11 world. The global field within which Western countries are now situated includes the possibility of terrorist attack involving mass civilian casualties, a fact that is shaping developments across the West and elsewhere. Police and intelligence agencies are being strengthened and redirected toward counterterrorism; governments and corporations are backing up key functions and facilities in case they are subjected to attack; civil liberties are under threat; Muslim minority populations live in increasing fear of unofficial and official harassment; and so on. While these developments have their own, local character in particular countries, they are occasioned by a common, wider context—a global field that includes the possibility of certain kinds of terrorist attack.

To explore further these two levels of analysis, and what a globalized war and society approach has to offer, the discussion below looks at the British imperial military system in India, how the world wars impacted on this system, and how it impacted on the world wars, as well as the consequences for Indian nationalism and independence. Throughout, both levels of analysis are attended to—how India and Britain as well as other countries were involved in "bilateral" relations of mutual constitution and the role India and the Indian army played in constituting a wider, global context that shaped developments generally. This chapter develops the general themes of globalization and war, preparing the ground for the remaining two chapters, on culture and war and on the War on Terror.

The World Wars and Indian Independence

In many popular imaginings, India won independence in 1947 from the British through a distinctively Indian, nonviolent political movement led by Mohandas K. Gandhi and the Congress Party. Such an image fits well with a nation-state ontology of world politics, in which "India" exists as a taken-for-granted place, already defined territorially, politically, and culturally. In fact, India and the other successor states to the Raj were constituted in large measure through their international relations, not least in respect of their very borders, which mark the farthest extent of British rule as well as the lines along which it eventually foundered. War plays a prominent role in the international histories of India. Successive waves of conquerors, as well as the armed and other resistances they faced, shaped "India" as cultural and political space. India itself has shaped the wider world in far-reaching and significant ways. This suggests it is necessary to attend to the role of the wider world context in shaping the dynamics of Indian independence as well as to Gandhi and the role of Indian populations in making their own local and international history. It so happens that the world wars and the manner in which the British organized their Indian armed forces played decisive roles in the end of empire in India. Equally, the Indian army played its own world historical role, and not just in securing British rule from the Near to the Far East. In both world wars, Indian manpower sustained the allied cause at crucial junctures in ways largely unrecognized in popular memory, nor in British or U.S. national military histories.

In the autumn of 1914, the small regular British army was exhausted and being bled white. It had fought continuously since August. As the generals tried to stabilize the line in the British sector after the first battle of Ypres, one corps in particular was in desperate need of relief. But there were no fresh, trained British or Commonwealth divisions available. Luckily for the allies, and especially for Paris, some Indian divisions arrived just in time and managed to hold one-third of the British sector until Christmas (Mason 1974, 412–14). Although Indian soldiers had trouble adjusting to the strange climate and to trench warfare, it is unlikely the line would have held without them. It is worth remembering that victory in war is rarely predetermined, yet the outcomes of wars are often of fundamental historical importance. Were it not for the fact that Britain had raised an army in India, the world might have witnessed a German victory in France in the opening months of World War I.

India occupied a constitutionally anomalous position in the British empire. It was neither a dominion nor a crown colony but a separate entity often referred to as the "Indian empire" and colloquially known as "the Raj." It included the territories of present-day India, Pakistan, Bangladesh, Sri Lanka, Bhutan, and Burma. Most of India was governed directly by the British government of India, while the rest, composed of over five hundred princely client states, was regulated by a variety of treaty arrangements, including subsidies to the rajas, many of whom maintained toy armies and other symbols of sovereignty. India was of enormous significance to British power in world politics from the eighteenth century onward: the Indian army served as an imperial fire brigade and strategic reserve of professional troops; arrangements favorable to Britain in trade and investment maintained British economic power even as British industry declined relative to its competitors; and India's strategic location was crucial for the projection of British power in the East. In order to enjoy the advantages of its Indian empire, however, Britain had to retain control. From the end of the nineteenth century, it could only do so in the face of an increasingly well-organized and assertive Indian nationalist movement (see Chandra et al. 1989; Collins and Lapierre 1997; Masselos 1991).

The course and direction of the nationalist challenge to British rule, however, was significantly influenced by international developments, not least the world wars, both of which were watersheds in the history of Indian nationalism (Voigt 1987). Total war involves intensive mobilization of society and economy. Established ways of doing things are overturned and existing patterns and structures disrupted, a situation particularly fraught with danger for colonial rulers. Yet Britain needed to draw on Indian economic and military resources to prosecute the wars. During World War I, Indian industry and agriculture were vital to the British war effort. In August 1914, the Indian army numbered just under two hundred thousand men, most of them long-service, professional volunteers. It would reach a wartime high of nearly six hundred thousand, with approximately 1.27 million men having passed through its ranks by the end of the war. Roughly one man in ten under arms in British and imperial forces in World War I was Indian, and there were nearly fifty thousand Indian soldiers among the 947,000 British and imperial war dead. By comparison, the United States suffered 116,000 dead in the "war to end all wars."

This mobilization of Indian society did not occur without consequences in India. There were food and other scarcities as commodities were shipped abroad, rises in prices and taxes, a clampdown on civil liberties and political activity, and intensive recruitment, involving use of force, for the ostensibly volunteer army. Sympathy for nationalist and revolutionary activities was on the rise, and there was some violence. The use of the Indian army in campaigns against the Ottoman Empire led to an increase in pan-Islamic politics in India. There were widespread expectations that in exchange for India's sacrifices during the war there would be an increase in India's political status afterward, at the least to the level of a self-governing dominion like Australia, New Zealand, and Canada at the time. As an educated Indian fighting in France put it in a letter home, "If we Indians bring back to India the flag of victory which we have helped win for our King George, we shall have proved our fitness and be entitled to self-government."[1]

Instead, the British sought to make cosmetic concessions to self-rule while ensuring that "the substance of British power remained untouched" (Voigt 1987, 12). As the war drew to a close, the British created a legislative assembly and a council with some elected Indian members in Delhi while also giving some ministerial powers to Indians in provincial governments. However, the relative power of the Indians was exposed as hollow as early as March 1919, when the Rowlatt Act was forced through the council in the face of opposition from all elected Indian members. It empowered the Government of India to take severe steps against "sedition," including summary trials, replacing wartime legislation to this effect that had expired. "This act of the Government was treated by the whole of political India as a grievous insult, especially as it came at the end of the War when substantial constitutional concessions were expected" (Chandra et al. 1989, 181).

Indian elites were well aware of the sacrifices India had made for

Britain during the war, and Britain's churlish postwar policy was to change the dynamics of the Indian nationalist movement. "Loyalty towards the Empire, the unquestioned attitude of the majority of Indian nationalists before and during the First World War[2]—even Gandhi did his best to enlist recruits for the Indian Army—could not be taken for granted after the war" (Voigt 1987, 8). Taking advantage of the new militancy in the nationalist movement sparked by the Rowlatt Act, as well as the contemporaneous Indian Muslim outrage at the dismemberment of the Ottoman Empire, Gandhi launched a civil disobedience campaign. Although he intended it to be peaceful, it turned violent in Delhi and the Punjab. In Amritsar in the Punjab, site of the most important Sikh temple, crowds attacked the town hall, the post office, telegraph wires, and Europeans on April 10, 1919. The Indian army was called in, and the city was placed under the control of Gen. Reginald Dyer, who prohibited all public gatherings. But on April 13 a large and peaceful crowd gathered in the Jallianwala Bagh to celebrate a harvest festival and protest the Rowlatt Act. Without warning, Dyer ordered a company of Gurkhas to fire on the crowd, ostensibly to disperse it, although he later said "it was not a question of merely dispersing the crowd, but one of producing a sufficient moral effect, not only on those who were present, but throughout the Punjab" (quoted in Omissi 1994, 218). According to British figures, nearly four hundred Indians were killed and 1,200 wounded, although other estimates ranged higher. The firing lasted for ten minutes, and 1,650 rounds were fired. The nearly one-to-one ratio of rounds fired to casualties testifies to the density of the crowd into which the Gurkhas discharged their weapons.

The massacre at Amritsar became both a symbol and a cause of the upheaval in nationalist, revolutionary, and other political activity that rocked India for the next twenty years, including the mass noncooperation movement of 1920–22 and the civil disobedience campaign of 1930–32. Indians at last achieved some real power through the Government of India Act of 1935, which placed the provinces under elected ministers who controlled all provincial departments, while giving all ministerial portfolios in the central government to Indians, except for defense and foreign affairs. However, British-appointed governors in the provinces retained "special powers" that allowed them to veto bills passed by provincial legislatures or reverse administrative measures taken by provincial governments if they affected minorities, British business interests, law and order, or the civil service. As after World War I, the British sought to make necessary concessions while retaining control of the core bases of their power in India. Lord Linlithgow, viceroy of India from 1936 to 1943, justified the 1935 act as "best calculated, on a long view, to hold India to the Empire" (quoted in Chandra et al. 1989, 448). The Second World War was to help prove Lord Linlithgow wrong; the arrangements of 1935 would not hold India to the British Empire for much longer than a decade.

The course and pace of Indian independence is just one route into the intermeshed history of India, Britain, and the world wars. Historians of Indian independence are often well aware of the role of the wider world, but the focus here is to place these interconnections front and center, to draw our attention to them, to make them the object of analysis. For it is in and through these connections that the wider world works its effects in particular places; conversely, it is through these same connections that India played its role in making the wider world. The next section considers the overall organization of "British" military power in India, how this shaped India, and how it mattered in world history.

India and the Colonial Military Order

It was not mere happenstance that the Punjab was the site of unrest after World War I. The Indian army was not recruited from all over India but from select populations defined as "martial races," many of them living in the Punjab, particularly Sikhs and Punjabi Muslims. The Punjab had a population of approximately twenty million, yet supplied more than half the combatant recruits during the First World War (Omissi 1994, 39; Voigt 1987, 9). Hence, while India as a whole did not supply large numbers of soldiers relative to population, the Punjab certainly did; the war left its mark on Punjabi villages in much the same way it did on British, French, and German villages—many men left and never returned home. The heavy reliance on the Punjab reflected a basic feature of colonial military organization—imperial powers typically relied on ethnic minorities to supply soldiers (Enloe 1980). When the manpower demands of world wars outstripped the normal recruiting patterns, the delicate balance between colonial rulers and colonial society was upset. The complex and dynamic interrelationships between colonial military organization, the world wars, and anticolonial, nationalist politics in India highlight different aspects of relations between the "local" and the "global" that need to be teased out.

At first glance, colonial militaries are paradoxical. Normally, military service is associated with loyalty not only to rulers but also to the political communities from which soldiers are recruited. The soldiers of national armies are often seen as patriots, men and women who serve their countries. However, as mentioned in the last chapter, regular military discipline and training has the ability to produce credible soldiers from any population. European soldiers in the eighteenth century were recruited from the dregs of society; yet, suitably trained, these men became magnificent soldiers capable of laying down their lives for their sovereigns. It is not so surprising that similar techniques worked on men recruited from colonized populations.

As European expansion into the non-European world intensified in the eighteenth and nineteenth centuries, and as Europeans increasingly became direct rulers of colonial territories rather than mere traders, the need for reliable armed forces became ever greater. They were required to protect European trade as well as Europeans themselves, to police local resistance to the European presence, and of course to bring yet further territories and peoples under European rule. European military systems generally proved very effective in the non-European world. Many mistakenly attribute this effectiveness to technology. In fact, Europeans did not acquire a decisive technological advantage until the second half of the nineteenth century, with the introduction of breech-loading and rapid-fire weapons. Before then, many non-European powers, such as the Ottomans, the Sikhs, and the Marathas, boasted powerful armed forces with artillery and rifles. The core of the European advantage was in fact regular military organization itself. Disciplined troops, trained in European style, were not only able to maneuver effectively on the battlefield but were more likely to stand their ground while taking casualties and to advance in the face of fire (Kiernan 1998 [1982],

34–35). As the British expert on colonial warfare, C. E. Callwell, remarks, "Irregular warriors seldom stand to receive a bayonet charge. Only a small percentage of such opponents will meet disciplined troops hand to hand" (1996 [1906], 376). Discipline enabled the Europeans to bring to battle and decisively crush the military power of indigenous rulers. It is this ability and willingness to fight decisive battles, despite the risks and bloodshed involved, that marks the "Western way of war" and its export to the non-European world (Hanson 1989; 2002).

There was no particular reason why the troops had to be Europeans themselves, especially since European troops perished rapidly in many colonies from disease and unfamiliar climate. It was far cheaper to raise and train forces locally, as both the English and the French discovered as they struggled for mastery in India in the eighteenth century. Training, uniforms, invented regimental identities, regular pay, and firm but fair discipline produced credible soldiers from Indian populations just as they did from European ones. This solution created the new problem of retaining the loyalty of colonial soldiers. Colonial rule always involved a small number of Europeans controlling far vaster populations from whom they extracted resources and labor. Arming and training the colonized to provide security was at once an efficient and a risky policy, as the British discovered in 1857 when some of their Indian army mutinied and nearly evicted them from the subcontinent.

By the mid-nineteenth century, the British had been territorial rulers in India for nearly a hundred years, steadily expanding their conquests. They had organized their colonial troops in three armies—the Bengal, the Bombay, and the Madras—but it was the Bengal army that was the strongest and most militarily effective, having vanquished the Sikhs in two hard-fought wars in the 1840s. While the Bengal army was composed of both Hindu and Muslim troops, most of the men were from similar economic and social backgrounds. They were the sons of a landed, high-caste gentry. In a variety of ways, British policy before 1857 began to undermine the status and economic position of these families. Land reforms began to remove their rights to collect taxes from agricultural land. Christian missionaries were actively trying to convert Hindus and Muslims, sometimes even those in the army. Provinces still officially ruled by local rajas were being annexed by the British. The Bengal army was newly designated for general service—meaning its battalions could be shipped far from home, across the seas—stoking fears of caste pollution and separation from families.

These and other factors created conditions in which the men of the Bengal army—from similar backgrounds, experiencing similar tensions—combined, mutinied, and launched a war to throw the British out. The British define 1857 as a mutiny, but Indians argue that the Bengal army was composed of prominent men in their communities who were leading a war of liberation against a foreign conqueror. Many peasants and other civilians joined the fighting against the British. It was a near-run thing initially, but the British defeated the mutinous troops and brutally suppressed the uprising. They did so with British troops, as well as with Gurkhas from Nepal and recently conquered Sikhs from the Punjab.

European military organization played an important role in facilitating British conquest and control of India, as it did in other countries brought under European rule. Soldiers were created out of colonized populations. At the same time, those soldiers often remained in more or less intimate contact with their own societies. Changes in colonial society carried the possibility of unhinging the social basis of the armed forces that European rulers relied upon, as in the years leading to 1857. Dilemmas of this sort were faced all over the colonized world. Each case was different in important, local ways. However, the overall context was that of a transregional colonial military order in which Europeans used a particular organizational technique to constitute armed forces from colonized populations (Kiernan 1998 [1982]). In order to understand the course of events, attention must be directed *both* to the particular local features and to the ways in which the wider context impacts on and shapes those local features.

Having defeated the mutiny, the British turned to the question of reorganizing their Indian forces so as to prevent a recurrence. The question was how to overcome the horns of the colonial military dilemma. If the British recruited from all over India, mixing castes, religions, and ethnicities in the same units, breaking down civilian identities, they risked creating an Indian nation—one that did not exist in diverse nineteenth century Indian society—in their own army. It was felt that such an army might be very difficult to use in internal security duties. On the other hand, were the British to allow a few minority groups to predominate in the army, British rule would become overly dependent on these groups—as with the Bengal army—and there would be no force capable of suppressing unrest among them. The British came up with a novel solution, one that proved quite durable until the world wars (Mason 1974, chap. 13; Cohen 1971, chaps. 1–2).

Colonial armies were excellent examples of the key principle of imperial rule *divide et impera*—divide and rule. In order to rule colonized populations, one gives certain minorities privileged positions in colonial administration and military service, while other groups receive special economic concessions, thus dividing the colonized against one another and the mass of their own people, enabling a few Europeans to rule vast numbers. Why not use this principle to govern colonial soldiers themselves? What the British did after the mutiny was continue to recruit select ethnic groups whom they termed "martial races." However, they carefully maintained ethnic differences in the army, keeping it divided by grouping men in companies of their "own kind" and catering to their religious, dietary, and other customs. As one colonial official argued at the time, it was necessary to "oppose class against class and tribe against tribe" in the army (Lawrence 1859, 229).

The reasoning was that religious and cultural differences among the ethnic groups, such as Sikhs, Punjabi Muslims, Pathans, and Hindu Dogras, would keep them from combining against the British. At the same time, no situation would arise that would render all the different groups of troops simultaneously unreliable, so should there be problems with one class of troops, the others would be available to check them. General Dyer was able to use Gurkhas recruited from Nepal to put down unrest among the Sikhs and Muslims of the Punjab. This application of divide and rule was to be extended right down to the battalion level (a unit of eight hundred or so men). Most battalions would be composed of companies from different ethnic groups, such that a battalion might have a company of Sikhs, one of Punjabi Muslims, one of Pathans, and one of Dogras. Each company was jealous of its position and of any perks and benefits *vis-à-vis* the other companies. The idea was that should there be unhappiness in, say, the Sikh company, members of the Punjabi Muslim company would report the fact to the British officers in order to curry favor. A few British officers were thus able to command a battalion of the colonized, even on internal security duties, with little fear that it would turn against them as had happened to the hapless officers of the Bengal army. The final line of defense was provided by the Gurkha regiments, which were composed only of Gurkhas, and by British troops stationed in India. A Japanese officer tasked to stir up unrest in the Indian army in the Second World War was warned by his superiors: "You must also note that there are different types of soldiers in the British Indian army. British Army headquarters have organized the Indian army in such a skillful manner that there is no possibility of an anti-British movement" (quoted in Ghosh 1969, 18).

The system was further strengthened by giving preferential advantages to the civilian communities from which the "martial races" came, thus tying these communities to British rule and giving the soldiers an incentive to stay loyal. Prime agricultural land was made available to veterans and their families, who consequently would send their children to the colors. Much of soldiers' pay, relatively high in comparison to other forms of employment, was remitted home, ensuring higher standards of living for their communities. Veterans, as well as their families and communities, had easy access to colonial administrative and judicial officials, ensuring a sympathetic hearing for their concerns. Regiments developed long-standing ties with particular communities from which they were recruited, creating personal and familial bonds between army and society. Another aspect of this military system was that the British relied on rural communities for their soldiers. The men arrived hardened by country life, familiar with firearms in many cases, and, most important, largely illiterate and detached from the centers of anticolonial, nationalist politics in the cities. Among the many dimensions of divide and rule at work, then, was country versus town. Urban nationalist agitators worked in fear of peasant lads from rural districts showing up under command of their British officers to put down any unrest with a "whiff of grapeshot." The insulation of the army from the Indian nationalist movement was further strengthened by the fact that the Congress Party was largely Hindu, while the army was heavily Muslim and Sikh.

The wider colonial military order was adapted to local Indian realities to create a durable military system. At the same time, this local system in part constituted the wider colonial order and impacted on other localities. The British Indian army emerged from the mutiny as a highly effective, well-trained, all-volunteer force of professional regulars. Except around the periphery, particularly the Northwest Frontier, India itself was largely pacified. The Indian army could therefore serve as a "fire brigade" to make up for military deficits in other parts of the British empire. For example, a succession of wars was fought in China from the 1840s on in order to open markets and maintain the European position there; very often, Indian battalions were called upon to form expeditionary forces for China. Indian forces were also widely used in the Middle East and in Afghanistan. The British had produced a surfeit of force in India, which they could use when trouble arose elsewhere. The Indian army was thus a crucial piece of a transregional British imperial military order, ensuring British supremacy at a number of different times and places. Lord Curzon, viceroy of India, noted the importance of the Indian army in this respect: "India has for long been one of the most important units in the scheme of British Imperial defense, providing the British Government with a striking force always ready, of admirable efficiency, and assured valour" (quoted in Merewether and Smith 1918, x). The utility of the Indian army was further increased by the fact that it, its expeditions, and even the British regiments stationed in India were all paid for out of *Indian* tax revenue.

The Indian army also had quite a significant impact on Britain itself and the military system there. As American presidents have from time to time discovered, imperial adventures are not always popular with democratic publics (Mack 1975). The public is generally very enthusiastic initially, when it is a matter of sending off small numbers of troops to conquer gloriously and civilize the "natives," but it tends to become rapidly disenchanted when long-term costs in blood and treasure become evident. A durable imperial system can afford to make only moderate military demands on the "home" population. The British empire would never have been so popular for so long with the British public if every single soldier who policed that empire had to be recruited in Britain. Thus the Indian army helped to make the empire politically palatable in Britain by reducing the demand for British soldiers and taxes. In this way, the British were able to maintain a very modestly sized national army while bringing and keeping a large portion of the planet under their control.

Both levels of analysis described in the introduction to this chapter are evident in this discussion of the British colonial military order in India. The ways in which militarized interconnections between India and Britain made each different kinds of places is much in evidence. This first, "bilateral" level of analysis between localities is evident in the British conquest of India, which not only made Britain wealthier but turned it into an eastern land power. Later, as India became a military reservoir for the British empire, Britain was able to get away with only a small professional army (and did until the twentieth century) while its European rivals built costly mass conscript armies. Meanwhile, India was reshaped in significant ways so that it could support its colonial army, not least in terms of the heavy tax burden its population bore, to the detriment of Indian economic development. Ethnic, caste, and rural-urban divisions were deepened, and a variety of expensive welfare policies—such as the agricultural canal communities for veterans—were put in place. The Indian economy supported the very army that held India, and many other colonies, in thrall to Britain. In these and many other ways, the military and other histories of India and Britain were intimately bound up with one another.

The second transregional or global level of analysis was evident in at least two ways. First, European military organization, and especially the fact that it proved "exportable" to the non-European world, was part of a wider context that made European colonial expansion militarily, politically, and financially possible. The regular military institution helped constitute the wider colonial order in which other localities became bound up. The Europeans had a technique whereby they could produce from local populations soldiers who were at least as good as, and often better than, those of the local rulers. This was an important factor in shaping and conditioning developments across much of the non-European world, even as it played out in specific ways in different locales. Once established, the Indian army, and its French counterparts from North and West Africa, itself became part of the wider colonial order, as it provided a check on anticolonial resistance from Iraq to China. Lord Curzon again: "During the past half century, the foreign campaigns in which [the Indian army] has been employed, greatly to its credit and glory, have extended from Egypt and even Ashanti on the West to China on the East, and have embraced most of the intervening countries" (quoted in Merewether and Smith 1918, ix).

Multiple relations between localities and between the local and the global are evident in the military system the British constructed in India. But the broader point is that the histories of widely disparate places cannot adequately be told without reference to this globalized war and society perspective. India and Britain are but one, albeit important, example of this truth. Having described this military system in its colonial heyday, it will now be easier to understand the difficulties it encountered in the world wars, wars of a size and intensity the Indian army was never designed to fight. Before turning to this topic, a sense of the experience of modern war for Indian soldiers will aid understanding of why this experience reverberated so strongly back home.

Indian Soldiers on the Western Front

As a young infantry officer in 1917 on the western front, the German soldier and author Ernst Jünger came under attack from an Indian unit. In his memoir *Storm of Steel,* he described his encounter with the Indians, "who had come far over the sea to run their heads against the Hanover Fusiliers in this God-forsaken corner of the earth" (1985 [1921], 152–53): "A row of shadows rose out of the darkness. Five, ten, fifteen, a whole lot of them. . . . They were fifty metres from us, thirty, fifteen . . . 'Fire!' For a minute the rifles rattled out. Sparks showered up whenever the storm of bullets encountered weapons or steel helmets" (151). Afterward, Jünger surveyed the Indian dead and wounded:

> Their fine bodies were in evil plight. At that short range infantry fire
> has an almost explosive effect. Many had been hit for the second time

76

when they had fallen, so that the track of the bullet passed along the whole length of their bodies . . . . We took the wounded up and carried them to our trench. They cried out as if they were being struck with spears, till the men had to stop their mouths and threaten them with their fists (153).

Two Indian wounded were brought in alive. An obvious move is available to colonial prisoners in metropolitan warfare: they can ingratiate themselves with their captors by disowning their colonizers. Jünger's Indians "strove to win . . . indulgence by shouting out all the time, '*Anglais pas bon!*'"[3] (153) The cosmopolitanism of the encounter, for Jünger, was all the more evident for the fact that the Indians spoke French: "Why these people spoke [it] I have never quite made out" he remarked (153). Jünger's small detachment had beaten back a much larger force of attacking Indians. During the engagement, he had seen off a flank attack led by "a giant with out-stretched revolver, swinging a white bludgeon" (151). Jünger returned to the scene to find the white officer lying amid some Indian bodies: "He had been shot in the eye. The bullet went out through the opposite temple and had smashed the rim of his steel helmet—which is now among my collection of sinister trophies. His right hand still grasped the club, stained with his own blood; his left a large Colt six shooter. There were only two live cartridges left in the magazine" (154–55).

So did one British Indian army officer meet his end. Jünger's anecdote offers some sense of the texture of modern, metropolitan warfare. He also provides a window on some of the cosmopolitan, culture-mixing aspects of the western front, often overlooked in accounts of clashing national armies. In one incident, Jünger engaged in conversation with a British officer across no-man's-land. Heavy rain overnight had flooded the trenches: "The occupants of the trenches on both sides had been driven to take to the top, and now there was a lively traffic and exchange going on in schnaps [*sic*], cigarettes, uniform buttons, etc., in front of the wire" (51). But then a shot rang out, killing one of Jünger's men in rather unsporting fashion and sending all the men on both sides scurrying back to their waterlogged trenches. This prompted Jünger to shout out to the British officer asking why his soldiers had so treacherously killed one of Jünger's. They began in English—halting on Jünger's side—but discovered they could converse more fluently in French. "We said a good deal to each other" (52). The British officer explained that the shot had been fired by the company on his flank, not by his own men. Later, as they talked, a German took a shot at the British officer, nearly hitting him in the head. "Il y a des cochons aussi chez vous," he shouted to Jünger—"there are pigs in your house too" (52). A British and German officer conversing across a battlefield in the language of European elites, expressing upper-class disdain at having to serve among so many unworthies—what could be more cosmopolitan?

As Jünger noted, the Indians had learned some French too. "I know very little English, but I have acquired a lot of French and can speak and understand it well," one Indian soldier wrote home.[4] Indian soldiers were often billeted with French civilians. French nurses attended to their wounds. On leave they traveled to Paris: "What is Paris? It is heaven!" another exclaimed in a letter.[5] Of course, as for soldiers among civilian populations the world over, there was also the possibility of sexual relations. Some worried about losing their religion if they slept with Christian women, but others wrote home asking for love potions to attract them: "The sort of medicine I want is that which would make a woman come to me directly she put it on."[6] Those in charge of censoring the mail of Indian soldiers noted that many French women had written "violently amatory" letters to their Indian lovers (quoted in Omissi 1999, 18). Evidently they did not all need potions.

At one level, these kinds of encounters are similar to those of any soldiers in a foreign locale. At the same time, the cultural and social divide between modern France and the Punjabi countryside yawned before the Indians. They drew comparisons between Europe and India, seeing their homeland as backward and, especially, impoverished. Just as scholars of contemporary cultural globalization emphasize, encounters with cultural difference lead to reassessments of home (Clifford 1997). Indian soldiers identified the differences they thought were holding India back, such as excessive spending on rituals, arranged and child marriages, and poor education (Omissi 1999, 19). "When I look at Europe, I bewail the lot of India" one wrote home.[7] The contrast between the social roles of Indian and

European women was striking to Indian soldiers, especially in wartime Europe, where women were filling jobs vacated by men at the front. "I know well that a woman in our country is of no more value than a pair of shoes and this is the reason why the people of India are low in the scale," commented one.[8] Another sent home the picture of an American female aviator to make a similar point. "I want you to study it and see what the women of Europe and America are doing. . . . The advancement of India lies in the hands of the women," he concluded.[9]

These are examples of a process that Roland Robertson, a sociologist of globalization, calls "relativization" (1992, 26–29). If you are aware only of your local circumstances, you have little basis to imagine things can be different. But as you become aware of the wider world, you can compare places relative to one another, critiquing them and assessing their chances for survival and flourishing in an interconnected world. Indian soldiers were driven to ask, how does India match up to Europe? Such comparison often focused on everyday experiences. Wounded Indians in hospital were particularly surprised that European nurses cleared away the contents of their bedpans, a task reserved for very low caste servants in India. Such simple novelties could draw the attention of acute observers to the role of caste in structuring relations in India. Some novel experiences required less acuity: an Indian soldier commented of French women that "contrary to custom in our country they do not put their legs over the shoulders when they go with a man."[10] Other soldiers compared Indian and European society. They tended to attribute Europe's wealth and what they interpreted as social harmony to extensive popular education. One wrote: "The people of Europe live in ease and comfort simply through education." He resolved to apply the lesson to his own family: "If I live to return, and if God gives me children, I will fashion their lives according to my new ideas."[11]

In many respects, British rule in India rested on the maintenance of traditional religious ideas, illiteracy, and caste division. Ideas about popular education, overcoming superstition, and Indian social and economic development could easily lead to a critique of British rule and to an anticolonial consciousness of the kind that would be much in evidence in interwar Indian independence politics. It is precisely travel and circulation—globalization—that generate this "relativization" and comparison. While small numbers of Indians had long traveled to England for education, World War I was the first occasion on which larger numbers had direct experience of Europe.

Army and Society

In the attack described above, Jünger was impressed with the fallen British officer's physique, his helmet, and his weapons. It would probably not have occurred to him that the dead officer had most likely been a man of some linguistic talent. In addition to English and whatever other European languages he had mastered in his schooling, he would have known Urdu—the lingua franca of the Indian army—as well as the local language and dialect of the particular class of men he commanded. For obvious reasons, the Indian army went to some lengths to teach its officers Indian languages, assigning personal tutors to newly commissioned officers when they first arrived in India. Along with knowledge of language went that of culture. In most battalions of the Indian army, each company was composed of men of a different religion or ethnicity. British officers commanding companies had to learn the religious and cultural practices of their men, how not to offend them, how to motivate them, and how to earn their respect. It was a regular practice to send young officers to their men's home villages to learn about Indian life.

Naturally, the cultural knowledge British officers acquired drew heavily on British images of the martial races, facilitated by ethnographic publications describing each ethnicity, caste, and religion. The British ensured that their Sikh troops, for example, conformed to "what the British conceived was proper Sikh belief and practice" (Metcalf 1995, 127). Nonetheless, this ethnographic knowledge was essential to the functioning of the army. Running a multicultural, multilingual colonial army was not easy; highly trained, experienced officers knowledgeable about cultural "sensitivities" were essential. Such men did not grow on trees, yet they would fall like leaves in the maelstrom of the western front.

Every ingenuity and every conceivable resource were exhausted by the authorities in the attempt to supply new officers to take the place of the fallen. A constant succession of gallant young gentlemen was drafted from India[12] and from home to fill the gaps in the ranks. . . . [E]ven where numbers were forthcoming, there was hardly leisure to establish in the necessary degree acquaintance and confidence [between officers and men] (Merewether and Smith 1918, 474).

In a national army, the fact that an officer was from a different province or state or county than his men was unlikely to make a significant difference, all other things being equal. British officers could command British troops, even those from Wales, and an American officer from Massachusetts could manage with soldiers from Texas. This made it easier for national armies to replace mass losses. But the complex ethnic organization of the Indian army meant that officers, especially the junior officers so important to fighting spirit, became specialists in—and often champions of—a particular class of troops, such as Pathans or Sikhs. Not only did the losses have to be replaced, but they had to be replaced in the correct proportions. This was true for soldiers, noncommissioned officers (NCOs), and officers alike. Pathan troops would be unhappy with Sikh NCOs, while an officer comfortable commanding, say, Gurkhas, would not be familiar with Punjabi Muslims. A battalion with roughly equivalent numbers of four different classes of troops would have to receive replacements equivalent to the losses in each different class or suffer a loss of fighting efficiency. Philip Mason put the point this way: "Where could be found a vast superhuman machine that would spit out a Rajput for every vacant place in a Rajput company, a Dogra for every Dogra? It would have to find officers who spoke Pashtu or Punjabi or Marathi as well as Hindustani, who understood the peculiar traditions of regiments of the most diverse origins" (1974, 341).

The scale of the problem confronting the authorities in India is evident in the casualty rates. Two Indian infantry divisions comprising together approximately twenty-four thousand men served in France for under a year. During this year around thirty thousand replacements were sent from India for these same divisions to replace the killed, wounded, and sick—a casualty rate well in excess of 100 percent over eight months (Merewether and Smith 1918, 478–79). "Regiments which had been accustomed to enlist 75 men per year now found that they needed a hundred men a month in the killing fields of Flanders and Mesopotamia" (Omissi 1994, 38). The remnants of an entire Indian division of twelve thousand men were forced to surrender to the Turks at Kut in April 1916. In seven months' campaigning in Mesopotamia, one battalion absorbed 1,600 replacements, twice its original strength (Mason 1974, 436). In an attack against Turkish forces in February 1917, two battalions lost in a single afternoon sixteen of seventeen British officers, twenty-eight out of thirty Indian officers (known as VCOs—see below), and 988 of the 1,180 men who went over the top (Trench 1988, 84).

The Indian army was at once a tool of imperial control, in India and abroad, and an *object* of imperial control—it was divided and ruled just like the rest of India. What insulated it from Indian nationalism—the heavy reliance on rural Punjabis and the careful maintenance of ethnic division—also made it vulnerable to the high casualties that were the hallmark of modern industrial war. Broadly speaking, two strategies were open to the British authorities in India in dealing with this situation, and both entailed dangers for the future of British rule. One was to recruit intensively among the martial classes, "scraping the bottom of the barrel" in terms of quality—health, stature, intelligence—and resorting to impressment when sufficient numbers were not forthcoming. This was the strategy favored in World War I and was one reason behind the unrest in the Punjab afterward. The other was to open the army to more classes of Indians and to break down partially the ethnic barriers within the Indian army, creating a larger recruiting base and more flexibility in deploying personnel. This strategy was pursued during the Second World War, when the Indian army was expanded to two and a half million men and widespread use of Indian commissioned officers was made. If the first strategy risked alienating those upon whom the British depended for manning their Indian army, the second strategy evoked the very danger British officials had cited when reconstructing the army after 1857—the development of Indian nationalism within the army.

Questions of recruitment highlight the connections between army and society. Armies are in one sense distinct, autonomous institutions bounded off from society in ways symbolized by the fences and guards around military bases. At the same time, soldiers are recruited from civilian society, they return to civilian society if they survive their service, and they generally remain more or less in contact with their families and communities while serving. Because the Indian army relied for its discipline and recruitment on close relations between the army and the communities from which soldiers came, these connections between army and society were further supplemented with generous and lengthy home leave where possible. The relations between army and society are a kind of transmission belt by which the army's experiences can affect the home front and developments on the home front impact the army.

For example, a central issue in relations between armed forces and society is the overall principle structuring recruitment, whether it is one of volunteering or conscription (Cohen 1985). Many commentators have argued that all-volunteer, professional armies are much better suited to imperial warfare and other "foreign adventures," such as interventions in the Third World. For one thing, short-service conscript soldiers are not generally sufficiently trained and experienced for the heavy demands of such warfare. But more importantly, conscription means that ever more families will become directly interested in the politics of such wars, perhaps pressuring political leaders to "bring the boys home." Many other parents and spouses will fear that their children and partners are next in line to be sent far from home to fight wars not perceived to be matters of national survival or even of vital interest.

In order to head off opposition to the Vietnam War among the politically influential middle and upper classes, President Lyndon Johnson exempted college students from the draft, a policy kept in place until 1970. College students played a prominent role in the antiwar movement, many fearing that service in Vietnam would follow graduation and the end of their deferments. One consequence of the prominence of privileged sons and daughters in the antiwar movement was resentment of the movement among the working class and minorities who, less likely to be in college, were more likely to be drafted. Some of them chanted, "End the fucking war and shoot the fucking draft dodgers," a slogan revealing of the complex relations between armed forces, different sectors of society, and the politics of foreign wars (quoted in Cohen 1985, 109). The army's experiences affect society, while events on the home front have impacts on the war front. As protests against the Vietnam War deepened in American society, the morale of the U.S. Army in Vietnam was sapped. As one helicopter pilot remarked, "It didn't help that the anti-Vietnam-war demonstrators were becoming prominent in the news. With the company in a black mood, the protesters' remarks were so much salt in our wounds. No one likes being a fool. Especially if he finds himself risking his life to be one" (quoted in Hynes 1998, 180). Here is interconnection between the home front and a field army half a world away.

In India, this connection between army and society was transnational and colonial in nature. The army's experiences had implications for colonial rule and relations between colonizer and colonized, while developments in colonial society could affect the fighting qualities of the Indian army. During the Second World War, between 1942 and 1944, large parts of India, including those from which the bulk of the soldiers were recruited, suffered widespread famine. The shortage of food and the runaway prices that resulted were compounded by a general wartime economic crisis. News of this famine reached the fighting soldiers through letters from their families and by other informal sources of communication, such as new recruits arriving or soldiers returning from leave. There is nothing quite so unsettling for a soldier, perhaps thousands of miles away, to hear of his family suffering at home—he can do nothing to help them. As such, reports on the morale of Indian soldiers during this period cite the famine as the main anxiety affecting the troops, and not without reason, for it killed approximately three and a half million Indians. A report from the censors of Indian soldiers' letters read: "Conditions in India are producing a progressively demoralising effect."[13] One soldier's relative wrote that "people are dying of hunger and if this goes on for another two or three months, then you won't find a single soul alive in our village."[14] Another soldier, frustrated at his inability to do anything, wrote back "For God's sake don't write me such letters, it drives me mad."[15] Interestingly, though, the famine in Indian society had other effects on the Indian army. The wartime economic crisis was so severe that many Indians volunteered for service seeking regular pay and food. The famine helped make the Indian army in the Second World War the largest all-volunteer force in world history.

The connection between army and society serves as a medium by which events and developments in each affect the other. Of more significance than the wartime famine in India was the process of "Indianization" of the officer corps that began in World War I. Before then, all commissioned officers in the Indian army had been British. An intermediate class of Indian officers, known as Viceroy's Commissioned Officers (VCOs), mediated between the British officers and the Indian soldiers and NCOs. VCOs were long-service soldiers promoted largely on a seniority basis. They were essentially equivalent to very senior NCOs in the British or American armies, such as first sergeants or sergeant majors, and were largely responsible for discipline. However, VCOs did command platoons, a post normally held by junior lieutenants in Western armies. In part because of officer casualties, the British began sending a very few Indians to their military academy at Sandhurst from 1917. After the war, Indian politicians began demanding a more extensive Indianization of the officer corps. They did so because they wanted to transform the colonial Indian army into an embryonic national army officered by Indians. This was seen as a prerequisite to becoming a self-governing dominion within the British empire, like Canada and Australia—and, of course, to independence.

The connection between Indianization and independence was not lost on the British, who resisted these demands bitterly. Moreover, the whole ethos of the Indian army was built around the notion of the indispensability of the British officer. The martial races were seen as dogged, loyal fighters but dim-witted and in need of guidance. Colonial society also had firm race barriers. British officers and colonial officials moved among elite, European society in India and had access to exclusive clubs, where most socializing among whites occurred. An Indian commissioned officer was an anomaly; his race marked him as an outsider, while his King's commission marked him as an insider. A final, and perhaps the strongest, source of resistance was racism. British officers could not stomach serving alongside Indians of equivalent status; indeed, the entire colonial enterprise was built on the notion that the colonized were a lesser form of human. Of the attitude of old colonial hands toward Indianization one Indian officer remarked, "They sat on club lawns, sipped *chota pegs*,[16] viewed with alarm, damned the government, cursed the climate, and abominated the impudent young natives who had the effrontery to consider themselves *pukka*[17] King's officers" (quoted in Evans 1960, 174).

At first the government of India proposed a scheme that would have taken forty-two years from 1925 to Indianize the officer corps, but even this was seen as going too far in London, where Winston Churchill, then colonial secretary, opposed it vehemently. In the end, an "eight unit scheme" was decided upon that restricted Indian commissioned officers to serving in one of six infantry battalions and two cavalry regiments. Even on this scheme, with just eight units to Indianize, it would take twenty-five years. From the point of view of British officers, this scheme had the "advantage" that none would ever have to serve under an Indian officer, as junior British officers were barred from joining any of the eight units. Indian commissioned officers serving elsewhere were encouraged to transfer to one of the eight units. Because about ten Indians a year were being commissioned from Sandhurst by the late 1920s, the eight units were quickly overstocked with Indian junior officers, who had to command platoons while their British equivalents elsewhere in the Indian army were commanding companies. As a retired officer of the independent Indian army and a historian of the Indianization process commented of the eight unit scheme, "This measure was nothing but apartheid or segregation of these officers and units" (Sharma 1996, xiv).

The result could only be a climate of racial tension among the British and Indian officers in the interwar period. As the last British commander in chief of the Indian army was to remark shortly after the Second World War, "[British officers] forget, if they ever knew, the great bitterness bred in the minds of many Indian officers in the early days of 'Indianization' by the discrimination, often very real, exercised against them, and the discourteous, contemptuous treatment meted out to them by many British officers who should have known better" (quoted in Connell 1959, 947). In one battalion, the British second in command regularly yelled abuse at Indian officers in front of the men, a very serious violation of military decorum and injurious to discipline. In another battalion, the British officers conducted themselves more professionally on duty but were hostile to Indian officers off duty, treating them as outcasts and refusing to let their wives dance with them at regimental functions. The officers' mess became a site of racial conflict. Indians argued that curry should be served, while the British insisted on British "cuisine," described by one Indian officer as consisting of "boiled, fried or roasted fish, chicken and scraggy mutton" (quoted in Narayan 1978, 72). Indians resented being forced to speak in English, while everyone argued whether European or Indian music should be played on the radio.

As Indianization progressed, these tensions lessened somewhat. Military life has a number of features that encourage cohesion and integration. Indian officers who were good at sports, could hold their alcohol, and were competent at their duties were likely to be accepted eventually. British officers were often surprised to find that their Indian counterparts were not allowed in many colonial social clubs and supported efforts to allow them in. The officers of one regiment resigned en masse from the Bangalore United Services Club when they discovered their Indian officers were not permitted to join. Early in the Second World War, Indian officers stationed in East Africa for the attacks on the Italians in Eritrea and Abyssinia were not allowed in clubs there; when this was brought to the attention of the British theater commander, he commented, "Who do these bloody people think they are? If Indian officers are good enough to fight for the King, they are good enough to be made members of any Club in the Sudan" (quoted in Narayan 1978, 130). The situation was rectified shortly thereafter when the commander threatened to prevent all British officers from patronizing the clubs.

The ways in which the presence of Indian commissioned officers scrambled the carefully maintained racial categories of colonial society are evident in a revealing story told by one Indian officer serving in the late 1930s. His unit, the 2/10 Baluch, was stationed in Peshawar, and the Indian officers were allowed into the club. However, the wives and daughters of British officers and other officials would get out of the club pool whenever an Indian officer went in. Our Indian officer developed a stratagem: "I collected my chaps, and we got beer and lashings of sandwiches and lay along the edge. When an English girl went in, we went in. And when she got out, we got out. So after a while she got tired of all this going in and getting out, and there was no more problem" (quoted in Fay 1993, 56). In such small, everyday ways, Indian officers were breaking down a variety of barriers, asserting their own rights, and developing confidence. The problem for the British was that none of these things boded well for continued British control of India.

Once the Second World War got under way, processes of racial integration in the Indian army accelerated markedly. There were a number of reasons for this. The Indian army was massively expanded, and of necessity the British started commissioning large numbers of Indian officers. At the beginning of the war there were 577 Indian officers in an army of two hundred thousand. By war's end, there were nine thousand Indian officers, many in senior positions. From a ratio of ten British officers to one Indian officer in 1939, there were by September 1945 only 4.1 British officers to each Indian one. Larger numbers of British "emergency commissioned" officers were needed too. These men were not drawn from the old colonial and Indian army families, as there were too few, but consisted largely of middle-class Britons. They had little direct experience of the empire and had not been brought up in an atmosphere of colonial racial segregation. As a group, they were far less likely to have extreme race prejudice and generally got on with their Indian counterparts. Battalions preparing for war spent a great deal of time away from colonial society and its divisive racial barriers and far more time in remote locations training hard. Under competent leadership, common work and hardship develop strong, comradely bonds, bonds intensified by the actual experience of war and the common danger that meant. As Indian officers proved themselves in battle and rose to positions of real authority, they earned the respect of fair-minded British officers.

During the Second World War, the Indian independence movement continued its activities on a number of fronts. Gandhi and the Congress Party demanded guarantees of independence in exchange for support of the war effort. When sufficient guarantees were not forthcoming, they demanded that the British "Quit India"; Gandhi and the Congress leadership were locked up, precipitating a widespread, if low-level, armed uprising across large portions of India between 1942 and 1944. A Congress radical, Subhas Chandra Bose, very popular with the rank and file of the party, worked with the Japanese and the Germans to raise an independence army from Indian prisoners of war held by the Axis. His efforts led to the formation of the militarily insignificant but politically potent Indian National Army from the large bag of Indian soldiers captured by the Japanese at the fall of Singapore in early 1942.

While worrying for the British, none of these challenges was alone fatal to their continued rule, especially if they could count on their old instrument of control and last line of defense, the Indian army. But the wartime expansion of the army and the incorporation of large numbers of Indian officers, recruited from middle- and upper-class families, meant that this was no longer the case. Generally speaking, these Indian officers offered only a conditional loyalty to the British. As one put it, "Although as Indians we were anxious to win the war against the Germans and the Japanese, we were equally anxious to have the British out of India so that we could be an Independent country" (Kaul 1967, 61). The British also discovered that good Indian officers favored independence. As the commander in chief of the Indian army noted, "It is no use shutting one's eyes to the fact that any Indian officer worth his salt is a Nationalist" (quoted in Connell 1959, 949). An Indian army led in large measure by Indians could never simply revert to being a loyal tool of the Raj. As an Indian brigadier noted at the end of the war, "We knew . . . the British Raj was irrevocably finished. We were impatient for the day when the Indian Army would serve its own country under its own leaders" (quoted in Evans 1960, 230). Meanwhile, the viceroy of India noted in his journal in December 1945, "It would not be wise to try the Indian Army too highly in the suppression of their own people" (quoted in Moon 1973, 197).

Independence came in August 1947, but amid widespread intercommunal violence as the heart of the Raj was split into India and Pakistan. It is a testament to the racially and ethnically integrative character of the military that Indian army units—composed of Hindus, Muslims, and Sikhs—policed to the best of their ability violence among adherents of these same religions, and then divided themselves in orderly fashion as Muslim troops left to form the Pakistani army.

This chapter has sought to capture the various ways in which the histories of the Indian army and Indian independence are international as well as local in nature. The very processes that constitute these histories are inherently transnational; the international is not just a "factor" or an "influence" in some essentially Indian history. The intertwined histories of India, Britain, and the Indian army provide a window on the global context of empire and colonial independence struggles; at the same time, the Indian army and all the transnational social relations it contained played its very important role in creating and maintaining that global context of empire and Western world power. Both India and Britain shaped one another as well as the wider world in profound ways. The history needed to tell this story is a global one, for it is in and through the connections between local and global—globalization—that this history was made. A local or national history can never capture the story.

This chapter has also opened up some of the questions raised by cultural approaches to globalization. New ideas occasioned by travel, the cosmopolitan aspects of colonial armies and wartime military service, and the political and military significance of identity were all highlighted. The next chapter takes these questions farther. International interconnection is generative of new meanings, new ways of understanding and conceiving oneself and others, and new meaningful practices. These meanings are part of what globalizing processes *are,* for it is through meaning—culture—that people experience and act in world politics in diverse ways.

WAR AND CULTURE IN
GLOBAL CONTEXT

Culture is about meaning, about how humans make sense of their lives and the world around them. It is not just about going to the opera (i.e., "high culture"), nor is it simply another dimension of the social, like the economy or the political system, safely left to the relevant academic discipline, in this case anthropology. The reason is that without meaning there would be no society or social relations of any kind. Even apparently straightforward social encounters— say, depositing a check at the bank—require complex sets of shared meanings between bank employees and customers, ranging from the abstract to the mundane. What is a bank? A check? Money? What are appropriate words of greeting? What are the tacit rules of conduct regarding waiting your turn in line? How does a checking account work? If you travel to another country and try to deposit a check, you discover that the shared understandings are more or less different and must be mastered before you can fully function. In the United Kingdom, for example, what is called a "checking account" in the United States is a "current account," and you do not sign the back of your "cheques" when you "pay them in." As a result of these different meanings, practices of banking in the United Kingdom are different than elsewhere. This is one way of saying that meaning is *constitutive* of social relations. Different meanings produce different societies.

So far in this book, globalization has been conceived as interconnections between locales and peoples, and war a form of such interconnection. What is the significance of culture for this way of thinking about globalization and war? It is in and through shared as well as contested meanings that people become conscious of the world, of the place of war in it, and of their interconnections with other peoples and places. One of the important ways in which global interconnections work their effects on society is through altering shared meanings, the meanings constitutive of what society is all about. The Indian soldiers on the western front described in the last chapter provide a good example. Travel to France and participation in the war changed their cultural horizons; it altered who they were, what they thought of India, of Britain and its empire, and so on. When they returned to India, these new understandings shaped how they conducted their lives, leading them to pay special attention to the education of their daughters, to join the independence movement, or to live out their time on a pension as respected war veterans. India became a different place in small and large ways. Culture is the medium or context through which interconnections worked their effects on India and elsewhere (Tomlinson 1999, chap. 1).

A consistent theme of this volume is that it is not sufficient to claim that globalization causes war and other violent conflict but rather that war itself is a form of interconnection. War is not only an example of globalization, it is one of the principal mechanisms of globalization, a globalizing force. If war is central to globalization, then so too are the meanings associated with war. This chapter will show that cultural frameworks derived from wartime experience are fundamental to the ways in which people come to an awareness of the world, of the place of their country in it, and of faraway regions. Especially at the popular level, war is one of the most important ways in which people are drawn out of their local concerns and made aware of their interconnection with other places, places where their sons or daughters may be fighting or where their nation has just suffered a crippling defeat.

Cultural frameworks shaped by war change over time and take different form in various contexts. In this book, globalization is conceived as a category broadly applicable to world politics across the centuries, not just since 1989 or some other recent date. It is necessary to look at the role of culture and war in different periods and different contexts. Of particular interest are constructions and images of the world as a whole and the ways in which different people locate themselves and their communities in this wider context. Three such contexts are addressed below. The first section below looks at the "national-international" world, an international system composed of potentially hostile nation-states, and at the significance of war in popular and elite consciousness of the world in such a setting. The second section focuses on "North-South" constructions of the world, looking at how war and the military shape constructions of "advanced" and "backward" peoples, as in notions of the "West versus the rest" or the First and Third Worlds. The third develops this line of thinking further, introducing the notion of military Orientalism, the ways in which constructions of the South as backward inform the military strategies pursued by Western powers in the non-European world. When these strategies go awry due to underestimation of the "natives," cultural crisis can ensue in the West. A discussion of the relations between American identity and the wars in Vietnam and Iraq offers an example. The fourth and final section is devoted to the place of war in consciousness of humanity as a political and ethical concept, as for example in expanded notions of "human rights" and the idea of a United Nations Organization that followed the collective human catastrophe of the Second World War.

Throughout, the chapter will engage Roland Robertson's important claims about globalization and culture (1992). Robertson argues that globalization is something relatively new, but he does so primarily on cultural not technological grounds. He argues that with the Age of Exploration and European imperial cartography, a genuinely global image of the world was made available to humanity. People became conscious of the world as a single place, as a finite globe, in ways not possible beforehand, when local maps had ended with dragons or other beasts around the edge. Over time, this consciousness of the world intensified and developed, as in contemporary concerns about global environmental crisis. This chapter seeks to "militarize" Robertson's insight by integrating war-related cultural phenomena.

War and Culture in a National-International World

"Globalization" is typically conceived as corrosive of the nation-state. A world organized around sovereign nation-states—a "national-international" world, in Shaw's terms (2000, 27–30)—is what globalization is supposedly replacing. The discussion of globalization in chapter 1 challenged this view in a couple of ways. One was to emphasize the role of states as agents of globalization as well as of globalization as a source of transformation of the state. Another was to suggest that one of the great advantages of the globalization concept was that it drew attention to the "thick" set of social relations that constitute world politics even in a world of nation-states. That is, rather than seeing states as self-contained and self-organizing behind sovereign borders, as discrete and separate entities, this approach conceives states and societies as embedded within and constituted out of all manner of international relations of connection and constitution, as in the case of Britain and India and the world around them.

Within such a perspective, there is no necessary opposition between nation-states, or other kinds of states, and globalization. Not only is there no opposition, but important cultural connections between nation-states and globalization come to light. In an important collection of essays, Akhil Gupta and James Ferguson raise the question of "place making" (1997). How is it that "German" culture comes to be associated with a portion of the earth's surface identified as "Germany," upon which people known as "Germans" live? Answers to such questions are complex; they include economic and political relations, language and literacy, as well as centuries of war and diplomacy. Gupta and Ferguson call the processes by which particular cultures and territories become associated with one another "cultural territorializations." Their key point is that territorializing a culture can only occur through constant interaction with the wider world. As anthropologists, they are concerned to critique a vision of the world as originally consisting of disconnected, separate peoples, each with its own original, unadulterated "culture," only later coming into contact with different peoples. Their work draws attention to the relational character of nations and other political identities. Nations come into existence in a cultural and social field of *other* nations and collective identities.

Gupta and Ferguson draw a telling example into service, that of the "Kalahari bushmen," often constructed as a primitive people with their own way of life protected by the isolation and vast distances of the Kalahari Desert (1997, 42–47). How did "bushmen" come to be the "Kalahari bushmen," they ask? It turns out that for as far back as there is evidence, those known as the "Kalahari bushmen" were in continuous interaction with others and that complex political and economic relations linked the Kalahari with the wider region before, during, and after colonialism.

> It is not possible to speak of the Kalahari's isolation, protected by its own vast distances. To those inside, the outside—whatever "outside" there may have been at any moment—was always present. The appearance of isolation and its reality of dispossessed poverty are recent products of a process that unfolded over two centuries and culminated in the last moments of the colonial era (Wilmsen quoted in Gupta and Ferguson 1997, 45).

It is through interconnection with others that "bushmen" came to be "Kalahari bushmen." Gupta and Ferguson conclude that the process of producing cultural difference—between Germans and British, for example—"occurs in continuous, connected space" within "a socially and spatially interconnected world" (1997, 45). If this is true of the "bushmen" and those around them, then it is certainly so in the dense cockpit of Europe.

What Gupta and Ferguson call "continuous, connected space" is what is termed the "thick space" of interconnection and mutual constitution in this book. There is no opposition between the globalization concept and distinct entities in world politics, such as nation-states; these entities are formed through processes of connection and constitution. Gupta and Ferguson are making a similar point with respect to cultural identities, which we are so used to thinking

)f as separate and distinct from one another. The question now be-
omes: What is the role of war and its associated cultural processes
ι the making of national and other identities?

In his classic statement *Writing Security,* David Campbell argues
that the representation of foreign danger is a key moment in national identity construction and transformation (1992). The perception that "we" are under attack leads to concern with who "we"
are and with who "they," the enemy, are. Conceptions of the "self"
require imaginings of an "other," and danger is an incitement to define the self against the other. In speaking of the communist threat
during the Cold War, American officials consistently emphasized
the distinction between the "free world" led by freedom- and God-
loving America and a "slave world" led by the atheistic, totalitarian
Soviet Union, which was intent on world domination. Representing
the Soviet Union as a threat and describing it in ways that were the
perceived antithesis of American identity served to (re)produce
dominant notions of what it meant to be an American and what
the United States stood for in world politics. At the same time, these
notions worked to discipline "un-American" Americans at home,
most famously in the McCarthyite Red Scare and the investigations
of the House Un-American Activities Committee. For example, to
have communist or socialist political beliefs, or to be a radical trade
unionist, was considered un-American and possibly pro-Soviet, despite the guarantees of freedom of speech and conscience in the U.S.
constitution. As Gupta and Ferguson comment, "'Community' is
never simply the recognition of cultural similarity or social contigu-
ity but a categorical identity that is premised on various forms of
exclusion and constructions of otherness" (1997, 13).

Identity construction in the face of perceptions of danger and
threat thus has a dual nature, serving both to define a dominant
identity and to "normalize" unruly people at home. As President
Woodrow Wilson and others in favor of taking the United States
into World War I sought to mobilize public opinion, they resorted
to branding their critics as "disloyal." In a speech to the Daughters
of the American Revolution in autumn 1915, Wilson called on all
"loyal" Americans to assail "disloyal" critics of his foreign policy,
suggesting that the loyal "haze" the disloyal, as in college fraterni-
ties. A disloyal citizen was defined by the president as one "who is

not to the very core of his heart an American" (quoted in Karp 2003 [1979], 239). The obvious implication is that "real" Americans supported Wilson's policies, calling into question not only the loyalty but the very identity of those who opposed entering the war. Wilson was playing on the specter of "hyphenated Americans," specifically "German-Americans." In this way, constitutionally legitimate criticism of the president's policies by American citizens could be branded un-American and pro-German. When a German-American audience cheered a non-German speaker who had criticized Wilson's prowar policies for betraying the American people, who were in fact overwhelmingly against going to war with imperial Germany, the prowar New York *World* newspaper reported that this kind of "disloyalty" was the greatest threat to America since the Civil War (quoted in Karp 2003 [1979], 238). As Shaw comments, "In a national-international world, antagonistic international relations reinforce separated nationalities" (2000, 28). But it is important to recognize that the divisions between these "separated nationalities" and other identity groups run both within and between nation-states. The role of war in shaping national identity and in popular imaginings of the world is further explored below in the discussion of Vietnam and Iraq and in the next chapter on the War on Terror.

War and Globality in a National-International World

The constitution, transformation, and normalization of national identities through representations of threat and danger is one way of thinking about globalization, war, and culture in a national-international world. A problem with using the globalization concept as a stand-in for the "thick space" of international relations is that a focus on the genuinely "global" can be lost. There is a difference between relations of "transregional interconnection"—such as between Europe, Africa, and the Americas in the early modern period—and a truly *global* stretching of social relations. In important respects, globalizations are always partial in terms of scale and consequences. Even the "global economy" is mainly centered on North America, Japan, and Western Europe. Equally, arguments about the development of a *common* global culture or society are overdrawn. However, as Robertson argues, there is a very important cultural sense in which globalization is genuinely global (1992). Ever since European explorers circumnavigated the globe, knowledge that planet Earth is a single, delimited, global space has spread ever more widely. People in China may be culturally distinct in diverse ways from many people in, say, Utah, but most humans with a modicum of basic education know that the globe is a finite space composed of different peoples and territories.

Robertson's argument is that relatively long-term processes of time/space compression increasingly make the global the frame of reference for human thought and action. It is in large measure on this *cultural* basis that he argues that "globalization" should be distinguished from mere transregional interconnectedness (Robertson 1992, 182–83). Societies and cultures became globally "contextualized," reflexively comparing their own ways to others, a process Robertson calls "relativization" (Robertson 1992, 26–29; Turner 1994, 111). Japanese modernizers in the late nineteenth century, for example, were acutely aware of other models of modernization, such as Germany and the United Kingdom, on which they based their new army and navy, respectively. During its economic boom years in the second half of the twentieth century, Japan itself became a model of economic development for others to emulate (Robertson 1992, 85–96).

Globalization does not necessarily produce global sameness but rather reflexive awareness of one's location in globalizing and modernizing processes as well as of one's prospects relative to others. "*Globality*—defined in the immediate context as consciousness of the (problem of) the world as a single place—appears increasingly to permeate the affairs of all societies and multitudes of people across the world" (Robertson 1992, 132). For Robertson, the compression of the world can lead to "an exacerbation of collisions between civilizational, societal and communal narratives" (1992, 141). Robertson here maps out possibilities for a theory of contemporary globalization and conflict, which locates ethnic assertion and violence within, rather than against, globalizing processes (e.g., Appadurai 1996, chaps. 7–8). Contemporary efforts to assert a local, "traditional" ethnic identity in the face of the global are an aspect of globalization, not a countervailing trend. "*Acting* (and thinking) globally is increasingly necessary in order make the very notion of locality viable" (Robertson 1992, 172).

For example, many indigenous peoples and ethnic minorities have formed the Unrepresented Nations and Peoples Organization, based in The Hague; it is one of several such organizations.[1] In order to protect local "cultural rights," peoples had to organize internationally. Indigenous Latin Americans acted similarly in the face of threats to their rights and localities, as Alison Brysk shows in *From Tribal Village to Global Village* (2000). The desire for a local identity and the search for a home are themselves globally diffused ideas that arise from awareness of difference and in reaction to modernization and rationalization processes. Organizing in order to secure a homeland is not necessary until that homeland disappears through, say, colonization or economic dislocation. The loss of one's homeland becomes all the more apparent when one learns that other indigenous peoples, as well as other kinds of communities, have their own homelands. An interest is then taken in how others (re)acquired their homelands, and in how one might do the same.

At the same time, for Robinson these processes prompt concern about humanity as a whole. Industry and science and their consequences for modernity, in particular the possibility of the destruction of humanity through nuclear war, global warming, or some other apocalyptic scenario, increase fears for the fate of humankind. Different ways of organizing politics, society, and economy are assessed relative to one another, as people become reflexively aware of alternatives and their potential global consequences. "Humanity" and the "world as a whole" become increasingly salient categories for human thought and action. But for Robertson, to be conscious of the world as a single place does *not* mean that there is a shared response to the problems posed, or even a shared analysis as to what those problems might be.

What is the place of war in Robertson's concept of globality? Cultural frameworks and understandings produced in and through war and military service are integral to the ways in which people experience their everyday lives and situate their localities in the wider world. The dependence of national identities on representations of threat from other nations is one way in which this is so. Robertson draws our attention, however, to a *world* of nation-states. National states and societies were globally consolidated in a world organized along national-international lines, an international system of sovereign nation-states. A global discourse concerning what it is to be modern and to have a modern society took shape around the nation-state. A basic aspect of this awareness of other societies in the global field—"relativization" in Robertson's terms, comparing your society relative to others—is consciousness of relative military power. Both elites and the mass of a population are often acutely concerned with their nation's relative military power, as, for example, in the United States and the Soviet Union during the Cold War. An "arms race" is only one of the historically pervasive consequences of such awareness and constitutes one form of military interconnection between societies.

Over the course of the nineteenth century, European and other powers made assessments of the "balance of power" largely in military terms. They sought advantage by increasing their forces as well as adopting new military technologies and organizational forms. In 1889, for example, the Royal Navy began a major building program justified by the notion of the "two-power standard," the idea that the Royal Navy had to be equal or superior to the combined forces of the next two largest navies, an excellent example of military consciousness of the world as a whole (McNeill 1982, 275). The 1889 program was in part inspired by a French naval buildup begun in 1888. Over the next two decades, British admirals became concerned about the Russian, Japanese, U.S., and, of course, German navies as well, and vice versa. Naval consciousness of the world took more explicit form with the publication of Capt. A. T. Mahan's *The Influence of Sea Power upon History* in 1890. Mahan argued that national prosperity depended upon a battle fleet to control the seas and secure trade routes to colonies and markets, claims that served admirals well in efforts to build up fleets in all the major naval powers.

If the late-nineteenth-century naval race gives some indication of military forms of "relativization" for elites, it also points to the powerful popular cultures of nationalist militarism that undergirded military preparedness. In both Britain and Germany, navy leagues agitated for further naval armament. Popular "jingoistic" awareness of relative military power and national military preparedness is one consequence of the link between danger and national identity. Numerous aspects of culture and society can be seen as relevant to military competition with other nations. The Boer War exposed the poor health and stature of working-class male youth in Britain relative to the hearty and rugged Boers, leading to public-health initiatives motivated by the need for cannon fodder of sufficient height and strength.

Military failures abroad could lead to cultural crisis at home. American prisoners of war (POWs) who voluntarily chose to remain in China after the Korean War provoked a crisis of confidence in American society over the strength and willpower of American boys in the face of communist "brainwashing" techniques (Biderman 1963). It was felt that only brainwashing could explain why American POWs would not choose to return home when offered the opportunity. One result was concern over "momism," the idea that American mothers were mollycoddling their sons, producing "momma's boys" who could not stand up to the rigors of war against communists. Childhood, it was argued, should become a kind of basic training, and much advice for parents was produced along these lines (Carruthers 1998). The outlandish and infantile warrior masculinity that characterized important segments of American popular culture in the 1980s, as in the Rambo film trilogy, can in part be seen as a result of the shock of losing in Vietnam, of which more below (Gibson 1994; Jeffords 1994). War, consciousness of the wider world, and the interactive processes that follow, are inherent in these "national" cultural phenomena.

The North-South Distinction

So far, we have attended to the role of war and culture in the formation and transformation of national identity as well as to military consciousness of the wider world—of the relative balance of power, of how the martial qualities of one's own nation measure up to the Japanese or the Prussians or what not. There is another way in which the world as a whole is envisioned, one in which war plays a large but often unappreciated role. One of the most pervasive ways of seeing the world is in terms of a distinction between an "advanced," modern world—the global "North"—and a "backward," underdeveloped world, the global "South." This distinction is spatial, in that the North and South are conceived as different places, even though parts of cities and impoverished rural areas in the North are more akin to the Third World while the "advanced" portions of Southern economies are seemingly part of the First World. The distinction is also temporal, in that the South is considered historically "behind" the North. Robertson characterizes the distinction between North and South as "geotemporal" in nature (1992, 151). Roxanne Doty identifies the following clusters of meanings around each pole: civilized, rational, and sovereign in the North versus uncivilized, instinctual, and dependent in the South (1996, 46). Naturally such distinctions between North and South take different historical and contemporary forms. The question for us is that of the role of war and its cultural construction in maintaining and transforming visions of a world composed of North and South.

The oldest form of the distinction between North and South, advanced and backward, is probably that between civilization and barbarism, perhaps first invoked between settled agricultural peoples and surrounding hunter-gatherers. Such distinctions encompass all dimensions of the social, as Doty makes clear. The "barbarians" lack learning, proper religion, civilized habits, and even appropriate clothes as compared to the putatively more advanced peoples. Warlike themes are not only ubiquitous in such constructions, they are central; the barbarian is almost always represented as warlike, as capable of pure, unreasoning violence. Such barbarians have threatened civilization from Roman times, when blond, axe-wielding giants from Germany unsettled the sleep of Roman children, to our own, when the figure of the "fanatical" Islamic suicide bomber haunts the West.

Force and war were central to the expansion of European powers into the non-European world from the sixteenth century onward. In cultural constructions of a world divided between Europe and its colonies, warlike imagery figured prominently. In his famous poem "The White Man's Burden," Rudyard Kipling represented "natives" as half child and half devil. The notion that they are children leads naturally to the idea that they require European guidance and tutelage in order to become modern, independent, and free—the moral burden of imperial power. The notion that they are half devil implies that the natives are not only potentially irrational, and so might resist such tutelage, but also dangerous. As Kipling puts it in "Fuzzy-Wuzzy,"[2] "You're a pore benighted 'eathen but a first-class fightin' man." Eliding the realities of domination and economic exploitation that characterized colonial rule, Kipling constructs colonial war as a species of humanitarian war. The phrase "savage wars of peace" was first used by Kipling in "The White Man's Burden." Natives-cum-devils must be defeated by force so that natives-cum-children can be civilized peaceably by the well-meaning Europeans.

Kipling's way of representing colonial war is historically pervasive and has continuing significance. Some important points need to be made. If we focus on the economic dimensions of imperialism, or of North-South relations in our own day, we are struck by the horrifying divide between a world of plenty and power—the North—and one of tremendous suffering and need, the South. However, if we construct the issue as one of dangerous barbarians in need of civilization versus rational, modern Europeans willing to sacrifice and fight in order to civilize the barbarians, the economic realities tend to fade from view. We are left with an exciting and adventurous morality tale in which a few disciplined Western soldiers fight off hordes of "half-devils" in exotic, tropical locales, and do so in the name of justice and humanity. In popular media and elsewhere, colonial war was most often represented in these terms, as in the *Boy's Own Paper,* adventure novels, and other publications, as well as radio and film produced in Britain during and after the empire (Mackenzie 1986).

That images of civilizing, colonial war recoup realities of domination and exploitation is a point with great relevance today. With the end of formal imperialism in the decades after World War II, colonies became sovereign states and, apparently, full members of the "national-international" world. Yet both in terms of political and economic relations, as well as in representations of danger and war, the old imperial distinctions between a civilized and an uncivilized world often reasserted themselves. Instead of a "white man's burden," there was "development" and "modernization" in which the global South sought to "catch up" to the global North, which provided aid and expertise (Escobar 1995). North-South distinctions overlaid a world apparently composed entirely of sovereign states.

The North provided the image of the modern, advanced, fully developed world to which all should seek to aspire, despite the horrors of the world wars, the Holocaust, the nuclear arms race during the Cold War and the continuing economic exploitation of both nature and other peoples. States in the global South were seen as "less developed countries," when it might reasonably be suggested that their citizens had much to teach those in the North. As Joas comments, Western "myths of progress lose all their credibility" in the face of the twentieth century's history of violence (2003, 11).

In other versions of the North-South distinction, Third World states are seen as not "real" states, as lacking in powers of governance, in national cultural cohesiveness, and so on—as "quasi-states," in Robert Jackson's term (1990). With the end of the Cold War, some of these quasi-states once again took on dangerous hues. The primary threat to the West was seen as emanating from "rogue" states, Third World states in which the "half-devil" had become dominant, as in the case of Saddam Hussein's Iraq. The U.S. military in the 1990s had its own "two-power standard," in that it prepared for the eventuality of having to fight two such rogue states at once (Klare 1995, 28–34). Other states were seen as "failed" states, taken over by a variety of cultural, economic, and political pathologies, such as ethnic and tribal conflict, warlords, and so on, all of which could spread to and destabilize neighboring states. Texts such as Robert Kaplan's influential *The Coming Anarchy* (2000) and Martin van Creveld's *The Transformation of War* (1991) represented the underdeveloped, backward South as dangerous, barbaric, and anarchic, a place where law and order had broken down into a state of nature, contrasted with the order, security, civilization, and progress found in the North. The systematic *connections*, historical and contemporary, between Northern wealth and Southern poverty and instability are not foregrounded; instead, the problems are blamed on the failings of those who live in the global South. While constructions of the North-South distinction such as Jackson's and Kaplan's mention the role of the colonial legacy in shaping a world with such horrifying divisions of wealth and power, they do not generally dwell on it (cf. Davis 2001). In this way, the utility of tropes of war and danger in eliding economic realities—for example, the net transfer of wealth from South to North, which continues to the present day—is once again evident.

Nowhere is this more so than in the debates around humanitarian intervention in the 1990s, as for instance in the form of UN peacekeeping missions. The notion that the West should pay reparations to the Third World for colonial and neocolonial economic exploitation has very little political traction in Europe or the United States. However, the idea that the West should "intervene" (in the terms of this book, the West has always already "intervened," in numerous ways) with military forces to prevent ethnic conflict, tribal massacres, or genocide is an idea that has wide support across liberal opinion. Here again, the idea of the West as a civilized, humane force in the face of the "half-devils" of the Third World occupies far more attention than the economic issues that arguably lie at the heart of much violence and instability in the global South (e.g., Hoogvelt 2001; Reno 1998). Poverty in the global South is directly linked to the economic policies of the North, such as European and U.S. agricultural subsidies. Certainly the West should intervene to avert genocide if it can. But here again images of civilizing, humanitarian war tend to dominate and shape our constructions of the North-South divide in continuing and important ways while averting our attention from the North's continuing economic exploitation of the South.

The United States and the United Kingdom invaded Iraq in the spring of 2003 for the announced purposes of disarming the devil Saddam—who turned out to be not very well armed—and civilizing his benighted children by turning the country into a modern democracy. Much political debate in the West focused on whether or not Saddam had weapons of mass destruction (i.e., was he dangerous?) and on whether it was possible, particularly under the clumsy guidance of President G. W. Bush's administration, to "civilize" the "children" of Iraq, who happened to live on the lands of the world's oldest civilization. The economic dimensions of the conflict, principally those involving Western control over the most important natural resource of all, were often seen as conspiracy theories held by those on the fringe of reasonable debate, such as the filmmaker Michael Moore or the longtime critic of American foreign policy Noam Chomsky.

The question "Did the United States really invade because of oil?" is somewhat misplaced, however. It is most likely the case that ensuring Western control over oil—say, by the creation and maintenance of friendly regimes in the region—is seen by U.S. elites and others as in the long-term interests of *both* the Middle East and the West. It is the West that has the appropriate model of liberal democracy and capitalism that in turn ensures economic development for the world. Thus, "appropriate arrangements" for the production and sale of Iraqi oil can be described, with a straight face, as part of the West's civilizing mission. There is no need for a conspiracy behind "humanitarian" propaganda, because in and through the North-South distinction American elites believe they are working for a better world for all, even when, indeed especially when, this involves invading countries from time to time.

It is nearly always the case that Western military action in the non-European world is represented as a species of "humanitarian war," warfare that seeks to liberate and civilize. Western self-interest is occluded among tropes of civilization and barbarism. As one British general remarked before a war of conquest in India in the nineteenth century, "We have no right to seize Scinde, yet we shall do so; and a very advantageous, useful humane piece of rascality it will be!" (quoted in Featherstone 1992, 16). That seizing Scinde was in British interests is clear by the comment that it would be "advantageous." Even though doing so is a form of "rascality," violating previous treaties, it was still seen as "humane." As with President Bush's invasion of Iraq, even when the West violates its own rules it does so for the highest of motives. There is a supposed harmony between Western interests and humanitarian purposes. America could defend itself from terror *and* install democracy in the Middle East by invading Iraq. In his second inaugural address, President Bush claimed that "America's vital interests and our deepest beliefs are now one."[3] As E. H. Carr remarked of the defenders of the British Empire, they "have been particularly eloquent supporters of the theory that the maintenance of British supremacy is the performance of a duty to mankind" (Carr 1946, 76).

This last discussion has focused mainly on how the West constructs the non-European world, and on the role of war and the military in these constructions. North-South war has been a historically pervasive category of conflict, whether during the era of European imperialism, the Cold War, or the humanitarian interventions of the 1990s. With the War on Terror, the primary threat to the West is now seen as emanating from the global South, and as suggested above, imperial representations of the "natives" and colonial war are once again being drawn into service (Gregory 2004). What is the effect of these representations on the West? The central theme of this book has been the *interactive, interconnected* nature of world politics. What happens when the "natives" reject "civilization" or the supposedly superior, modern Western armies fail to defeat the barbarians? What are the consequences for culture and politics in the West in such circumstances?

Military Orientalism

Edward Said's classic *Orientalism* dealt with the body of knowledge through which Westerners came to know and describe the Orient (1979). A crucial theme was how "the Orient has helped to define Europe (or the West) as its contrasting image, idea, personality, experience" (Said 1979, 1–2). On the one hand, Orientalism was a body of knowledge essential to Western dominance and authority over the Orient. On the other, Orientalism entailed a set of comparisons in which the West was privileged, as in the North-South distinction, to which it is very closely related. The West is defined in terms of rationality, progress, democracy, and economic development, qualities in which the Orient was always found lacking (Turner 1994, 22). The West defined itself against the Orient; it required the Orient in order to be the West. As Said comments, Orientalism has less to do with the Orient than it does with the West (1979, 12).

Within the discourse of Orientalism, the West is always in a superior position. Orientalism "puts the Westerner in a whole series of possible relationships with the Orient without ever losing him the relative upper hand" (Said 1979, 7). What is so in discourse is not always so on the battlefield. In 1896, the Italians mustered one of the most powerful colonial expeditionary forces ever seen in Africa in order to conquer Ethiopia. It was composed of sixteen thousand Italian and colonial troops and fifty-two artillery pieces. At Adowa, on March 1, 1896, the entire force was surrounded and wiped out by the Ethiopians. Some 262 Italian officers and four thousand Italian soldiers were killed, along with almost all of their colonial troops in this single greatest military disaster in European colonial history (Mockler 2003 [1984], xxxix–xxxxii).

The consequences of this defeat for Italy extended beyond the frustration of colonial schemes of conquest. For one, Prime Minister Francesco Crispi's government fell. Moreover, Italian identity, as with Western identity generally, was based on the superiority of Europeans over natives. How could this identity be reconciled with defeat at the hands of the inferior? In order to preserve Orientalist constructions, images of Ethiopia had to be altered in a positive direction. Most absurdly, in order to recoup in imagination the ignominy of being defeated by black men in reality, the view was propounded that Ethiopians were in fact Caucasians (i.e., white) darkened by exposure to the equatorial sun. Harold Marcus, a historian of Ethiopia, describes further transmutations in representations of Ethiopia in the West after the victory at Adowa:

> Whereas previously Ethiopians shared sloth, ignorance, and degradation with their African brothers, they suddenly became energetic, enlightened, and progressive. The Orthodox church, often reviled by visiting white clerics as debased and corrupt, now was seen as a proper vehicle of the Holy Spirit and the true keeper of Ethiopia's national spirit. Menelik [emperor of Ethiopia], earlier regarded as a barbarian princeling, became the epitome of monarchical virtues. . . . The Ethiopian army, hitherto composed of a cowardly rabble, was suddenly pictured as a magnificent force of heroic marksmen (2002, 100–101).

As Said reminds us, however, Orientalism is mostly about the West. Refiguring the Ethiopians as worthy opponents could not fully repair wounded Italian pride. Precisely because Orientalism informs European colonial ventures, when those ventures meet with defeat there is a possibility for a kind of cultural "blowback" (cf. Johnson 2000). How do Orientalist categories inform Western strategy in the non-European world? What are the consequences for society, culture, and politics in a Western power that has suffered defeat in the non-European world? These are the core questions of military Orientalism. Adowa remained a sore point for the Italians, and restoring Italian greatness as well as expanding its African empire were important and popular planks in Benito Mussolini's rise to power. He sought to repair the stain on Italy's honor with his invasion and conquest of Ethiopia in 1935–36, one of the key events on the road to World War II in Europe.

Military Orientalism identifies a linkage between Western military strategies in the non-European world and constructions of Western identity. The assumed superiority of the West is placed at risk in battles against supposedly inferior, irrational, weak, and uncivilized opponents. When these opponents fail to be defeated as expected, there are cultural as well as political and military consequences. This interconnection between strategy and identity, conflict and culture foregrounds the interactive dimensions of war. Societies become interconnected through the medium of war with effects that range widely in time and space. In order to explore military Orientalism further, as well as take a more fine grained look at the relations between war, culture, and identity, the following turns to two of America's key engagements in the non-European World: Vietnam and Iraq.

From Vietnam to Iraq

The Tet offensive in early 1968 is one route into the intertwined, global histories of the Vietnam War and proved to be a key moment in American politics and culture. It occurred three years after the introduction of American ground combat forces into South Vietnam. The United States had claimed steady progress during those three years. At the end of 1967, the American commander, Gen. William Westmoreland, reported that the "friendly picture gives rise to optimism for increased success in 1968" (quoted in Lewy 1978, 75). In fact, Westmoreland was considerably underestimating enemy strength, as communist general Vo Nguyen Giap's countrywide offensive was about to show.

Giap was seeking to bleed the Americans in order to convince them to come to peace terms favorable to Hanoi, ignite popular uprisings against the South Vietnamese regime, and drive a wedge between that regime and the United States (Karnow 1984, 548–49). Following the U.S. government's predictions of light at the end of the tunnel, Tet came as a rude shock to the American public. Events such as the widely publicized attack on the U.S. embassy in Saigon by Viet Cong sappers amplified the effect. The press corps in South Vietnam had grown to 464 by the time of Tet. Much of the fighting before Tet had occurred at night and in remote areas where few journalists tended to go. With Tet the fighting was not only in daylight but in populated areas, setting the stage for journalists and television crews to report a seemingly chaotic mosaic of desperate combats (Carruthers 2000, 116).

The irony was that, in strictly military terms, the Tet offensive was a serious defeat for the Vietnamese communist forces. They were unable to mount a major offensive again until 1972. American commanders had long waited for enemy forces to concentrate and fight in large formations, where superior U.S. firepower could fix and destroy them. But the increased tempo of operations meant that American casualties soared, while nightly news reports were full of savage fighting. As a result, between the beginning of the offensive at the end of January and the middle of March 1968, nearly one American in five switched from the "hawk" to the "dove" position, according to Gallup Poll data (Lewy 1978, 434). In those same six weeks, President Lyndon Johnson's approval ratings plummeted, endorsement for his handling of the war falling from 40 to 26 percent (Karnow 1984, 559). It was at this point too that Walter Cronkite turned against the war. Public trust in the veracity and authority of the U.S. government was shaken in ways that were never fully recouped.

After the war, Giap commented with benefit of hindsight that with Tet "we wanted to carry the war into the families of America" (quoted in Karnow 1984, 557). Via the medium of the war, Giap and his forces reached out and exercised a constitutive role in U.S. society and politics. With Tet and President Johnson's decision not to seek a second term, Vietnam became a central, if not the dominant, issue in American politics, and its cultural consequences began to proliferate. In turn, the altered social and political landscape in the United States reacted back on the war, as U.S. commanders were obliged to move with renewed intensity toward "Vietnamizing" the war and seeking an exit for U.S. forces. Constitutive circuits ran in and through the societies at war, conjoining them and shaping developments on the home fronts and at the war front. Among other effects of Tet, Johnson called a halt to the bombing of much of North Vietnam, while the Saigon regime suffered a grievous blow to its prestige in the countryside.

The constitutive circuits of America's involvement in Indochina spiraled out in time and space, extending far beyond the war and even the combatant societies. The importance of the Vietnam experience for American politics, society, and culture in the last quarter of the twentieth century is difficult to overestimate. The extent, diversity and significance of Vietnam War–related cultural phenomena in U.S. society are quite extraordinary (e.g., Bates 1996; Dittmar and Michaud 1990). As Susan Jeffords argues, the rise of Ronald Reagan and a new conservative hegemony in the United States was in part accomplished through the rewriting of the Vietnam War in popular and political culture (1989). In such narratives, Washington was typically figured as consisting of "liberals" and "bureaucrats" who had stabbed the American field army in Vietnam in the back, preventing it from winning.

Vietnam was indeed a searing experience for the American national security establishment, and the U.S. Army in particular. As Colin Powell remarks in his memoir, "Many of my generation . . . vowed that when our turn came to call the shots, we would not quietly acquiesce in halfhearted warfare for half-baked reasons" (1995, 149). Whether the U.S. effort in Vietnam was "halfhearted" is disputable, but certainly "lessons" were learned that shaped future U.S. force projection, and hence the character of future wars. The strategy adopted to evict Iraqi forces from Kuwait in 1990–91 was an embodiment of the Vietnam-derived Powell/Weinberger doctrine. A different application of the lessons of Vietnam shaped American involvement in Bosnia and Serbia (Ó Tuathail 1996, chap. 6). "You don't want to be Lyndon Johnson," one of President Bill Clinton's advisors told him, "sacrificing your potential for doing good on the domestic front by a destructive, never-ending foreign involvement" (quoted in Morris 1997, 245).

The idea that the Vietnam experience has made the U.S. public less willing to support military adventures abroad is known as the "Vietnam syndrome." Conventional understandings of the Vietnam syndrome posit a gap between the perceptions of decision makers at the highest level of government and of the public. The idea is that political leadership and their expert advisors know what is to be done, but their hands are tied by a public composed of "complacent" citizens, or miscomprehending liberals, or whatnot. However, the strategy the United States pursued in Vietnam reflected a conception of the communist threat and the Cold War world that was in many respects shared between military and political decision makers and the public (Brands 1993; Robin 2001). The basic vision was of a world divided between two blocs, one slave, one free, and of the communists as a threat to the American way of life. In 1971 one of the leading U.S. defense intellectuals, Bernard Brodie, observed that the "felt necessity" of opposing the spread of communism was a "determinant" of strategic policy analysis (1971, 6–7; cf. Barkawi 1998). This image of the Cold War was reproduced in numerous popular cultural sites throughout the Cold War, not least in Hollywood (e.g., Carruthers 1998). It went without question that the denizens of the free world *wanted* to be free. Subversion emanated from the Soviet bloc countries and infected the free world, as in *The Manchurian Candidate* (dir. John Frankenheimer 1962) or, with aliens standing in for communists, in *Invaders from Mars* (dir. William Cameron Menzies 1953) and *Invasion of the Body Snatchers* (dir. Don Siegel 1956). Threats to the free world were represented as arising from external sources even when they manifested themselves internally.

Accordingly, insurgencies in the free world, such as that in South Vietnam, were read as evidence of external attack rather than as consequences of the social and political upheaval that gripped the Third World in the wake of the Second World War (Kolko 1988). "What Chairman Khrushchev describes as wars of liberation and popular uprisings," Secretary of Defense Robert McNamara remarked, "I prefer to describe as subversion and covert aggression" (quoted in McClintock 1992, 174). Among strategic analysts and political decision makers, such an outlook contributed to the view that insurgencies primarily could be handled *militarily*, that the key was to block external sources of support, eliminate sanctuaries in neighboring countries, and to isolate, fix, and destroy the insurgent combat forces with superior firepower. While the United States also supported a "hearts and minds" campaign in Vietnam, both during and after U.S. involvement, the "big-unit war" received primary attention among the U.S. military, in American politics, and in popular representations of the war—as, for example, in *Hamburger Hill* (dir. John Irvin 1987) and numerous other films that focus on U.S. Army units or, latterly, on the American POW/MIA issue. The fact that the "big-unit war" was often counterproductive for pacification efforts aimed at winning the support of South Vietnamese peasants, a point frequently made in critical analyses (e.g., Lewy 1978; Race 1972), has very little resonance in most popular representations of the war. A hegemonic construction of American identity informed many elite and popular visions of the war. This meant that untoward developments on the battlefield had the capacity not only to unhinge elite strategies for the conduct of the war but also to disturb general constructions of national identity and purpose.

Tet exposed a distinctive weakness in this construction of American identity and its dependence upon a particular vision of the meaning of the Cold War in the Third World. Americans like to believe that their country is a beacon for "freedom loving" peoples everywhere. Peoples who are "unfree," such as those under communist rule, still love freedom but are enslaved by totalitarian elites and their ideologies and security services. When America wages war it likes to think it does so in order to bring freedom to these enslaved peoples by liberating them from totalitarian rule, the American version of the civilizing mission. In essence, it is not the Vietnamese or Iraqi people the United States is at war with but rather those elites who dominate ordinary Iraqis and Vietnamese, who themselves would live in freedom if only they had the chance. Curiously, Americans often envision themselves as the real *allies* of those they are at war with.

The Vietnam Syndrome and the Threat to U.S. Self-Perception

The groundwork is now in place to grasp the real surprise the Tet offensive held for the U.S. public. Tet was, and appeared to be on television screens, a general popular uprising against the Saigon regime and its American backers. It was no longer possible to evade the fact that "the people" were against the "freedom" the United States was offering; indeed, they were quite evidently laying down their lives in large numbers to oppose American purposes in Vietnam. This constituted a direct assault on the self-perception of many American citizens and their view of the role of the United States in the world. Even many in the antiwar movement retained this basic vision; they simply—and naively—transferred their support to Hanoi, imagining the regime there as the true embodiment of "the people." The initial framing of the conflict in Vietnam, as one primarily about communist subversion from outside, led to the adoption of an ineffective and counterproductive military strategy, one pregnant with the promise of defeat. This defeat then became a more general crisis for the body politic, a form of cultural blowback, because it challenged the identity relations and ideological constructs that had inspired intervention in the first place. Popular cultural representations of the Vietnam War were a key site for the playing out of this crisis, which gave rise to the idea of a Vietnam syndrome.

The Vietnam syndrome is conventionally assumed to consist of an unwillingness of the United States to suffer casualties in foreign imbroglios that do not obviously involve its national interests. There are various versions. For some, it is not an actual unwillingness to accept casualties on the part of the public but the perception that this is the case among the political class, which is then inhibited in using military power abroad for fear of being punished at the next election. Such accounts are confused. Any notion of a Vietnam syndrome of this kind must contend with the fact that the United States was willing to suffer over fifty thousand killed in action and inflict with its allies over a million civilian and military deaths in a country few Americans had even heard of prior to 1965. Such figures do not reflect an unwillingness to shed blood. The issue of American casualties in Vietnam was not the fact that they were being suffered but rather the perception that they were being suffered to no useful purpose, that the war was unwinable, and for many, that it was wrong as well (Karnow 1984, 558–69; Kolko 1985, 322–24).

A far more important Vietnam syndrome is in fact at work. At the level of elite ideology and popular memory, the history of the war has been radically rewritten, such that its meaning has served to re-empower the militarized American internationalism evident today in Iraq. The crux of this rewriting is to assert that *really*

America always was on the side of "the people" in Vietnam, who are now abandoned to communism, but that nefarious forces in Washington, as well as "liberals" and "hippies" in the country at large, prevented America from completing its mission. What was not so in practice is achieved in imagination, like Italians discovering white men in Ethiopia. The neoconservative clique that exercised such influence over the thinking and decision making of the first G. W. Bush administration had its roots in the Vietnam era. Its members were originally muscular liberal internationalists in the Democratic Party, who fled to the Republicans when what they perceived as isolationism and an unwillingness to use force in pursuit of values infected the Democrats. The view was that whatever went wrong in Vietnam, it was right for America to use force to pursue its values, which are synonymous with liberty and freedom around the world. After Vietnam, as two prominent neoconservatives argue, "the suspicion of American power inherent in contemporary liberalism now became a reflexive opposition to the exercise of American power in the world" (Kaplan and Kristol 2003, 57). Overcoming the American experience in Vietnam is about removing inhibitions to the use of force to achieve freedom. It is the invasion of Iraq in 2003 rather than the Persian Gulf War of 1990–91 that marks this overcoming.

Crucial to these constructions of the meaning of America are representations of oppressed peoples abroad who want to be free. As President Bush said of the role of the United States in the Cold War, America "provided inspiration for oppressed peoples. . . . They knew of at least one place—a bright and hopeful land—where freedom was valued and secure. And they prayed that America would not forget them, or forget the mission to promote liberty around the world."[4] American identity is actually dependent upon a vision of the world, or at least part of it, as enslaved. As with European colonial wars, America's wars too are a form of humanitarian war, intended to liberate those who cannot liberate themselves, the "children" of communism, of rogue or failed states, or of Islam. In Vietnam, these children turned out to be "first-class fighting men" (and women)[5] who had their own ideas about liberation. Because of the dependence of American identity on representations of, and ideas about, the Vietnamese people, when these ideas were overturned by events, cultural crisis ensued. Overcoming this crisis required restabilizing American identity, refiguring peoples in the South as in need of America's aid and America as their last best hope. That is, the history of the Vietnam War had to be rewritten, and that is exactly what happened in American popular and political culture (Jeffords 1989).

A stream of films, novels, and television series have (re)shaped memory of the war in Indochina, especially for Americans who came of age after the war and whose knowledge of it is based almost entirely on popular culture. Broadly speaking, the rewriting of the war is a movement from the world of *The Deer Hunter* (dir. Michael Cimino 1978) to that of the Mel Gibson vehicle *We Were Soldiers* (dir. Randall Wallace 2002). By the time of the latter, as Marilyn Young remarks, "Vietnam has become a war of which Americans can feel proud" (2003, 261). Young argues that the mechanism through which this is achieved is the recycling of World War II themes into new wars, with the primary focus being on the combat troops themselves, fighting for each other. The action of *Deer Hunter* moves between war front and home front, where complex family lives are riven apart by the psychological consequences of war. In *We Were Soldiers*, the home front is primarily represented by beautiful, Christian, and loyal wives in idyllic suburban-style base housing, waiting to hear news of their equally attractive, religious, and loyal husbands at the war front. Young notes the political work that can be achieved through cinematic focus on the community of warriors. Principally, the question of "why are they fighting that war in the first place" is more easily deferred. Also, it becomes possible to portray American soldiers as the principal victims of war, through close attention to their travails, wounds, and deaths.

Even with a tight focus on the troops, however, such films still depend on at least implicit constructions of suffering, oppressed peoples waiting to be liberated by Americans from the enemies of "freedom." Filmic and other representations of Vietnam, while borrowing World War II themes, also recycle older images of colonial warfare. In a variety of media, representations of colonial warfare emphasize the multitudinous as well as savage and warlike character of "native" armed forces. The classic example is the fight at Rorke's Drift in 1879, where about three hundred British soldiers fought off a four-thousand-strong Zulu *impi*. Even at the time, the British government sought to emphasize this defensive victory in order to obscure the serious defeat that had just occurred at Isandhlwana, where part of a large British force invading Zululand had been nearly annihilated by the main body of the Zulu army (Morris 1965). Since then, Rorke's Drift and its ilk have continued to serve similar purposes, turning defeat into victory and attack into defense.

Rorke's Drift was memorialized in the film *Zulu* (dir. Cy Endfield 1964), as well as in numerous other literary and pictorial representations. Such representations play on the emotive power of this kind of engagement, where rational, disciplined, but outnumbered white soldiers stand against waves of "savages." These images have found their way into numerous Vietnam films, where the Vietnamese communist forces typically attack in human-wave formation—as, for example, in *The Green Berets* (dirs. Ray Kellog and John Wayne 1968) when the Special Forces base camp is overrun. In the context of Vietnam and other postwar interventions, this colonial dimension does important work. A widespread feature of contemporary films that represent U.S. military involvement in the extra-European world, as well as elsewhere, is that they heavily emphasize the role of heroic small groups of special operations troops or even individuals, as in the *Rambo* trilogy, in desperate combat against hordes of non-Europeans.

The saga of Jessica Lynch, captured by Iraqis and then "rescued" by U.S. Army Rangers and Navy SEALS, resonated with these themes, which perhaps explains some of the popularity of the Lynch affair, including its dramatization in a television movie. In the movie *Saving Private Lynch* (itself a reference to the popular World War II movie *Saving Private Ryan* [dir. Steven Spielberg 1998] which also invoked the trope of outnumbered Americans on the defense), the use of dim lighting emphasized the darkness of the Iraqi other. Lynch and Diane Sawyer further perpetuated these stereotypical images in a *Primetime* interview aired on November 11, 2003. Taking the engagement in which Lynch was captured out of the larger context of U.S. invasion, Sawyer introduced footage of the ambush by stating that the Americans had been heavily outnumbered and outgunned in a battle that raged for an hour. As in the examples above, Westerners are represented as outnumbered, and hence the underdog. It also means that the action easily takes defensive form, when it is the United States that attacked Iraq.

When Western powers make war on the extra-European world, they typically do so through heavy reliance on firepower, preferably delivered from the air, in ways that minimize the risk to Western soldiers. However, in Indochina, where the United States was on its way to using over twice the total tonnage of munitions it used in all of World War II, John Wayne in *The Green Berets* is represented as leading a small band of heroes against hordes of Vietnamese communists (Kolko 1985, 189). Bombing people from a relatively safe height does not make for very good films, and dramatic devices are necessary to set up suitable scenarios. In order to create a situation pregnant with the possibility of heroism and cowardice, *Courage under Fire* (dir. Edward Zwick 1996) used a downed helicopter crew surrounded by Iraqi forces, so that the local balance of forces in the film did not reflect the actual balance of forces in the Persian Gulf War. Similarly, *Behind Enemy Lines* (dir. John Moore 2001) used a downed pilot, conveniently making possible heroism in Bosnia, where the United States in particular mostly refused to risk the lives of its soldiers despite its humanitarian rhetoric. The various Vietnam MIA/POW films also concern small special operations teams or individuals, as in *Uncommon Valor* (dir. Ted Kotcheff 1983), *Missing in Action* (dir. Joseph Zito 1984), and *Rambo First Blood Part II* (dir. George P. Cosmatos 1985).

The focus on small groups of outnumbered soldiers, generally on special operations missions, powerfully lends itself to defensive representations of Western military action. The reality of a global North that relies on military power, chiefly exercised through relations of "advice and support" of clients, to maintain a political and economic order in the Third World conducive to its interests is not only obscured but reversed. It is here that representations of oppressed peoples are drawn into service. Crucial to the moral universe of *The Green Berets* is the peasant village that lies outside the base camp, where John Wayne's men use humanitarian aid and a soft touch to try and convince the village chief to bring his people over to the government side for their own safety. The village is then punished for its cooperation by the Viet Cong, the chief killed and his young daughter horribly mutilated. In this way the insurgents are seen not as the saviors of the people but their oppressors, while the Americans are the people's real ally in defending themselves against an external imposition. This political reversal is completed in the final act of the film, which sees John Wayne and his men seizing a Vietnamese communist general. The general is represented as corrupt and decadent, driving about in a sports car and living in a mansion with a mistress, who turns out to be a double agent. Such a representation would be far more appropriate for a general serving the Saigon regime than for communist commanders, who typically worked in very primitive and difficult conditions. The effect is to complete the picture of the communists as brutal and parasitic toward an innocent people whose only hope is that America will maintain the will to save them.

The crossover between contemporary war and colonial war is fully complete in *Tears of the Sun* (dir. Antoine Fuqua 2003), starring Bruce Willis. Here again the focus is on a small band of American special operations forces fighting off large numbers of attackers, in this case Nigerian Muslims, who are represented as part savage native and part storm trooper. Willis's men decide to disobey orders in order to save some Christian refugees, among whom, it turns out, is a Christian prince who represents the future of Nigeria. The moral universe of this film consists of hard-bitten Western soldiers, who nonetheless listen to their consciences in order to save the natives; other Westerners, principally missionaries and doctors, providing humanitarian aid to the natives; bad and vicious natives; and good, innocent, although sometimes weak natives whose only hope for salvation lies with Willis's muscular humanitarianism. In the final scene, American air power obliterates the Muslim storm troopers in a flash of napalm, bringing the full weight of the United States behind militarized humanitarianism, but not before some of Willis's men have died heroically on their mission of justice. Absolutely crucial to the entire narrative, in *Tears of the Sun* as in *The Green Berets,* is the figure of the oppressed, indigenous people awaiting salvation from the West. Historically speaking, however, it is not generally "salvation" that has arrived in the extra-European world from the West.

The real Vietnam syndrome in elite ideology and popular memory is the process through which the verdict of Tet—that the United

States was not on the side of "the people"—is erased and America reinstated as the defender of the oppressed everywhere, willing to use its military power to liberate them. Such imaginative work was essential to laying the ground for the most recent American venture in Iraq. The rewriting of the Vietnam war was crucial to enabling politically the conquest and occupation of Iraq for purposes of liberating the oppressed Iraqi people. President Bush has himself made the connection directly. In a speech about American efforts to bring democracy and freedom to the Middle East, he cited Vietnam as one place where "Americans have amply displayed [their] willingness to sacrifice for liberty."[6]

The Iraqi people have a central role to play in this narrative, they must want to be free. Accordingly, the resistance to U.S. occupation, which became increasingly evident to Americans on the nightly television news, was represented as somehow not emanating from "real" Iraqis. The fiction that the resistance in Iraq consisted mainly of "Saddam loyalists" and "foreign terrorists" was invented, for to admit otherwise was to switch from discourses of liberation to those of occupation. "We're working hard with freedom-loving Iraqis to help ferret these people out before they attack," President Bush said.[7] The American administrator in Iraq, L. Paul Bremer, referred to those behind a series of bombings in Baghdad in October 2003 as "cold-blooded killers . . . a handful of people who don't want to live in freedom."[8] The main goal of the "killers" is "to intimidate Iraqis from building a free government and to cause America and our allies to flee our responsibilities."[9] Nothing less than the very identity of "America" is at stake in these constructions of the Iraqi resistance, as it was in representations of the Vietnamese people. "America" is that country that fights to bring freedom to oppressed peoples. When those peoples do not behave as expected or resist American efforts, the meaning of "America" is called into question, and efforts must be made to explain away the contradiction, as Bremer does in the quote above. Similarly, after the handover of "sovereignty" to an Iraqi regime under Iyad Allawi, U.S. and coalition forces in Iraq began referring to the insurgents as "Anti-Iraqi Forces," conflating Iraqi patriotism with the American invasion and occupation. As with the British empire and mankind, the interests of America and Iraq are synonymous, and so anyone opposing American purposes in Iraq is by definition "anti-Iraqi."

The problem is that this framing of the situation in Iraq, despite its resonances with American elite and popular self-perception, is dysfunctional in military and strategic terms. The implication is that the sources of resistance are to be found *not* in a complex political, cultural, and social context fuelled by conquest and occupation but rather in an identifiable group of "cold-blooded killers," who must be ferreted out and destroyed. As in the Cold War, subversion is seen as coming from the "outside," not from the people the United States seeks to free, when in fact it is the United States that has invaded Iraq. When the "ferreting out" comes in the form of heavy-handed use of military force, it contains the potential to generate further popular Iraqi resistance. As the father of a young Iraqi girl killed by a U.S. air strike exclaimed, "I am going to kill America" (quoted in Conetta 2003, 2). Despite its compatibility with American identity, this framing of the conflict in Iraq, as in Vietnam, promises military reverses, because it inspires counterproductive strategies. Such reverses then can become more general crises for the body politic in and through the constitutive circuits connecting war front and home front.

Like the Vietnamese, the Iraqi people are not playing their assigned role in the American narrative. Iraqi nationalism and popular resentment of the occupiers is evidenced by daily attacks, fed by civilian casualties inflicted during the initial conquest and by the lack of American fire discipline afterward, among other factors. The realities of the battlefield intersect with identity constructions through the interconnectedness of publics at war. American identity is caught up in the external reach of the U.S. state and its role in the extra-European world. This identity depends upon a stable vision of the other as consisting of a minority of oppressors and a mass of innocents. But if the other fails to behave as expected, as during Tet, the American self is potentially shaken, as occurred from 1968.

It is curious, this dependence of the most powerful country in human history on a particular vision of others, as oppressed peoples awaiting salvation through American arms. Such dependence would not show up in any standard assessment of the international balance of power. The American economy is the largest in the world and its military the most powerful by several orders of magnitude. Yet attention to the links between war and identity in the context of an interconnected world reveals how and why defeats in faraway places can become central moments in domestic politics and culture, moments that can shape and drive events at home and abroad in the future.

War and Humanity

In reflecting on the modern experience of war it is difficult to evince much optimism. This chapter has dwelled on the all too evident dark side of war and culture. We have looked at the role of war and the military in feeding national chauvinisms and arms races, in dividing the world between civilization and barbarism, and in the cultural crises and renewed militarism that follows defeat in the non-Western world. Students of war, especially those who take seriously its tragedy, are often drawn to cyclical theories of history. The cultural dynamics of war seem everywhere to fit similar depressing patterns, inspiring further militarism, further conflict, more killing and ruined lives—Mussolini's invasion of Ethiopia followed defeat at Adowa, as U.S. intervention in Iraq followed that in Vietnam.

Students of war, though, are also attracted to their subject matter, and not only because it allows prurient access to violence and powerful weapons. In war, humans behave in an appalling manner. At times, soldiers rape and pillage at gunpoint, exact revenge on enemies who have surrendered, cower in foxholes while their friends fight and die around them, and take pleasure in inflicting pain and death. But humans also perform extraordinary, sublime acts on the ugliest of battlefields. In battle, soldiers often make the ultimate sacrifice for their comrades. Where else in human endeavor does such generosity occur so regularly? Upon a landscape of unrelenting human tragedy, soldiers sometimes manage kindness, even gentleness, for each other, for civilians caught in the fighting, and, yes, even for enemy soldiers, who suddenly seem simply human. At one point or another, many combat soldiers realize that they have much in common with those across no-man's-land, the enemy, as they too are doing a tough and deadly job. This is a moment of empathy, of human recognition across all the myriad divisions of war—of nations, of race and culture, of religion. So there is some cause for hope here.

It is important to emphasize that both constructing war as something that divides humanity and that has the potential to unify it rely upon interconnection between combatants of the kind discussed in this chapter. War involves interconnection between peoples and places, whether experienced by soldiers actually fighting one another or by civilians on the home front following events from afar. In postwar memory and constructions of war, as in the films discussed above, this interconnection lives on after the fact. The enemy, in wartime and later on, is always constituted in and through meaning in ways that relate the self to the other. War produces cultural resources that can be used both to vilify the enemy and glorify the self, or to find common human ground between combatants. In either case, it is precisely the interaction and interconnection occasioned by war that gives rise to such cultural constructions. Paradoxically, even when constructions of war are mobilized to divide and separate humanity, as in narratives of the War on Terror as a "clash of civilizations," they can do so only through relation and comparison, through connecting constructions of the self to those of the other. This dependence of the self on the other is evident in America's ongoing relations with Vietnam and Iraq. Also evident is the fact that these mutually interdependent constructions of self and other can change over time.

In the Second World War, the British, their Indian army, and other colonial troops, fought a savage and difficult campaign in Burma against the Japanese. A British officer, who must remain nameless here, saw and heard much of Japanese cruelty during several years of fighting in Burma. He contrasted his own attitude as that of a civilized professional soldier with the behavior of the Japanese. The Japanese rarely took prisoners, they often killed those they did take, and POWs who did survive were horribly mistreated. These stories, true enough but often exaggerated during the war, in many cases inspired cruelty on the part of British and Indian soldiers toward the Japanese, creating a self-reinforcing cycle of barbarity (Barkawi 2004). Having experienced Japanese brutality firsthand, and lost many of his men, this British officer said that for most of the war he had no feelings of human empathy whatsoever toward the "Japs." In defensive positions, after a Japanese attack was repulsed, he would leave their moaning and dying wounded outside his perimeter to suffer and think nothing of it, denying them even the grace of a quick death by bayonet or gunshot where possible. But toward the end of the war he came upon some Burmese villagers who, having seen that the Japanese were in retreat, were exacting their revenge on a Japanese soldier. They were ramming bamboo up his anus, and his horrifying, all too human screams echoed through the jungle. In the face of this pain and torture, the British officer realized for the first time that Japanese soldiers were human too. Shotgun justice was administered; a Burmese villager paid with his life for the moment of empathy, while the Japanese soldier, unlike so many of his comrades, was quickly put out of his misery.

This moment of human recognition and empathy is not an unambiguous one, as the Burmese villager would attest if he could. Nonetheless many soldiers come to recognize a common ground with enemy soldiers, between self and other, during the war or upon reflection afterward. Contemporary Western societies are marked by a great deal of racial and cultural discrimination, as in concern over immigration and asylum seekers in Holland, the United Kingdom and France or continuing discrimination in the United States against African-Americans and other minorities. Why is it harder in peaceful, civilian society to recognize something evident to many soldiers in much more extreme contexts? There is something about the combination of human depths and heights in war that makes possible compassion even across the yawning divide of race war, as some American soldiers are discovering today in Iraq. Not everyone crosses this divide to shake hands with the enemy, but some do. After the Second World War, many British veterans formed the "Burma Campaign Fellowship Group," traveling to Japan to meet their former enemies and hosting them in the United Kingdom, in a spirit of reconciliation and friendship. Of the possibilities for human unity and racial harmony glimpsed in war, not least in the multicultural Indian army itself, but so easily eclipsed in peace, a great memorialist of the Burma campaign cried, "What *is* Man, that he can give so much for war, so little for peace?" (Masters 1961, 162)

Amidst deadly conflict and personal suffering, it is possible in wartime to recognize our common humanity, even that of our tormentors. This is not the only, thin source of hope that war offers. War, and most especially the deadliest and largest war there ever was—the Second World War—can be experienced as a collective human tragedy. Wars might be fought by nations, but it is human beings who everywhere pay the price. While many thinkers long have seen war as one of humanity's greatest common problems, after World War II as after World War I, many politicians and ordinary people were ready to agree. Great international institutions, principally the United Nations, were established in a collective effort to regulate war and other political violence. While the UN is an institution of sovereign states, it also embodies efforts to set universal standards—"human rights"—for the treatment of people everywhere. Here is a new and powerful form of Robinson's insight of globality, the problem of managing our collective planetary affairs of war, peace, and violence. The nuclear arms race during the Cold War convinced many that the possibility of nuclear war was an unparalleled threat to the world as a whole. An international peace movement took shape around resistance to nuclear weapons.

Especially since the end of the Cold War, the UN system has sought actively to intervene in conflicts to alleviate human suffering, bring warring parties to the peace table, and punish those involved in war crimes. An invigorated system of international humanitarian law has sought to try war criminals in international tribunals and ensure that tyrants are not left in peace. These, too, are not unambiguous moments of common human recognition. All too often, war criminals turn out to be "barbarians" and "natives" in new guise, while their "civilized" equivalents, such as Henry Kissinger and Ariel Sharon, suffer only the indictment of hostile editorials in leading newspapers (Hitchens 2002). Meanwhile, junior functionaries in the Bosnian Serb war machine are tried in The Hague for crimes against humanity at a special tribunal, or militias in Sierra Leone are seen as the very peak of human barbarity because they cut off the limbs of their victims rather than obliterate them with cluster bombs in the manner of Western air forces.

Nonetheless, and despite this reappearance of the North-South distinction, war's horror is an incitement to all concerned to put an end to it, to see it as a common problem rather than a normal instrument of politics. In this sense, war is fundamental to the recognition of globality of which Robinson speaks. Paradoxically, war that so divides humanity also leads to the realization that these violent divisions are themselves a common problem, about which we must do something. Humanity is much less far down this road than many liberal advocates of the UN and international law believe. Indeed, it may well take further collective catastrophes equal to or greater than the Second World War before we realize, if we ever do, that war is all too often a bigger problem than any it is called upon to solve. But whether or not humanity overcomes the tragedy of war, the resort to violence to settle disputes, war will continue to impel concern with humanity as such. And in this sense, as in so many others, war is a globalizing force.

"TERROR" AND THE POLITICS OF GLOBAL WAR

The experience of war can prompt an overcoming of the differences that divide humanity and lead to recognition of the enemy, the other, as a fellow human being. But all too often "humanity" is invoked in war in different guise. One side purports to fight in its name against a barbarian other. Humanity is used as an ideological concept, as part of the war of ideas that accompanies the actual fighting. As Carl Schmitt explains:

> When a state fights its political enemy in the name of humanity, it is not a war for the sake of humanity, but a war wherein a particular state seeks to usurp a universal concept against its military opponent. At the expense of its opponent, it tries to identify itself with humanity in the same way as one can misuse peace, justice, progress, and civilization in order to claim these as one's own and to deny the same to the enemy (1996 [1932], 54).

Schmitt introduces us to the political character of war. Especially in the liberal West, war is often conceived in legal or ethical terms.

Was the U.S. and British invasion of Iraq in 2003 illegal? Is it right for the UN to intervene with force to stop "crimes against humanity" such as occurred in Rwanda in 1994? Is it wrong not to do so? Whatever the legal or ethical character of the wartime use of force, it is always political. But what does it mean to say that war is political, and how is this meaning qualified by the global?

For Clausewitz, war is political in that political leaders pursue their objectives through use of force. Such objectives might be "material" in nature, such as a province rich in natural resources, or ideal, such as the spread of civilization or democratic institutions. Typically the two are combined, despite the insistence of many realists that they be kept rigorously apart and material interest govern policy. Adolf Hitler invaded Russia for its wealth and resources and to rid the world of the "Judeo-Bolshevik" menace. President G. W. Bush's administration invaded Iraq for its oil and strategic value and to implant "freedom" and "democracy" in the Middle East.

Realists emphasize material interest, because properly understood it encourages prudent compromise where possible. Imagine two rational leaders nearing a clash over a rich province, one calculating that a speedy and decisive war might pluck a ripe plum, the other devising ways to frustrate the opponent's intentions. The possibility for negotiation and compromise remains very much at the forefront. If the balance of forces are such that a war will be successful, the other side may conclude that it is not worth fighting. Avoiding the cost of war for the stronger party may be worth allowing the weaker side to retain a few counties of the province. Hubris and miscalculation always threaten to scupper such rational compromises reflecting the relative balance of power, but the common currency of interest can provide the basis for negotiation.

Clausewitz emphasized pursuing limited objectives through force for another, related reason. Unlimited objectives fed war's tendency to serve itself, to generate ever more war, while limited objectives were more likely achievable through the careful application of violence. Modern ideologies such as fascism, communism, and liberalism often entail unlimited and universalist goals for war and other uses of force. The degree and manner in which these tendencies are historically realized has varied. But when coupled with modern mass politics and the need for popular support of war aims, the conditions are present for war to be framed as an ever-escalating clash between competing ideological visions. Here a second, classical meaning of the political is at work—competing conceptions of the "good life," of the right ordering of society and its rule.

Classical realism sought a balance between political ideals, such as safeguarding a democratic way of life at home and abroad, and the vital interests necessary for such ideals to be realized in practice. These might include natural resources, access to markets, and the military balancing of other powers. It may well be necessary to occasionally violate cherished ideals in order to secure their long-term survival and flourishing; in politics, especially those concerning war, it is axiomatic that the ends can justify the means. A problem with war, and force more generally, is that it is a blunt instrument for the pursuit of ideals. Violence generates resistance and further violence. The uncompromising and ultimately impossible nature of some ideals can lead to ever more violence in their pursuit, in part because they often require the complete humiliation and submission, or even extermination, of the enemy, at least some of whom are more likely to fight to the last breath in such circumstances.

The notion of a war to end terror illustrates some of the problems involved. "Terror" is often a weapon of those who lack other weapons, who believe their voices are not heard and whose desires go unrealized. It is a brutal and often counterproductive weapon to be sure, but a weapon of the weak nonetheless. To insist that terror stop prior to serious political engagement—as, for example, the Israelis often ask of the Palestinians—is to request the weaker party disarm in the face of the strong, when it is precisely the taking up of arms that drew attention and perhaps support to its cause. For the strong, who can never protect themselves entirely from terrorism, an effective strategy requires a judicious combination of political and coercive means. Engagement and compromise with those the terrorists claim to represent whittles away at the legitimacy of terror. Further terror attacks in such circumstances can lead to a reduction in support from friends and cause the stronger party to withdraw valuable concessions—or step up counter-terror operations. To respond to terror with engagement and negotiation requires realization that justice lies on both sides and that the conflict is in part about how the strong have exercised their power at others' expense.

Framing the conflict in terms that deny any humanity to the enemy, as a struggle of opposing ideals or values, sets in train an opposite dynamic. If the terrorists are viewed by the strong as evil fanatics beyond the pale of civilization, as people who cannot be reasoned with or engaged in any fashion, the tendency is to rely wholly on military and other security means, legitimated in a Manichean rhetoric of absolute right versus absolute wrong. This combined offensive in word and deed is escalatory in nature, producing a similar reliance on force and the eschewing of dialogue on the other side. The number of victims rises all around, including civilians killed as "collateral damage" and those targeted directly by terror.

An important reason that clashing worldviews are not as amenable to compromise and resolution as disputes conceived in terms of material interest is that adherents *see* the world differently, they identify different phenomena as good or bad, and they give events different, often opposing meanings. Opponents often are fighting *different* wars and so misunderstand what the war is about for the other side. History and even geography are imagined differently. For the Chinese for example, World War II was the "Anti-Japanese Resistance War," and it began in 1931, not 1939 or 1941 (Fujitani et al. 2001, 3). Many Americans believe the War on Terror began on September 11, 2001 when their country was attacked. But Europeans have long been fighting terror, in the form of the Irish Republican Army (IRA), the Basque Fatherland and Liberty group (ETA), the Red Brigades, and others. Osama bin Laden dates the beginning of hostilities differently from either the Americans or the Europeans. In a videotaped statement released on October 7, 2001, he declared that for over eighty years Islam had been "tasting . . . humiliation and contempt . . . its sons . . . killed, its blood . . . shed, its holy places . . . attacked."[1] "Eighty years" has little resonance in the West, but it is a reference to the breakup of the Ottoman Empire and the ceding of the territories of the old caliphate to the control of Western mandates and thereafter, in many cases, to regimes friendly to the West. For bin Laden, hostilities began when Muslims passed under the rule of those he regards as crusaders and infidels. The fact that U.S. troops remained in Saudi Arabia after the 1990–91 Persian

Gulf War, another reason cited by bin Laden for 9/11, was for him only the latest iteration of Western intervention in the Middle East, which as he sees it includes Israel.

A clash of worldviews through the medium of armed force raises the question of the relative power of each side and of the different kinds of power they wield, for power in its many forms also is a core dimension of the political. In the War on Terror one side's power to strike fear into ordinary citizens' lives is juxtaposed with the other's conventional military strength. Each side's ideas and messages appeal differently to various audiences. How do these kinds of power measure up? What are their distinctive advantages and disadvantages in particular situations and contexts? In an escalating war between worldviews perceived as unalterably opposed, the very processes of war driving out those who seek a middle ground, one last dimension of the political is very much in evidence, one identified by Schmitt (1996 [1932]). For him, politics comes into play when a state—and the nation and worldview it represents—is under existential threat, that is, a threat to its very existence. In such situations, there are friends who assist and enemies who seek its end; the distinction between the two is the heart of politics.

In many ways, the War on Terror has reinvigorated the state and put an end to claims that states were disappearing from history, such as those that marked the initial euphoria over "globalization." Rather than oppose globalization to the state, this book seeks to contextualize a world of territorial states in the "thick space" of mutual interconnection. It is possible to be attentive to the continuing power and significance of states while also acknowledging the ways in which world politics exceed territorial states. While it is fought in and through a world of states, many of the terms invoked in the War on Terror are not reducible to nation-states, such as Islam, civilization, the West, democracy, and bin Laden's idea of a new caliphate extending from Afghanistan to the Persian Gulf. At risk of tautology, worldviews construct different worlds, worlds that vary spatially as well as chronologically. When did the War on Terror begin? Is it a war between Islam and the West, or between civilization and terrorist outlaws? Who—and where—are our friends and enemies?

Various answers to these questions are offered by participants, answers that imagine the War on Terror differently in space and time. These geographical and historical imaginaries are part and parcel of what the War on Terror is and how it will develop around the world in decades to come. Thinking politically and globally about the War on Terror involves taking seriously these different worldviews and how they interact with armed conflict itself. It is important to remember that even as these clashing worldviews emphasize difference and separation, as between the West and Islam, they require interconnection and interaction with one another precisely in order to establish this difference and separation. In this and other ways, the War on Terror serves to review and integrate the themes of this book. Like worldwide conflagrations before it, from the Seven Years' War to the Cold War, the War on Terror plays out globally, with events in one locale affecting other places in a chain of interconnection across time and space.

The discussion below begins with the view from Mindanao, one of the many places where a preexisting conflict became caught up in the War on Terror, and goes on to consider the idea that the War on Terror is a clash between civilizations. The following section takes up the claim that the War on Terror is a war *for* civilization, another prominent framing of the conflict. The final section considers some of the important ways in which the War on Terror is shaped by the globalization of the Israeli-Palestinian conflict, in particular the adoption of Israeli conceptions of the terrorist enemy and appropriate responses by important elements of the U.S. national security establishment. Throughout, the chapter highlights the ways in which the global circulation of people, goods and ideas make the War on Terror what it is.

The View from Mindanao

One of the most common ways of understanding the War on Terror is in terms of the latest iteration of a long-standing conflict between the West and Islam. This is a particular way of imagining the histories and geographies of world politics. The American political scientist Samuel Huntington remarks, "The twentieth-century conflict between liberal democracy and Marxist-Leninism is only a fleeting and superficial historical phenomenon compared to the continuing and deeply conflictual relation between Islam and Christianity" (1996, 209). Six years earlier, in a widely read article, Bernard Lewis referred to Islam as "an ancient rival against our Judeo-Christian heritage, our secular present, and the worldwide expansion of both" (1990, 60).

Some of the difficulties of this way of thinking about the War on Terror become apparent in the slippage between "the West" and "Christianity," as well as in Lewis's realization that Western expansion is connected to Islamic hostility. But most problematic is the idea that "civilizations"—whether Islamic, Christian, or some other—persist through world historical time as unitary entities capable of having "ancient rivalries." A brief visit to a minor front of the War on Terror, the island of Mindanao in the Philippines, helps explore the dynamic interaction between long-term histories of Western expansion and the Islamic world, an interaction at the root of current conflict but not in the way that the "clash of civilizations" school imagines. Invoking Christian or Islamic civilization is one of the ways in which worldviews come to play a role in the War on Terror and, indeed, work to escalate its violence on both sides. But such invocations do not fully account for either the causes or the nature of the conflict.

Long before what we now call "globalization" and imagine as the "inevitable" spread of Western culture, Islam already was a world religion. "The classical *dar al-islam* [land of Islam] was . . . a 'transhemispheric civilisation' and probably the most successful, long-lasting and far-reaching example of archaic globalization" (Bennison 2002, 80). When the Spanish arrived in the Philippines in the sixteenth century, they discovered two well-developed Muslim sultanates and identified their inhabitants as "Moors," transplanting to East Asia Spain's own experience of a seven-hundred-year struggle at the other, western end of Islamic globalization. War broke out, with the Sultan of Maguindanao urging his "Moros" to resist as their only hope of retaining freedom. For three hundred years, resistance continued in one fashion or another. When Spain turned over the Philippines to the United States in 1898, Mindanao was still not pacified; it became a major site of U.S. anti-guerrilla operations that, in the Philippines as a whole, had claimed around a quarter of a million lives by 1902—no small conflict by any measure (Boot 2002,

125). By comparison, total British civilian and military deaths in the Second World War were around 388,000. The Moros were never completely defeated, and many of them greatly resented being integrated by fiat into the new state of the Philippines when the United States granted independence in 1946. They carried on fighting, and now the Moro National Liberation Front and the Moro Islamic Liberation Front find themselves caught up in a new Western wartime construction, the War on Terror, and once again U.S. advisors are in Mindanao. In conjunction with the United States, the Philippines began an antiterror campaign in 2002. At least a hundred people were arrested without warrants, and dozens of them remain in custody in 2005, many still awaiting formal charges.[2] As one contemporary Moro fighter remarks, "My parents taught us that unless we are free as a people, we shouldn't do anything else during our lifetime but to be in this *jihad*."[3]

A literate Moro fighter might well imagine modern history much differently than is usual in the West. After all, he is the inheritor of a once great and proud world civilization driven underfoot by Spanish and American barbarians and their local cronies. He is also the product of a very different military tradition, that of the weak against the strong. Westerners fulminate about hostage taking, bombings, ambushes, and other "cowardly" and "terroristic" tactics, as President G. W. Bush remarked of the militias opposing the invasion of Iraq in the spring of 2003. Some see such tactics as indicative of different civilizational forms of warfare. In the wake of 9/11, the military historian Sir John Keegan drew a distinction between Western and "Oriental" traditions of warfare: "Westerners fight face to face, in stand-up battle . . . [observing] rules of honour. Orientals . . . shrink from pitched battle . . . preferring ambush, surprise, treachery and deceit" (quoted in Gregory 2004, 58; see also Hanson 2002). But only a moment's reflection is necessary to realize that Moro fighters and those like them would stand no chance if they played by the rules established by the strong, standing up to be shot down by the superior firepower the powerful are always able to employ. Theirs is necessarily a war of the shadows, and Westerners do no different in similar situations, as the American Revolutionary War and the French resistance in the Second World War, for example, establish.

What might 9/11 have meant for this fictional, literate Moro fighter? Watching those towers fall on a satellite television deep in the bush, or perhaps viewing some gloating al-Qaeda video of the events of that day, he might well have realized that something had just happened to his own little war, that it had become part of something bigger. There is an important sense in which Third World resistance movements, even while skillfully developing distinctive military traditions, were less resourceful politically, playing a game set up by the West and its system of international relations. Ever since the French Revolution, resistance movements such as that on Mindanao have sought independent statehood as legal equals with the Europeans, mutually recognized by other sovereign states. At the same time, they accepted the European notion that the title to statehood is rooted in the nation, a notion that sets Moros against Filipinos, Arabs against Muslims, Zulus against South Africans, and Kurds against Iraqis, Turks, Syrians, and Iranians. Such Third World struggles have been primarily local and national in purpose, whatever support they and their opponents may have drawn from abroad.

At a stroke, bin Laden changed this far more effectively than decades of Soviet and Chinese pronouncements about communist internationalism ever did. Bin Laden is no respecter of sovereign borders. For him, dividing up the Islamic world into separate countries is a tool of Western control, the classic tool—divide and rule. As the al-Qaeda website noted in reference to Afghanistan's president, hand picked by the United States, "A 'Karzai' regime exists officially in all the Muslim countries. All rulers are crowned in the Karzai way."[4] Elsewhere, bin Laden asks: "Who are the ones who implanted and established the rulers of the Arabian Gulf? They are none other than the Crusaders, who appointed the Karzai of Kabul, established the Karzai of Pakistan, implanted the Karzai of Kuwait and the Karzai of Bahrain and the Karzai of Qatar and others" (quoted in Anonymous 2004, 150–51).

Bombastically put, but consider the origins of many Middle Eastern countries, carved out by the Turks, the British, and the French, centered on specially selected sheikhs, sustained by oil money and U.S. as well as British military and police assistance, supplemented by the occasional covert operation when someone untoward made it to power or threatened to. Iran is the paradigmatic case. In the early 1950s, in an effort to head off Soviet influence in the Middle East and to reverse the nationalization of Iranian oil, the United States derailed a republican and nationalist experiment in Iran by helping to overthrow the Mosaddeq government in a CIA-supported coup. The United States then armed and supported the increasingly brutal rule of the shah of Iran as its policeman in the Persian Gulf (Hollis 2004; Prados 1996, 91–98). There is more than a little truth in bin Laden's account of the "Karzais." President Karzai even has a foreign bodyguard, supplied by the U.S. private military firm Dyncorp.

Moros can recognize their own history of imperial subjugation and foreign influence in bin Laden's critique. Aside from direct Spanish and American colonial rule, the Moros suffered under the U.S.-supported Marcos regime for decades. A Moro fighter might now choose to imagine himself as a participant not in a local struggle for a nation-state of his own but in a transregional war designed to bring about a new caliphate in the old *dar al-islam*. He might not do so, he might carry on in the old way, but he could join the new struggle. It is this new possibility that al-Qaeda and its various loosely affiliated organizations, networks, and individuals have put on the table. As a recent report from the International Crisis Group notes, "The most significant threat of all for the Philippines and the wider region is the possibility of international terrorism and domestic insurgency becoming ever more closely interwoven and mutually reinforcing."[5] A potentially global resistance movement has been called into existence, made possible by the centuries-old spread of Islam around the world and the histories of colonial and neocolonial domination Muslim peoples have endured.

One way of conceiving the War on Terror is in terms of a global Islamic insurgency, an insurgency that exceeds the al-Qaeda organization per se but that develops out of its example and ideology (e.g., Anonymous 2004; Burke 2003). Bin Laden has some relatively local concerns, such as overthrowing the Saudi monarchy and evicting U.S. forces from the Arabian Peninsula as well as the wider Arab world. But his actions speak to a larger circumstance. The presence of large numbers of Muslims in the West as well as in all the poor regions of the world, with the exception of Latin America, potentially provide a large popular base for Islam's growing militant resistance. Vital to a global insurgency of this kind will be the mobilization and organization of Islamic militants around the world.

The key to mobilizing this popular base is the increasing belief that the West is truly engaged in a war against Islam, that the West is fighting Islam everywhere. Might it not seem to a Moro fighter that this is indeed the case, as he catches sight of U.S. special operations forces on patrol in his backyard, hears of the Palestinian struggle, watches the wars in Afghanistan and Iraq, and discovers that the Americans even remembered to include some obscure Muslim brothers in remote parts of China on their lists of enemies?[6] Might he not decide to start returning the favor and begin establishing transnational connections with other, like-minded groups, coordinating operations and orienting them toward the larger, global struggle? Al-Qaeda again: "It must also be noted that in its war with America, the Al-Qa'ida organization adopted the strategy of expanding the battle arena. . . . This strategy has priceless advantages; the enemy who had only his country to defend realized that he now must defend his enormous interests in every country."[7] Here we have a glimpse of this conflict's potential for widespread and long-term destruction, very far from being fully realized as yet.

A Clash of Civilizations?

How does the notion of a global Islamic insurgency compare with the idea of a clash of civilizations as a way of imagining the War on Terror in time and space? In Huntington's influential formulation, civilizations are clearly delineated on maps, and they persist through world historical time as distinct cultural essences based primarily on religion (1996, map 1.3, 26–27). Conceived in this way, the problem of war between civilizations involves the disputed borderlands between them: "Wherever one looks along the perimeter of Islam, Muslims have problems living peaceably with their neighbors" (Huntington 1996, 256). Huntington goes on to argue, on the basis of quantitative evidence of Muslim involvement in violent conflict, that Muslims in general have a distinctive propensity for violence (1996, 256–58).[8] "The underlying problem for the West is not

Islamic fundamentalism. It is Islam, a different civilization whose people are convinced of the superiority of their culture and are obsessed with the inferiority of their power" (Huntington 1996, 217). This idea that something is wrong with Islam that leads it to war with the West has wide currency. As the *Newsweek* columnist Fareed Zakaria said of bin Laden and his followers, "They come out of a culture that reinforces their hostility, distrust and hatred of the West" (quoted in Gregory 2004, 22).

In many ways, bin Laden shares Huntington's view of two unalterably opposed civilizations in conflict: "The world has been divided into two camps: one under the banner of the cross, as Bush, the head of the infidels said; and another under the banner of Islam."[9] Like Huntington, bin Laden thinks the conflict started some time ago: "The struggle between us and them began centuries ago, and will continue."[10] Naturally, bin Laden does not accept the idea that the violent tendencies of Islam are to blame for the conflict but casts his struggle in defensive terms. In his 2002 letter to the American people, bin Laden responded in this way to the question of why he attacked the United States: "The answer to that question is very simple. Because you attacked us and continue to attack us" (quoted in Anonymous 2004, 131). For President Bush, the United States was attacked on 9/11 because al-Qaeda hates Americans simply because of who they are. Speaking to a joint session of Congress on 20 September, 2001, he explained: "Americans are asking, why do they hate us? They hate what we see right here in this chamber—a democratically elected government. . . . They hate our freedoms—our freedom of religion, our freedom of speech, our freedom to vote."[11] Similarly, bin Laden's view is that the West hates Muslims because of who they are: "We say that all the Muslims that the international Crusader-Zionist machine is annihilating have not committed any crime other than to say God is our Allah" (quoted in Anonymous 2004, 130).

Despite these similarities, there is an important difference between bin Laden's and Huntington's versions of clashing civilizations. As is clear from bin Laden's discussion of the "Karzai regimes" quoted above, he has a concept of informal empire. Whereas Huntington has borderlands between civilizations, for bin Laden the West is already *in* the Muslim world: "The west's occupation of our countries is old, but takes new forms."[12] Indeed, this "occupation" is precisely what exercises him. Huntington's notion of separate civilizations leads easily to his view that civilizational conflicts are about culture and identity, about who Muslims and Westerners simply *are* and always have been: "So long as Islam remains Islam . . . and the West remains the West. . . . [T]his fundamental conflict between two great civilizations and ways of life will continue to define their relations in the future even as it has defined them for the past fourteen centuries" (Huntington 1996, 212). On Huntington's account, Western imperialism is effectively over (1996, 210, 212), but for bin Laden it is very much in existence.

The United States is currently attempting to establish friendly regimes in Iraq and, with NATO, in Afghanistan. Along with Britain, it has a long and ongoing history of intervention in the Middle East, much of it designed to establish and protect client regimes as well as secure access to oil (Kolko 2002; Mamdani 2004). Quite aside from issues of culture and identity, such intervention and informal imperialism provide ample political reasons for bin Laden and other Arabs and Muslims to wage war on the United States. For bin Laden, Arabs are unable to pursue their conception of the "good life." U.S. intervention and hostility to Islamic regimes poses an existential threat to his conception of how politics and society should be organized. Americans need only imagine how they would react if their country were subject to informal control from abroad—no doubt much as they reacted in 1776. None of this is meant to justify bin Laden's attacks or endorse his vision of the "good life," but it does suggest that more is at issue than some essential, unalterable identity conflict between two cultures.

If the West is already in the Islamic world, Islam is also in the West, and this poses further, more fundamental difficulties for Huntington's understanding of separate civilizations. Some fifteen million Muslims lived in the European Union prior to its recent eastward expansion (Goody 2004, 11). Many al-Qaeda members, particularly those who conducted the 9/11 strikes, spent considerable time in Western countries and were educated in Western universities. Others, such as Richard Reid, the unsuccessful shoe bomber, were Westerners who converted to Islam. At stake here is more than the fact that Huntington's "borderlands" run right through the heart of the West. Given so much interchange between "Islam" and the "West," how can it be said that they have remained essentially separate cultural formations for "fourteen centuries"? What "Islam" and the "West" *are* is in part the result of the interaction between the two.

This book uses the globalization idea to elaborate a view of the international as a distinct social space of interconnection and mutual constitution. Islam and the West have in part constituted one another through their long history of interaction. Jack Goody points out that:

> Islam has been of great importance not only to but in Europe itself ever since the eighth century, in terms of its political, military and religious presence as well as for what it has contributed to technology, architecture, classical scholarship, mathematics, chemistry, agriculture, the use of water, philosophy, political science, travel literature and indeed literature more generally (2004, 8).

Neither the West nor Islam can be understood without reference to the other. The West was produced out of a history of interaction, assimilating crucially important inventions and ideas from the more advanced East prior to 1800, while appropriating Eastern resources in the era of colonialism thereafter (Hobson 2004). Just as the West developed in relations with Islam, so the reverse is true. The role of the West in making the modern Middle East is apparent not only from the political map and the existence of Israel but also in the state structures and nationalist ideologies the Arab world appropriated from the West.

Appreciating this history of interconnection and mutual constitution is crucial to understanding the War on Terror, for bin Laden's "Islamic fundamentalism" and the al-Qaeda organization are in fact modern, hybrid creations of Islam's encounter with the West (Roy 2004). The Egyptian thinker Sayyid Qutb, one of the central intellectual influences on modern Islamic fundamentalism, lived in the United States for three years, a period that was central to the development of his ideas (Mamdani 2004, 55–56). Qutb's brother Muhammad was bin Laden's teacher at King Abdul Aziz University in Saudi Arabia. All three men viewed the West as suffering from a "great spiritual famine" (Gray 2003, 23, 77). Much of their thought is a reaction against Western modernity and an attempt to outline a new, Islamic modernity, for they did not want the same fate to befall their societies.

The West was not only an initial impetus to their ideology; they also utilized a variety of quintessentially Western ideas. "Qutb's writings are filled with horror of the West, but he also borrowed many of his ideas from Western sources" (Gray 2003, 24). Qutb was influenced in particular by Marxism-Leninism, taking the concept of a revolutionary vanguard and the idea that the world could be remade through an act of will, both important intellectual bases of al-Qaeda. His notion that Islam could serve as a universal ideology of emancipation in modern conditions is a distinctive combination of Islamic and Enlightenment thinking (Mamdani 2004, 56–60). Gray notes that while it is tempting to see a regime like the Taliban, of which bin Laden approved, as "medieval," in its total effort to re-make society in line with an ideology the Taliban "had more in common with Pol Pot" (Gray 2003, 79). "Traditional," medieval Islam had allowed the Bamiyan Buddhas to survive.[13] Similarly, the Otto-man Empire and the Moorish kingdoms in medieval Spain were in many ways exemplars of toleration of diverse cultures and religions. Bin Laden's spare, uncompromising and absolute version of Islam is very much a modern creation, comparable in some ways to the Protestant reaction against Catholicism.

If al-Qaeda's ideas could develop only in and through relations with the West, the organization itself is even more obviously of the modern world, not simply a product of "Islam." It is a contemporary, global, and networked enterprise, with a flattened hierarchy and cel-lular structure characteristic of drug cartels and some multinational business companies. It is comfortable with computer technology, science, and modern communications, and it has a knack for manip-ulative use of news media. As the U.S. State Department realized as early as 1995, "These trans-national terrorists benefit from modern communications and transportation, have global sources of funding, [and] are knowledgeable about modern explosives and weapons" (quoted in Burke 2003, 10).

In its ideas and its organization al-Qaeda is a hybrid creation, but it also has even more direct debts to U.S. foreign policy. Bin Laden's central role and his organization developed out of the U.S.-supported resistance to the Soviet-backed regime in Kabul. In the largest-ever CIA operation, the United States provided some three billion dollars in aid to the *mujahedin* in Afghanistan in the 1980s. It included the provision of approximately a thousand shoulder-fired Stinger antiaircraft weapons, some of which may still be in al-Qaeda's inventory.[14] With Washington's approval, Saudi intelligence poured in another two billion dollars, and the chief of Saudi intelligence picked bin Laden to lead the foreign legion of Arab fighters in Afghanistan (Kolko 2002, 48–49).

It is precisely through diverse forms of interaction between peoples and places around the world that "Islamic fundamentalism" and al-Qaeda came into existence; they were mutually constituted out of relations of interconnection. Currents of Western, Arab, and Islamic cultures and histories, modern technologies and communications, and the policies of various regimes and great powers combined to form crystallizations, among them bin Laden's and al-Qaeda's particular way of being modern. Attempting to disaggregate these phenomena and squeeze them into boxes marked "Islam" and "the West" will not aid understanding of the dynamics of the War on Terror. Much will remain opaque if the conflict is viewed only as a clash between two diametrically opposed civilizational identities. But if this view is correct, that the participants in the conflict, indeed the conflict's very nature, can only be understood through hybrid categories of mutual constitution, why is there so much talk on both sides about identity, about Islam and the West?

In Huntington's view, civilizations are relatively static cultural formations that persist and develop through historical time. Otherwise, it would make no sense to speak of a fourteen-centuries-long conflict between something called "the West" and something else called "Islam." Conflict occurs on this account because of differences in belief, in religion, in identity between civilizations: "The great divisions among humankind and the dominating source of conflict will be cultural" (Huntington 1993, 22). What Huntington overlooks is the utility of violence and war in *remaking* identities. The very idea of contemporary militant Islam, and of the *jihadi* as an available identity for young Muslim men (and some women) around the world, has its roots in struggle, most particularly if not originally in the war in Afghanistan against the Soviets (Devji 2005).

Through various media, this identity was globalized, in part because it spoke to the experiences of many Muslims in diverse social and cultural locations, whether the sons of wealthy Saudi princes, disaffected South Asians living in the United Kingdom, or Moro fighters on Mindanao. 9/11 was not only the product of this identity and the actions it endorses but also gave it a potent and powerful new image, made it *attractive* to many who feel disempowered and humiliated in a world dominated by Western and American modernity. "It is," as John Comaroff remarks, "in situations of struggle and times of trouble that the content of ethnic self-consciousness is (re)fashioned" (1991, 670). An excellent example of this is the increase in Islamic belief among formerly relatively secular populations, as among Sunnis in contemporary Iraq.

In and through conflict, bin Laden and his allies are attempting to fashion a new Islamic identity, to remake Islam in *their* image. They do so through spectacular acts of violence and the propagation of interpretations of these acts through the Internet, the release of video tapes, and other media. In many respects, bin Laden and his specific organizational network are no longer required for this identity to propagate. As the commission set up by the U.S. Congress to investigate the 9/11 attacks concluded, a "radical ideological movement in the Islamic world" is gathering strength "and will continue to menace Americans and American interests long after Usama Bin Ladin and his cohorts are killed or captured" (National Commission 2004, 363). The key point is that the conflict itself works to instantiate and radicalize this identity ever more widely. This returns us to a basic war and society theme: just as society and culture shape war, war in turn shapes society and culture. What it means to be American is also changing through the medium of violent conflict, discussed further below.

In many ways then, Huntington has it the wrong way round. It is not conflicts of belief between civilizations that lead to war so much as it is war that refashions cultures. What Huntington misses is the fluidity of identity, and the power of discourse—such as bin Laden's speeches—as well as actions to evoke sentiments of belonging to *new* groups that did not previously exist in the same form, such as contemporary militant *jihadis*. As Bruce Lincoln comments, a social grouping is composed "of people who feel bound together

143

as a collectivity and, in corollary fashion, feel themselves separate from others who fall outside their group" (1989, 9). Boundaries of affinity and estrangement between groups are not natural or given by the "civilization" one is born into, as Richard Reid and other converts such as the "American Taliban" John Walker Lindh demonstrate. Al-Qaeda offers new identities for Arabs as well as recent Muslim converts, identities assembled out of diverse cultural resources. These new identities, which involve reworking old ones, are fashioned by the evocation of sentiments of belonging and estrangement. Violence and blood sacrifice provide powerful resources for such sentiment evocation, as American national unity in the immediate wake of 9/11 demonstrates.

The emotional power of violence and its casualties need not be used to evoke sentiments of ever more extreme chauvinism on both sides, although this always remains the likely possibility in wartime. Gen. William Boykin, deputy undersecretary of defense for intelligence in the Bush administration, has said, "We in the army of God, in the house of God, the kingdom of God, have been raised for such a time as this," elsewhere referring to the Islamic enemy as "Satan."[15] But the dead in the World Trade Center can speak for hybrid identities, rather than for Christianity, American nationalism, or Western civilization. As Paul Gilroy has written of them, "The ordinary dead came from every corner and culture, north and south. Their troubling manifestation of the south inside the north . . . destabilizes the Manichean assumptions that divide the world tidily into 'us' and 'them'. . . . Their untidy, representative diversity might . . . be valued as . . . a civic asset that corrupts the sham unity of supposedly integral civilizations" (quoted in Gregory 2004, 57). In his speech to Congress on September 20, 2001, President Bush spoke of "the citizens of 80 other countries who died with our own" and avoided conflating bin Laden and al-Qaeda with Islam as a whole: "The terrorists practice a fringe form of Islamic extremism that has been rejected by Muslim scholars and the vast majority of Muslim clerics—a fringe movement that perverts the peaceful teachings of Islam."[16] Here is a different frame for understanding the War on Terror, as a conflict between civilization and terrorist outlaws rather than one between civilizations. In the speech to Congress President Bush claimed that "the civilized world is rallying to America's side. They understand that if this terror goes unpunished, their own cities, their own citizens may be next." Elsewhere, he has spoken of the "terrorist threat to civilization."[17] In the next section, this way of framing the conflict is considered, one that identifies "terror" and "terrorists" as the enemy.

A War *for* Civilization?

Alongside the West versus Islam is another construction of friends and enemies in the War on Terror: civilization versus terrorism. The definition of terrorism used by the U.S. government refers to "premeditated, politically motivated violence perpetrated against noncombatant targets by subnational groups or clandestine agents, usually intended to influence an audience."[18] The notion of "noncombatants," or civilians, is key to this construction of "terror." The basic idea is that civilians are "innocent" and that directly targeting them to get media attention or pursue a political goal is outside the rules of civilized warfare and conduct of politics. It is one thing for civilians to be killed as "collateral damage" in the course of legitimate wartime operations directed at enemy forces or war-making infrastructure. It is quite another to set out deliberately to kill civilians who themselves are not directly responsible for whatever it is that the terrorists are opposing. In doing so, it is claimed, terrorists place themselves beyond the pale of civilization and become enemies of all civilized peoples. What is at work in this construction of friends and enemies? How is it related to the West versus Islam frame? How does it shape the dynamics of the War on Terror?

Terrorism of the sort referred to in the U.S. definition can be useful for the weaker side in asymmetric conflicts. Palestinians had trouble drawing attention to their cause until they started hijacking planes and engaging in other acts of terror in the 1970s. But in many of those actions relatively few civilians were killed, in part because of awareness that this would lead to bad publicity. The IRA regularly issued warnings before many of its bombings in the mainland United Kingdom, precisely to keep the civilian toll relatively low while gaining maximum publicity and causing disruption. By contrast, al-Qaeda operations, those of groups affiliated with it as well as other "new terrorists," often set out to kill the maximum number of people possible. Here, the publicity generated can work against the terrorists, although its spectacular nature can draw in new recruits from among the disaffected and humiliated.

Terrorism like this can be seen as an evil beyond redemption or understanding. As former Israeli prime minister Benjamin Netanyahu argues, *"Nothing* justifies terrorism. . . . [I]t is evil *per se"* (1995, 21). His reasoning is simple. The definition of civilized warfare is that it tries to proscribe deliberate attacks on "defenseless civilians"; the notion of a war crime only takes on meaning in this context. In completely ignoring the line between combatants and civilians, in its "uninhibited" and "brazen" resort to violence, "terrorism attacks the very foundations of civilization and threatens to erase it altogether by killing man's sense of sin, as Pope John Paul II put it" (1995, 21–22).[19] Any attempt to excuse terrorism, to justify it, or to take seriously the reasons for it proffered by terrorists themselves is to participate in this erasure of civilization: "For if anything is allowable, then even the gassing of a million babies in Auschwitz and Dachau is also permissible," intones Netanyahu (1995, 21).

The idea that the civilized make war with a distinction between combatant and civilian, and that those who do not make this distinction are uncivilized, fits with long-established Western constructions of lawful and just war. As Victor Davis Hanson explains:

> The real atrocity for the Westerner is not the number of corpses, but the manner in which soldiers died and the protocols under which they were killed. We can comprehend the insanity of a Verdun or Omaha Beach, but never accept the logic of far fewer killed through ambush, terrorism, or the execution of prisoners and noncombatants. Incinerating [by aerial bombardment] thousands of Japanese civilians on March 11, 1945, is seen by Westerners as not nearly so gruesome an act as beheading on capture parachuting B-29 fliers (2002, 97).

This view tends to dismiss as "collateral damage" the losses inflicted on civilian populations in Iraq and Afghanistan, while feeling Western losses to terrorism—for example, the far fewer killed on 9/11 itself—particularly deeply. "We in the West call the few casualties we suffer from terrorism and surprise 'cowardly,' the frightful losses we inflict through open and direct assault 'fair'" (Hanson 2002, 97).

Such an attitude is a recipe for continual escalation, as those "frightful" losses tend to inspire more "terrorism" and "surprise" from the other side. An al-Qaeda operative, Omar Bakri Muhammad, was asked if there was any difference between civilian casualties suffered in an attack on military targets and attacking civilians directly. He replied:

> We are not hypocrites. We don't say: "I'm sorry, it was a mistake." We say: "You deserved it." We assume the purpose is to kill as many people as possible, to spread the terror, so that people in the West think: "Look what happened to us!" and realize that every time they send beautiful Apache helicopters and F16 aircraft, the purpose is to kill women and children. How many people died in Afghanistan? They carpet bombed day and night, and a number was never released. One hundred sixty thousand? Who were those people? In Madrid [where al-Qaeda-affiliated cells struck commuter trains on March 11, 2004] were there 196 or 197? They were counted one by one.[20]

Muhammad dramatically overestimates the numbers killed in Afghanistan, but the power of his point remains. While counting the victims of terror meticulously, the United States publicly denies keeping a count of Iraqi or Afghani civilian casualties. As bin Laden remarks, "The Islamic nation must also know that the U.S. version of terrorism is a kind of deception. Is it logical for the United States and its allies to carry out this repression, persecution, plundering and bloodletting over these long years without this being called terrorism, while when the victim tries to seek justice, he is described as terrorist?"[21]

The hypocrisy Muhammad and bin Laden point to was evident in an incident that grew out of Russia's wars in Chechnya. In early September 2004, Chechen rebels took over one thousand parents and children hostage in a school in Beslan, North Ossetia in the Russian Federation. After a two-day standoff, an apparently accidental explosion in the school gym where the hostages were held triggered a fierce and confused firefight. When it ended, well over three hundred hostages were dead, about half of them children. Hundreds more were injured, many seriously. During and after the crisis, news media around the world were filled with heart-wrenching pictures and stories of grief-stricken parents. Because of the late summer heat and lack of ventilation, many of the children held hostage had shed their clothes. Pictures of half-naked children fleeing the scene at the climax of the crisis or lying dead with bullet wounds or burns, often severe, were all the more poignant. Only a month before, Chechen rebels had blown up two passenger aircraft in Russia, killing eighty-nine people.

Around the world, there was outrage at the targeting of a school and its children. The pope condemned the "vile and ruthless aggression on defenceless children and families," while the archbishop of Canterbury was struck by "the depth of energy that people can put into such evil."[22] President Bush went to the Russian embassy to express his sympathy "for the victims and the families who suffered at the hands of the evil terrorists. . . . The atrocities that took place in the school were beyond comprehension. Many in America, and I know many in Russia, simply cannot conceive the hearts [sic] of a person that would mow down innocent children."[23] President Putin of Russia struck a similar tone: "We encountered not mere murderers but people who used weapons against defenceless children. . . . [W]hat happened . . . is a crime of terrorists, inhumane and unprecedented in its cruelty."[24]

At the same time, while saying he could not speak of Beslan without tears coming to his eyes, President Putin made a set of political moves characteristic of the War on Terror. He used the Beslan crisis as an opportunity to announce a centralization of power in the Russian Federation, giving himself the power to appoint regional governors who had previously been elected, leading to real concern about a return to autocracy in Russia.[25] He also increased funding for security, with $3.66 billion in additional funding for the Defense Ministry alone.[26] Additionally, he sought to link the Chechen rebels to "international terror."[27] Without providing evidence, President Putin and other Russian officials argued that international Islamic groups were sustaining the war in Chechnya and that several "Arabs" had been among the hostage takers in Beslan.[28] The dynamics of the War on Terror are global in character, shaping different spaces and populations in similar ways.

Expressions of horror at the deaths of so many children are easily understood, and satellite news coverage lends such tragic events an immediacy and emotional intensity not dissimilar to that evoked by a powerful film, all the more so for being real. Yet, perspective is necessary. Russia has fought two wars in Chechnya recently, one from 1994 to 1996 and the second from 1999, which is still going on in 2005. Both involved the occupation of Chechnya by Russian regular forces in the face of widespread resistance, leading to the nearly total destruction of the Chechen capital, Grozny, by air and artillery bombardment as well as through heavy fighting. Conservative estimates of the dead from the first war are around 180,000, most of them Chechen civilians. Total deaths from 1994 to the present are around a quarter of a million, with one estimate placing the number of dead children at forty-two thousand.[29] Among the dead were the wife, two daughters, brother, and seven other relatives of Shamil Basayev, the Chechen commander who masterminded the Beslan operation.[30] War remakes people as well as societies in its own image.

Many of the key dynamics of the civilization versus terrorism frame are evident in the Beslan tragedy and its aftermath, dynamics that play out in common ways in different places such as Chechnya, Israel/Palestine, or Iraq. This frame depends on the idea that "terror" is an unconscionable evil, yet in practice it works to highlight certain evils (Beslan's dead children) while obscuring others (the tens of thousands of dead children in Chechnya). As one civilian who has suffered under Russian bombardment in Chechnya remarked of her experiences, "They didn't show any of that on television."[31] Presidents Yeltsin and Putin did not set out to harm children in the way that Basayev's men did, but this distinction based on intentions rather than outcomes is much less stark than that of "evil terrorists" versus civilization. The nominally Muslim identity of Chechnya and the increase in Islamic fundamentalism there as a consequence of ten years of war and violence allowed President Putin to link the incident to international Islamic terrorism, regardless of the lack of evidence of any serious foreign Islamic role. An obvious advantage of this move for Putin is that it distracts attention from the facts that Chechnya has been fighting for its independence from Russia and that Chechen terrorism is a direct result of Russia's two invasions and brutal occupation of Chechnya. As Basayev said in response to Russian allegations of international *jihad,* "Chechens fight only against [Russia] for their freedom and independence."[32] Chechens, like others in similar situations, have turned to insurgency and terrorism as the only available weapons of the weak. In this sense, terrorism has much in common with a Clausewitzian definition of war—the use of force to pursue political ends. Terrorist actions and the responses to them by military, police, and intelligence forces are a kind of fighting or mutual combat.

There is a second and ultimately more important aspect of President Putin's articulation of Russia's struggle against Chechen terrorism with the global War on Terror. The notion of a War on Terror implies that there is something like a unitary, global terrorist enemy, that terrorists everywhere are allied with one another in some way. Vice President Dick Cheney was asked if Beslan would encourage the Russians to join the United States in fighting terrorism more aggressively around the globe. He responded affirmatively, saying, "I think what happened in Russia now demonstrates pretty conclusively that everybody is a target, that Russia, of course, did not support us in Iraq. . . . They've gotten hit anyway."[33]

Cheney's logic—that someone or something is targeting everybody everywhere—is very curious but very typical of the War on Terror. Chechen operations, with a single minor exception, have been limited to Russia and began well before 9/11 and the invasion of Iraq. Not everybody is a target, only Russians and whoever happens to be in the way. Cheney implies that there is a link between terrorism in one place and terrorism everywhere, that this imaginary unitary enemy hit Russia even though it had not supported the United States in Iraq, as if in wanton cruelty. What Basayev and his men did has everything to do with what Russia has done in Chechnya and very little to do with the United States and Iraq or 9/11. Yet the notion of "terror" as an enemy allows Cheney to occlude this obvious fact. In the wake of Beslan, Prime Minister Ariel Sharon of Israel called for an international anti-terrorist alliance. Echoing Cheney, he said of the Russians, "They understand now that what they have is not a local terror problem but part of the global Islamic terror threat."[34]

As with Putin and his Chechens, Sharon has long sought to represent Israel's enemies not as Palestinians seeking self-determination and making use of weapons of the weak, but as "terrorists." Also like Chechnya, Israeli security operations in the occupied territories over the course of the two *intifadas* have killed more Palestinian civilians than Palestinians have killed Israeli civilians in deliberate acts of terror. In the al-Aqsa *intifada* that began in September 2000, 2,746 Palestinians have been killed as of 2004, among them 550 minors. During the same period, Palestinians killed 208 Israeli civilians living in the territories and 424 civilians in Israel itself.[35] Around three Palestinians die for every Israeli.[36] A similar pattern is evident in the U.S. response to 9/11. On that day, just under three thousand were killed. By October 2004, estimates of Iraqi civilian casualties range between ten and fifteen thousand, while the most conservative estimates suggest around two thousand Afghan civilians have been killed since U.S. operations began there in October 2001.[37] Bin Laden remarks of this imbalance: "Under what grace are your victims innocent and ours dust, and under which doctrine is your blood blood and our blood water?"[38]

Underneath the civilization-versus-terrorism frame is the nature of armed conflict between weak and strong powers, in which justice does not necessarily belong only to the latter. While the weak may use terror, the firepower of the strong is also horrifying, and it is usually more deadly. As is clear from the examples above, the civilization-versus-terrorism frame is not very far from the clash of civilizations, as behind terror, in the view of many, is Islam. It is Islam that seemingly connects the many different terrorist outrages around the world together. Many of the terms of the War on Terror are derived from the Israeli-Palestinian conflict, and increasingly the United States is using the language, tactics, and strategy that Israel uses in its fight against the Palestinians and other resistance organizations. The relations between Israel and the United States are another example of international interconnection and mutual constitution, relations that are shaping the War on Terror globally. In order to understand how the civilization-versus-terrorism frame works and influences the current global conflict, it is necessary to delve into Israeli constructions of the terrorist enemy.

The Globalization of the Israeli-Palestinian Conflict

This book conceives violent conflict as a form of interconnection between antagonists. The effects of conflicts can proliferate widely in time and space and can shape events far beyond their original context. One way in which this can happen is through the generalization of a certain conception of the enemy. During the Cold War, the United States perceived its enemy as "communism." This definition of the enemy was fungible; it could be applied nearly anywhere around the world. Parties to conflicts in the Third World, be they Vietnamese nationalists, Congolese anti-colonialists, or peasants struggling against landowners in any of a number of countries, found themselves defined and acted upon as "communists" by the United States. Tiny Nicaragua, for example, or even tinier Grenada could be constructed as existential threats to the American way of life, because the very existence, and certainly the popularity, of "communists" even in faraway places challenged the universality of the American model, a universality central to American self-conceptions.

During the Cold War, no amount of explaining that Third World conflicts had their own local sources or that they had systemic sources other than U.S.-Soviet confrontation, such as decolonization or the world economy, would serve to convince hawks in the United States that American prestige and credibility were not at stake in Angola, or Indonesia, or Timbuktu. "Communism" connected all these conflicts. The significance of the Israel-Palestine conflict for contemporary world politics is that for the United States, the common enemy in the War on Terror, in Iraq, in Afghanistan, in the Philippines, and elsewhere has come to be defined in and through categories derived in large measure from the Israeli-Palestinian conflict. Of particular significance is the notion that terror itself is the primary enemy and that putting an end to it takes precedence over any other political objective—including that of addressing the cause for which the terrorists fight. The Bush administration and its neoconservative ideologues have powerfully articulated this enemy with core aspects of American identity and purpose, in ways strongly reminiscent of the Cold War. As a result, through the close relationship between American identity and U.S. foreign policy, especially in wartime, ideological categories derived from the Israel-Palestine conflict are playing a central role in shaping the present world crisis and the coming long decades of struggle it portends.

In identifying the enemy as terror and in insisting on the cessation of terror prior to meaningful negotiations, hard-line Israelis, as well as violent Palestinian responses to their policies, have shaped the Israel-Palestine conflict in distinctive ways. The notion of terror as itself the enemy serves to obfuscate the sources and nature of violent resistance, making any other strategy than "no appeasing of terror" appear irrational, for to give in to terror is to encourage more terrorism. A spiral of terrorist attack and harsh reprisal is set in train, one that encourages the digging in of heels on both sides, delegitimizes negotiation and compromise, and inspires further and ever more violence. Using terror to frame the enemy "other" results in particular strategic and identity dynamics. These dynamics are now evident in the developing War on Terror, in the fighting in Iraq, and in U.S. constructions of these conflicts. Some of the core ideas and interpretations of events that have driven American leadership and that have been popularized through various media are derived directly from and modeled on those of the Israeli right.

In 1995, former Israeli prime minister Benjamin Netanyahu published a slim volume entitled *Fighting Terrorism: How Democracies Can Defeat Domestic and International Terrorists,* some of which was quoted above. Netanyahu's concise treatment encapsulates the state of the then-developing field of terrorism studies and demonstrates the unusual ideological utility of "terror," "terrorism" and "terrorists" as representations of enemies and their violence. This utility rests in part on the facility with which terror can be articulated to diverse conflicts, particularly those involving the violence of the weak against the strong, creating an imaginary alliance among all those who use terror. Netanyahu also makes a very important move, although he is by no means the first to do so: he articulates Israel with the West and identifies terror as the common enemy of both, as in the terror-versus-civilization frame. If Israel is at war against terror, rather than against occupied Palestinians or Arab states, security relations with the United States are that much warmer, as terror can become America's enemy too, as it can be Russia's, and so on.

"Terrorism is back," Netanyahu's book begins. Rather than defining the term, he lists examples: the 1993 attack on the World Trade Center, the Oklahoma City bombing, "terrorist attacks from Beirut to Buenos Aires," a Paris subway bombing, and the Aum

Shinrikyo attack in Tokyo (1995, 3). What is left entirely unclear—in fact, is never addressed in the book—is why such diverse
events, actors, and uses of violence should be grouped under one
category, even one he goes on to subdivide between domestic and
international. What, exactly, "is back"? Even if one granted for sake
of argument that these uses of violence fell under a common classification, it would be ridiculous to suggest—as Netanyahu implies—
that these instances were the work of some common enemy. This
move, the implication that the use of a "tactic" is indicative of an
"alliance" of some kind among all who use it, lies at the origins of
any notion of a War on Terror.

On its own, this move is so transparently absurd as to be unsus-
tainable. It amounts, as some wag remarked, to declaring war on all
airplanes rather than Japan after the attack on Pearl Harbor. What it
requires is a vision of a unitary enemy behind acts of terror, and this
enemy is radical Islam, yet slippage is left to insist that one is not at
war with Islam, or Palestinians per se, only terror, and this is the
key difference with the clash-of-civilizations frame. In laying out the
rise of militant Islam and its terror threat, Netanyahu's book serves
as a "road map" to the War on Terror that was to follow six years
after its publication. All of the major terms of debate are present,
beginning with references to Charles Martel's defeat of raiding "Sar-
acens" at Poitiers in 732, invoked to establish the supposed long-
running, primordial hostility between Islam and the West (Netanyahu 1995, 82–83). Terrorism and dictatorship—the latter an expansive category into which Netanyahu places the Soviet Union,
authoritarian Arab states, Iran, and so on—are associated in ways
that make nondemocratic regimes threatening by their very existence: terrorism "is not an incidental characteristic of dictatorships;
it is their quintessential, defining attribute" (1995, 75).

Through this mechanism, Netanyahu links terrorism to Arab
state sponsors and counsels hostility toward these states. This is the
same logic that appeared in President Bush's pronouncements immediately after 9/11, in which he insisted that the United States
would make no distinction between terrorists and the states that
harbored them. Netanyahu identifies Gaza as the archetypal terrorist
enclave, arguing that Israel's participation in the Oslo peace process
created this enclave—drawing the lesson that negotiation and com-

promise with terrorists are counterproductive and that terrorist en-
claves should be directly occupied by security forces. Finally, his
penultimate chapter speculates on the possibilities of terrorist use of
WMD, in particular an Iranian nuclear weapon, sketching out the
presumed relations between "rogue states" and WMD that marked
justifications for the invasion of Iraq.

Throughout the text, in his discussions of past, present and future, Netanyahu links Israeli security concerns to Western security
concerns. This sounds somewhat forced in his account of the "So-
viet-Arab terrorist network" and the "Soviet-PLO axis," or in his
ham-fisted efforts to liken Baathist pan-Arabism to Hitler's pan-Ger-
man nationalism (e.g., 1995, 60, 62, 85). However, as he moves into
the 1990s, this articulation of Israel with the West via common enemies becomes progressively more plausible. This plausibility is
achieved through the logic of a simple syllogism. Terrorism/militant
Islam is hostile to Western democracy; Israel is a Western democracy; therefore, Israel and the West share a common enemy. Netanyahu argues that Islam was hostile to the West long before Israel
came into existence, and that therefore no one should assume that
if Israel did not exist or was forced to make peace with the Arabs
and Palestinians, hostility between Islam and the West would evapo-
rate. He emphasizes: *"The soldiers of militant Islam and Pan-Arabism
do not hate the West because of Israel; they hate Israel because of the
West"* (1995, 87). Overall, we are left with an articulation between
terror, Islam, and dictatorship, on the one hand, and the West, democracy, and Israel on the other. Netanyahu manages deftly to work
the 1990s themes of a "democratic peace" into his imagined geography of a war on terror, in which Israel is the West's front line against
the "rest." The suggestion here is not that Netanyahu's book represents a plan that was later followed by the United States or that, in
and of itself, it was directly influential. Rather, the book represents
an effective blending of the ideas that would provide the ideological
framing of the War on Terror after the shock of 9/11.

What Netanyahu calls terror can be an effective weapon in the
hands of those who lack other weapons. It is hardly surprising that
the powerful would seek to discredit such a weapon in moral terms.
Doing so has the additional advantage, one upon which Netanyahu
eagerly seizes, of silencing any justification for using such a weapon

in the first place, on the grounds that by assertion, nothing can justify it. What Netanyahu has outlined is a kind of principled deafness by which the powerful righteously refuse any dialogue with their opposition until the latter disarm, even though it is the very taking up of arms in the first place that made the strong pay attention. The utility of such a position for sections of the Israeli right, which wish to remain in possession of Gaza and the West Bank regardless of consequences for the Palestinians living there, is obvious; its value for the West in the War on Terror is much less evident.

Netanyahu's ideas reflect a particular milieu of security thought and practice in the 1990s. As Stefan Halper and Jonathan Clarke have argued, many of the ideas developed in the 1990s by neoconservatives and others became policy after 9/11, in particular the notion of spreading democracy to the Middle East by force (2004). G. W. Bush had never intended to be a foreign-policy president, and he had explicitly rejected the idea of "nation building." After the strikes on New York and the Pentagon, President Bush required not only a plan but an overall paradigm, and the neoconservatives and their allies in his administration were ready with one. They seized the moment almost immediately. Richard Clarke, National Coordinator for Counterterrorism in the Bush administration until March 2003, relates how when he returned to the White House on September 12, 2001, "I walked into a series of discussions about Iraq. . . . I realized . . . that [Secretary of Defense] Rumsfeld and [Deputy Secretary of Defense] Wolfowitz were going to take advantage of this national tragedy to promote their agenda about Iraq" (2004, 30). Although the CIA was already certain al-Qaeda had conducted the strikes, Wolfowitz was insisting—in line with long-held views about state sponsorship of terror, like Netanyahu's—that al-Qaeda must have had assistance from Iraq. He even resurrected the idea, long discredited outside of neoconservative circles, that Iraq had been behind the World Trade Center bombing in 1993. "Later in the day, Secretary Rumsfeld complained that there were no decent targets for bombing in Afghanistan and that we should consider bombing Iraq, which, he said, had better targets" (Clarke 2004, 31). While the plan to go to Afghanistan first prevailed, Bush insisted that Clarke and his team "go back over everything, everything. See if Saddam did this. See if he's linked in any way" (Clarke 2004, 32).

This emphasis on Iraq seemed bizarre to Clarke in the wake of an attack on the United States by al-Qaeda: "Having been attacked by al Qaeda, for us now to go bombing Iraq in response would be like our invading Mexico after the Japanese attacked us at Pearl Harbor" (2004, 30–31). But it made perfect sense in the context of the neoconservative agenda worked out in the 1990s. That agenda had long included regime change in Iraq (e.g., Perle 2000). There was simply nothing, at least initially, in the state-centric neoconservative outlook that could take on board something like the global network enterprise that is al-Qaeda. Related and more important is the turn to the "distinctly American internationalism" of Lawrence F. Kaplan and William Kristol (2003). This involves the use of American power aggressively to further "freedom" abroad, exactly the policy that the neoconservatives argue was an unnecessary casualty of the debacle in Vietnam (Kaplan and Kristol 2003, 65–67, 115–18). A liberated Iraq was to be the bridgehead of "freedom" in the Middle East, regardless of whether or not this was an appropriate response to the threat posed by al-Qaeda and its affiliates, or worse, of the fact that it might generate more terrorism. As Vice President Cheney put it before the invasion, with Saddam removed, "the freedom-loving peoples of the region will have a chance to promote the values that can bring lasting peace" (quoted in Kaplan and Kristol 2003, 100). In this way, an attack by a nonstate actor on the United States, an actor the United States had been instrumental in creating, is turned into a neocolonial occasion to bring democracy to Middle Eastern states by force.

"The Israelization of America"

It is in this context ("democracy versus dictatorship") that the U.S. War on Terror is most easily articulated with Netanyahu's vision of an embattled "Western" Israel fighting the same fight. In early April 2003, with the invasion of Iraq under way, the Project for a New American Century (a neoconservative "educational" organization) sent a letter to President Bush on Israel and the War on Terror.[39] It was signed by many prominent neoconservatives, as well as by other U.S. security analysts. The letter opens by identifying Israel as a liberal democracy under attack by "murderers who target civilians," insisting that "we Americans ought to be especially eager to show our solidarity in word and deed with a fellow victim of terrorist violence." The differences between the armed resistance of occupied Palestinians and al-Qaeda's strikes on the United States are here erased through the magic of "terror." The letter urges the president to accelerate his efforts to remove Saddam Hussein from power, citing the fact that "Saddam, along with Iran, is a funder and supporter of terrorism against Israel." Pressuring Israel to negotiate with Yasser Arafat is likened to pressuring the United States to negotiate with Osama bin Laden or the Taliban leader Mullah Omar, while the Palestinian authority is described as a "cog in the machine of Middle East terrorism." In these constructions, it becomes increasingly difficult to separate out U.S. from Israeli interests; they appear as one and the same. "No one should doubt that the United States and Israel share a common enemy. . . . You have declared war on international terrorism, Mr. President. Israel is fighting the same war."

But in fact, the United States had already come to be fighting Israel's war, or at least as Netanyahu and his allies might envision it, taking out one of Israel's most implacable enemies in Iraq and threatening Iran and Syria, the next two largest worries for Israeli security planners. The United States was attacked by al-Qaeda, not Iraq. Yet, the notions of state sponsorship of terror, of the link between "dictatorship," Islam, and terror, and of regime change as the solution came to overshadow the actual group that had attacked the United States, against which a limited war could and should have been waged, rather than an expansive, never-ending War on Terror. All of these terms were packaged together by Netanyahu and others long before 9/11. Just before the first anniversary of that day, President Bush told some members of the U.S. House of Representatives: "The war on terrorism is going okay; we are hunting down al Qaeda one-by-one. . . . The biggest threat, however, is Saddam Hussein and his weapons of mass destruction. He can blow up Israel and that would trigger an international conflict" (quoted in Woodward 2004, 186).

It is not as surprising as it should be that the president of the United States would downplay to the U.S. Congress an enemy that had directly attacked the United States in favor of one that might harm Israel. As Senator J. William Fulbright remarked in 1973, "On every test on anything the Israelis are interested in [in] the Senate . . . the Israelis have 75 to 80 votes" (quoted in Reich 1984, 190). If anything this tally increased after 9/11. In November 2001, eighty-nine senators wrote to President Bush urging him not to restrain Israel from "using all [its] might and strength" against Palestinian terrorism (quoted in Allin and Simon 2003, 130). This occurred at a time when many sensible commentators were urging Israeli restraint because of the utility of the Israel-Palestine conflict for al-Qaeda propaganda—that is, for the enemy that had only recently inflicted a heavy attack on the U.S. homeland. Many mistakenly attribute American support for Israel to Jewish influence and the pro-Israeli lobby. To be sure, this lobby is effective and powerful, but it would not be nearly so effective if were it not advocating policies that a broad range of Americans see as in U.S. interests and as reflecting U.S. purposes in the world.

The question becomes why so many Americans find it both congenial and necessary to make common cause with Israel. The reason is that they define the meaning and identity of America in ways that make Israel a "friend," and supporting this friend a test of American character and strength. This occurs in several ways: some religious, as when Israeli possession of Jerusalem is seen as a vital prerequisite to the second coming of Christ; some strategic, as when Israel is seen as a loyal ally against the Soviets or radical Islam; and some Kantian, in that they invoke a fraternity of democratic republics. Here again we have an example of the ways in which identity is constructed relationally, in the thick international space of mutual constitution.

None of these different strands linking American identity with Israel are exclusive of one another, and each predates 9/11. They also frequently have purchase across the political spectrum. In a famous 1977 article critical of Israeli policies, George Ball wrote, "Not only must Americans admire Israel, there can be no doubt that we have an interest in, and special responsibility for, that valiant nation" (quoted in Reich 1984, 178–79). As early as 1969, Gerald Ford had declared that "the fate of Israel is linked to the national security interests of the United States," while Eugene Rostow warned in apocalyptic terms that

it is unthinkable that the international community could stand idly by
. . . if Israel were in danger of destruction. The moral and political con-
vulsion that such an event would engender is beyond calculation. It
could spell the end not only of the Atlantic alliance, but of liberal civilization as we know it (both quoted in Reich 1984, 179).

During the Reagan era, Israel was designated a major non-NATO
ally of the United States, and relations between the United States
and Israel were characterized by frequent dialogue and consultation,
including the establishment of a U.S.-Israel free trade area in 1985.
An agreement to intensify political, security, and economic cooperation between the United States and Israel in 1988 began by reaf-
firming "the close relationship between the United States of America
and Israel, based on common goals, interests, and values."[40] In April
1996, President Clinton and Prime Minister Shimon Peres reaf-
firmed U.S.-Israel strategic cooperation and signed a U.S.-Israel
Counter-Terrorism Cooperation Accord, setting up a joint task force
to oversee the implementation of the agreement.[41] The U.S. and Israeli militaries developed close relations ranging from arms procure-
ment to trips for American service academy cadets and midshipmen
to Israel.[42]

The hard facts about U.S.-Israeli relations are less important than
the sentiments of affinity and emotional attachment of which they
are indicative. The effective evocation of sentiments of affinity cre-
ates a bond, a sense of shared identity and purpose across international space. Representations of war and sacrifice can intensify these
bonds, and in doing so they create an imagined geography of conflict that informs policy in fundamental ways. For example, consider
the notion of the "Western Allies" in the Second World War and the
associated tropes of liberation through war and conquest. President
Bush recently invoked these tropes to the graduating class of the
U.S. Air Force Academy, quoting General Eisenhower's message to
the troops who were about to invade Normandy: "The hopes and
prayers of liberty-loving people everywhere march with you."[43] Bush
was attempting to articulate his War on Terror with both World War
II and the Cold War, likening something called "the ideology of terror" to "the murderous ideologies of the 20th century."[44] There is
much at work in these tropes of the West and the Second World

War. The downplaying of the Soviet contribution to victory is routine, as evidenced recently in the sixtieth anniversary memorialization of D-Day, where media commentators regularly identified the Normandy campaign as the "turning point" of the war, ignoring the larger and more decisive struggle at Stalingrad. But more important here is the curious disassociation of Nazi Germany from "the West." As Martin Lewis and Kären Wigen observe, imagined geographies are vehicles "for displacing the sins of Western civilization onto an intrusive non-European Other in our midst" (1997, 68). Germany only returns to the West after being schooled in democracy by the United States and its allies.

The sometimes expanding, sometimes contracting "West" was very much in evidence in the invasion of Iraq. In U.S. policy pronouncements and in much American news commentary, the West was reduced to an Anglo-American rump, with some assistance from Spain, for a time, and Eastern Europe. Most of Western Europe was considered to be undeserving of fully fledged membership in the West, precisely because of its unwillingness to engage in military action for purposes of liberating a potentially "free people." Robert Kagan's very widely read and influential *Paradise and Power* exemplifies this move (2003). Israel, however, does much better in these terms. "You've worked tirelessly to strengthen the ties that bind our nations—our shared values, our strong commitment to freedom," President Bush told the American Israel Public Affairs Committee (AIPAC) in May 2004—something very difficult to imagine him saying sincerely in regard to France, for example.[45]

After 9/11, many Americans, rather than seeing Israeli occupation of the West Bank and Gaza as an underlying cause of terrorism, viewed Israel as an allied republic under assault from the same enemy. In the immediate aftermath of the strikes on New York and Washington, the number of Americans who said their sympathies lay with the Israelis rather than the Palestinians increased to 55 percent from 41 percent the previous month.[46] Even more, the fact that the United States had been grievously wounded by this same enemy was represented as creating a new bond between the United States and Israel, leading to greater empathy with Israel's plight. In April 2002, as Israel was on the offensive in the West Bank, Deputy Defense Secretary Paul Wolfowitz told a rally of American supporters of Israel and Prime Minister Sharon, "Since September 11, we Americans have one thing more in common with Israelis. On that day, America was attacked by suicide bombers. At that moment, every American understood what it is like to live in Jerusalem or Netanya or Haifa."[47] Later that same month, the House Majority Whip Tom DeLay told AIPAC that Israel should not give up "Judea" and "Samaria"; he described Israel as "the lone fountain of liberty" in the Middle East, referring to the Palestinian authority as a "holding company for terrorist subsidiaries."[48] This "Israelization of America" was evident in Bush's speech to AIPAC in 2004 as well.[49] Invoking the purported common experience of the United States and Israel, President Bush remarked, "We experienced the horror of being attacked in our homeland, on our streets, and in places of work. And from that experience came an even stronger determination, a fierce determination to defeat terrorism and to eliminate the threat it poses to free people everywhere."[50] This warmth of feeling is reciprocated in Israel. Israelis, unlike nearly every other country in the world, backed the reelection of Bush over his Democratic challenger in November 2004, by over two to one.[51]

That Israel and the United States face a "common enemy" begs the question of who this enemy is. In Bush's AIPAC speech he makes the obligatory concession to reality that "not all terrorist networks answer to the . . . same leaders," but he then insists that "all terrorists burn with the same hatred" of people who love freedom and that all terrorists kill without shame or mercy, counting their victories in the number of dead innocents.[52] As with Netanyahu, the "terrorism is evil" line is not sufficient on its own, and so Bush goes on to list a number of instances of terrorist attack, spread widely over time and space, that share only one thing—the nominally Muslim identity of the perpetrators, nominal because at least one case is the work of secular Palestinian nationalists. Bush's list includes Nicholas Berg, beheaded in Iraq; Daniel Pearl, killed in Pakistan; Leon Klinghoffer, killed in the Mediterranean; and "blood on the streets" of Jakarta, Jerusalem, Casablanca, Riyadh, Mombasa, Istanbul, Bali, Baghdad, and Madrid. "Every terrorist is at war with civilization, and every group or nation that aids them is equally responsible for the murders that the terrorists commit," Bush concludes.[53] Vice President Cheney produced a similar list in October 2003, referring to a "global campaign" waged by a "terrorist network" ranging from Casablanca to Bali.[54]

The degree to which al-Qaeda represents a tightly controlled hierarchy or a looser network of more or less affiliated organizations, or both in different times and places, is a question open to dispute (Burke 2003; Duffield 2002). Equally, the notion that various resistance organizations might draw from a similar pool of personnel as well as financial and ideological resources can also be debated. But Bush and Cheney offer expansive views of a common enemy, in ways strongly reminiscent of Cold War representations of a unitary and global communism. On their account, "civilization," of which the Anglo-American-Israeli rump is the main defender, is at war with what they see as a widespread pathology of Islam. To arrive at this vision, they must erase the differences between, for example, the despair of long-term occupation and desire for revenge that inspires Palestinian suicide bombers; Jemaah Islamiya's strike in Bali in October 2002; and Moro resistance in the Philippines that has been under way in one form or another since the sixteenth century. Strategically speaking, it would seem to be in the U.S. interest to *disarticulate* these various conflicts by addressing their direct sources, including past and present American policies. But in terms of U.S. identity, it is precisely the expansive vision of civilization's enemy that resonates.

There is some slippage and mobility in the notion of what "civilization" is being defended. Is it "the West"? It is notable that in Rostow's formulation, the fate of the Atlantic alliance and of "liberal civilization" hangs on the willingness of the "international community" to aid Israel. A feature of the diplomacy surrounding both the Israel-Palestine conflict since 9/11 and the war in Iraq is increasing tension between the United States and Western European powers, including the United Kingdom, over Palestine. The warm language of common cause consecrated by blood sacrifice that U.S. leaders reserve for Israel, and the intensity of pro-Israeli feeling among many Americans, is difficult to find in relation to Europe, with the exception of Britain. "The American people join me in expressing condolences to Prime Minister Sharon and all the people of Israel, and in reiterating our common dedication to the cause of fighting terrorism," President Bush stated after a suicide bombing in Haifa in

October 2003.[55] When the Israelis killed the commander of Hamas's military wing in a July 2002 F-16 strike, the CIA station chief in Israel telephoned the chief of staff of the Israeli Defense Forces and the director of the Shin Bet to say, "Great job."[56] The imagined geography at work here is not the familiar one of "the West" but something new, perhaps "post-Western" in John Gray's term, of which two intensely religious societies are the core: the United States and Israel (2002, 128–30).

More recently, there has been close cooperation between Israel and U.S. forces over Iraq. Israeli military and intelligence officials have trained U.S. counterparts preparing to go to Iraq, in part to develop a program, modeled on Israeli operations in the occupied territories, of targeted killings designed to dismantle the Iraqi insurgency.[57] British advice to adopt a "hearts and minds" approach has been much less warmly received by the Americans.[58] The British have a much more successful record in counterinsurgency than either the Israelis or the Americans. As has been pointed out, Israeli tactics in the occupied territories have created isolated cells led by young, often inexperienced and aggressive individuals not subject to central control. More generally, the Israelis have little prospect of winning hearts and minds in the occupied territories, and so a coercive, militarized strategy is the only one available to them. Iraq is a much different conflict, and despite the presence of foreign elements interested in spoiling a positive outcome, a "hearts and minds" strategy seems a rational way forward, one fully concordant with announced U.S. purposes to liberate and rebuild Iraq.

The problem is that in the U.S./Israel vision of "terror," the enemy is not conceived as someone whose heart and mind is potentially winnable. Rather, the enemy is conceived as a dedicated, fanatic terrorist. One of the planners involved in the U.S.-Israeli counter-terror initiative in Iraq is Lt. Gen. William Boykin, the evangelical Christian quoted above who likened the Muslim world with Satan. Elsewhere he has claimed that Islam wants to "destroy us as a Christian army" and that it hates America "because we are a nation of believers."[59] To be sure, many American officers have a more subtle account of both the War on Terror and the nature of the insurgency in Iraq than does Boykin. But Boykin's vision is far more compatible than theirs with American identity as the defender of "free peoples" under attack from "armed minorities" who must be found, fixed, and destroyed. The tendency at all levels in the United States, from the military to the public, will be to see as particularly rational and appropriate policies and strategies that fit with this identity. As a senior British army officer remarked of U.S. soldiers in Iraq, "[they] view things in very simplistic terms. It seems hard for them to reconcile the subtleties between who supports what and who doesn't in Iraq. It's easier for their soldiers to group all Iraqis as the bad guys. As far as they are concerned Iraq is bandit country and everybody is out to kill them."[60]

The U.S./Israel vision of the enemy is a recipe for continued escalation of the War on Terror, in ways that increasingly take on the form of a clash of civilizations—as a product rather than cause of the conflict. Neoconservative ideologues eagerly seize on this possibility. Daniel Pipes, whom President Bush has appointed to the board of the U.S. Institute of Peace, speaks of a long-term conflict between the West and militant Islam. Like Bush, he sees Islamism as a "totalitarian movement that has much in common with fascism and Marxism-Leninism."[61] Such claims, repeated in Bush's address at the Air Force Academy, are now commonplace in U.S. political discourse. But Pipes's "West" is not what it seems at first take: "The Europeans, with their low birth rates, have brought in immigrants from Islamic countries. Indicators suggest that Europe is gradually becoming part of the Muslim world." He sees Christianity and Islam on a collision course, competing for converts and territory: "The main centers of Christian vigor are now in Africa, Latin American and Asia."[62]

This medieval language of religiosity and conversion is at odds with standard accounts of a secular and rational Western modernity. Gray argues that unlike the United States, Western Europe is "post-Enlightenment," in that it has largely given up on the idea of a "universal civilization," as well as the armed imposition of this civilization on "natives." The United States, in the view of Gray and others, is diverging across a range of indicators from Europe. Not only do more Americans go to church, but their Protestantism is the most fundamentalist in Christendom. "Just under 70 per cent of Americans believe in the devil, compared with a third of the British, a fifth of the French and an eighth of the Swedes. . . . America's secular traditions are weaker than Turkey's" (Gray 2002, 126). The United States locks up an extraordinary percentage of its population in prison, particularly African-Americans. Americans proudly own guns. The United States is becoming more Latin and Asian, and more oriented toward the Pacific. Its capitalism is largely devoid of social-welfare protections common in Europe and even in post-Thatcher Britain. Both Old World disdain and wonder are evident in Gray's survey of contemporary American exceptionalism: "Every one of the fifty state governments in the United States has agreed to accept Federal funding to advance the absurd project of promoting sexual abstinence among American teenagers"(2002, 126).

War and conflict are opportunities for voices within communities to redefine and refashion dominant identities. Such is the case in the War on Terror, for America, for Islam, and for the West. These processes are inherently international and take place in and through the thick space of mutual constitution, even when they emphasize separation and difference. Separation and difference can be constituted only in and through relations with others; Europeans, Americans, and Israelis define themselves against and with one another. Much commentary has focused on the diplomatic tensions between Europe and the United States over Iraq, but less attention has been paid to the kind of increasingly fundamental divergence—across a range of social, cultural, and political dimensions—that Gray identifies. The War on Terror is both an example and agent of this divergence. For many Europeans, terror is a problem to be managed, something they have lived with, something that is not eradicable, and something to which the primary response should be increased policing and intelligence. For many Americans, terror is an evil against which a crusade must be waged. In this they have in part taken their cue, their language with which to conceive the enemy, from a certain, now dominant, strand of Israeli and neoconservative thinking. The tragedy in the making is that the battlegrounds of the War on Terror will come increasingly to resemble those in Israel-Palestine. "Close your eyes for a moment, and you can imagine that the [U.S.] Marines in Karbala are Golani infantry in Tul Karm."[63] Iraqi imaginations need no prompting: They already refer to American soldiers in Iraq as "Jews."[64]

AFTERWORD

This book appropriates the globalization concept and redefines it as a general property of the "international," as relations of interconnection and mutual constitution. It looks at armed force and war through the lens of globalization, arguing that by means of the interconnections it occasions, war is transformative of world politics and of the people and places it reaches out and touches. Throughout, the text foregrounds interconnection and the play of relations across often widely divergent spaces and populations. In these ways, the book opens up the international as a distinct social space of connection and constitution and anatomizes the place of war and the military in this space.

Chapter 1 began with the popular understanding of "globalization" as a set of ostensibly inevitable processes occurring in the world economy. The basic claim was that the intensification of international trade and investment had reached a point at which national economies dissolve into a global economy. The nation-state, it was argued, was in terminal decline, subsumed by a global free market and its flows of people, goods, and ideas across increasingly irrelevant borders. At the same time, modern communications technologies intensified these flows, collapsing time and space, loosening the bonds between culture and place, and supposedly making possible a unitary global society. Drawing on liberal visions of the pacifying tendencies of free trade, many saw "globalization" as not only the grave digger of the state but also of war, at least in the "globalized" world.

This conception of "globalization" was critiqued along a number of dimensions. States are in fact agents of globalization, and the global economy is fundamentally dependent upon state regulation. Much of this regulation occurs at the international level, leading to the transformation of local states. Far from being peaceful, establishing "free trade" often requires war, while the modernizing processes it sets in train can generate further armed conflict. Visions of a unitary global economy, society, and culture are belied by horrific divides of wealth and power between North and South and a growing world conflict commonly perceived as a clash between Western and Islamic civilizations.

The notion that "globalization" is essentially about the intensifying circulation of people, goods, and ideas wrought by modern communications technologies is also subjected to critique. While it is true that this circulation is increasing in the contemporary world, such circulation and the interconnections it sets in train does not require modern communications. Telegraphs, sailing ships, and horse-drawn transport served to connect and transform places long before satellite TV and the Internet arrived on the scene. Precisely such connection and transformation, the mutual making together of interconnected places, is in fact the heart of the globalization concept used in this book. Liberated from neoliberal assumptions and technological determinism, it serves as a useful guide to thinking about the international as a space of connection and constitution. This space is multidimensional in nature and is not limited to economic processes but includes social, cultural, political, and military relations as well.

If enthusiasts for "globalization" wrote premature obituaries for the nation-state, students of war, as chapter 2 shows, all too often made a fetish of it. Whether in the disciplines of military history, strategic studies, or international relations, studies of war generally took for granted an image of the world as composed of nation-states. Moreover, in the social sciences generally, war was conceived as a breakdown of interchange and circulation between combatant parties, as a deviation from normal, peaceful relations between societies. Part of the price of this way of conceiving world politics is that the role of war in creating and transforming a world organized along nation-state lines is easily overlooked. Histories of imperial war and of colonial and other transnational armed forces can fall from view.

From a war and society perspective, war can be seen as an occasion for interconnection, as a form of circulation between combatant parties. In and through war, societies are transformed, while at the same time societies shape the nature of war. War is refigured as a globalizing force, as a multidimensional form of connection and constitution between peoples and places. The peoples and places so connected were not only nation-states and national peoples but also imperial states and the peoples they subjugated or attempted to subjugate. In the Cold War, the superpowers and their societies become bound up with histories of intervention in the Third World. Today, it is civilizations that are putatively interconnected in and through war. Global histories of war and armed forces are opened for inquiry, histories in which wars and their effects play out across wide spaces and have consequences for world politics long after the guns fall silent.

Chapter 3 explored one such global history, that which arose out of Britain's involvement in South Asia. British and South Asian history became intertwined in part through the raising of a British Indian colonial army. This army shaped Indian history, by helping to conquer India and holding it for the British; it shaped British history as well, and the histories of many other places, by allowing Britain to rule a world empire with only a small army of its own. Through its vital role in two world wars, the British Indian army influenced the outcome of the great conflagrations of the twentieth century. At the same time, in a variety of ways, the use of the Indian army abroad helped seal the fate of the Raj at home. As chapter 3 argued, globalizing the war and society approach involves attention not only to social transformations occasioned by war in particular countries but also to transregional and worldwide military orders, and to historical transformations in the organization and use of force that make possible certain societies, politics, and cultures in different times and places. The Indian army helped to make possible a British empire at the same time as it changed the course of British, Indian, and European history. As this book has argued throughout, peoples and places are tied together through interactive dynamics, and such interaction and interconnection is what globalization is all about.

One of the ways in which the illusion of a world composed of separate and discrete places is maintained is through the idea that cultures are distinct, self-generating, and sealed off from one another—at least until disrupted by "globalization." Chapter 4 took a different approach. It argued that even in a "national-international" world, people required other cultures and nations against which to define their own. Nations come into existence in a cultural and social field of *other* nations and collective identities. The international is a thick space of cultural interaction even when populated by nation-states. Many of the meanings and ideas that circulate in this space concern war and the military. Perceptions of danger from abroad are incitements to define—and police—dominant identities at home. Both leaders and the general public are often acutely concerned with their nations' relative military power. More generally, conceptions of civilization and barbarism and of the West, and the rest, have important military dimensions. The idea of the West as a muscular liberator and civilizer is one of the ways in which the brutal history of imperialism, exploitation, and domination of the non-European world is obscured. At the same time, militarily underestimating the "natives" can lead to defeat and to cultural and political crisis in the metropole, as in the Vietnam syndrome.

Militaries and war are also sites of culture mixing and hybridity. Military traveling cultures expose soldiers to the foreign and lead them to reassess their ideas about home. Soldiers returning from abroad transmit new ideas and practices to their native lands. War itself can be experienced as a collective human tragedy and prompt identification not with one's nation or particular group but with humanity as a whole. In the post-1945 era, ideas about human rights, the prevention of genocide and other crimes against humanity, and humanitarian intervention and peacekeeping all derived much of their moral energy from the bloodshed of the Second World War.

Chapter 5 addressed the global history of a war in the making, that of the War on Terror. As with other wars discussed in the preceding pages, the War on Terror links distant places and peoples together and is transforming societies and cultures through interconnection. Particular attention was paid to the politics of the War on Terror and to the escalatory logics involved in notions of a war fought for civilization or between civilizations. Participants and ideologues on both sides say they are fighting in the name of a civilization conceived as distinct and separate from the enemy. Yet, as the chapter showed, neither the West, Islam, nor al-Qaeda can be understood without reference to the constitutive interconnections between all three.

Categories derived from the Israeli-Palestinian conflict, most importantly an understanding of "terror" as the enemy and of the strategies that flow from this approach, play a role in shaping the War on Terror. This is just one important example of how that war has conjoined preexisting conflicts together and of how local conflicts can influence events far beyond their immediate focus. The intensifying bonds between Israel and the United States, and the increasing importance of religion in the War on Terror on all sides, are yet further examples of how war occasions transformations in society. At the same time these transformations react back on the war, framing it in uncompromising, eschatological terms that can lead only to further violence. Like the Cold War before it, the War on Terror promises to be the governing influence in world politics for decades to come. Only a perspective sensitive to connection and constitution can grasp how the War on Terror will develop and how it will shape events in many distant locales, even as it is shaped by them.

This book has used war and the military as an occasion to rethink the concept of globalization. One of the things it demonstrates is that no matter how globalization is understood—as economic globalization, as transregional interconnectedness, or as consciousness of the global—war and the military play far more important roles than extant studies of globalization indicate. In a sense, this is a specific instance of a more general problem. While matters military are of enormous significance for politics and society, past and present, most scholars in the humanities and social sciences know very little about armies and war. Specialists in these latter topics return the favor. With important exceptions, studies of military affairs are most often conducted in isolation from their relation to and significance for wider social and political context. This dialogue of the deaf produced the structural conditions in the academy for pacified forms of globalization studies.

By mapping where war and the military intersect with globalization studies, this book has sought to lay the basis not just for studies of military globalization or of war as a form of interconnection, or even of how globalization is productive of conflict. Rather, what is needed is an assessment of the ways in which war is centrally implicated in processes of globalization. While Shaw's call for a "*war-centred* social theory" perhaps overstates the case, his basic point is that war is a central determinant of social and political relations (1988, 28). To the extent this is true of globalization, no adequate account of globalization can attend to economic or cultural or social dimensions without also taking into account war, and vice versa. War and armed conflict very often have been the leading edge of transregional interconnectedness. Maintaining such interconnection in the face of resistance has often required repeated use of force, while the circulation of people, goods, and ideas in world politics has often taken military forms. Most importantly, war itself is a principal form of interconnection between peoples and places, and it is in this sense a globalizing force. All of this suggests that war needs to be taken far more seriously in globalization studies. This book has taken some initial steps in that direction.

NOTES

Preface

1. Oriental and India Office Collection [hereafter OIOC], L/PJ/12/654, Middle East Military Censorship Fortnightly Summary Covering Indian Troops, no. 144, March 24–April 6, 1943.

2. Labour's electoral victory was said to be the only victory of the British Army Education Corps, perceived to be a hotbed of socialists and other intellectuals by some regular officers.

3. OIOC L/WS/1/1506, India Command Weekly Intelligence Summaries, August 31, 1945 and October 12, 1945.

Chapter 1: The False Dawn of "Globalization"

The title of this chapter is borrowed from John Gray, *False Dawn: The Delusions of Global Capitalism* (London: Granta Books, 2002).

1. Jennifer Lee, "High-Tech Scrutiny Set for U.S. Travellers," *International Herald Tribune,* August 25, 2003, 2.

2. Phil Bloomer, "Europe's Subsidy Junkies Stay Hooked," *Observer Comment Extra,* June 29, 2003, politics.guardian.co.uk/print/0,3858,4701211-102273,00.html [accessed September 8, 2003].

3. For a set of essays that seek to place American history in transnational context, see Thomas Bender, ed., *Rethinking American History in a Global Age* (Berkeley: University of California Press, 2002).

4. President G. W. Bush, Commencement Address, University of South Carolina, Columbia, South Carolina, May 9, 2003, www.whitehouse.gov/news/releases/2003/05 [accessed May 10, 2003].

Chapter 2: Behind "Globalization"

1. For an excellent brief introduction to Clausewitz's life and thought, see Michael Howard, *Clausewitz* (Oxford: Oxford University Press, 1983).

2. In saying "again," Clausewitz is referring to ancient "barbarian" tribes, where every man was also a warrior.

3. Another important factor to remember in interpreting casualty statistics of this sort is that many infantry soldiers might be wounded more than once. Any soldier receiving a wound serious enough to be evacuated from his unit will show up in the statistics. Over the course of the war, a soldier might receive one, two, or even three such wounds, each of which would count, as would his subsequent death in combat. This again emphasizes the fact that casualties were overwhelmingly concentrated among the combat troops, for whom debilitating wounds or death were likely the only possible routes out of frontline service.

4. Hitler's boast was untrue. As many as three million European Jews survived the Holocaust.

5. Eric Pape and Michael Meyer, "Dogs of Peace," *Newsweek* 142, no. 8 (August 25–September 1, 2003): 26–28.

6. Pape and Meyer, "Dogs of Peace," 26–28.

7. Rodolfo F. Acuña, "Immigrants Could End Up Fighting War in Iraq," *Miami Herald* online, Herald.com, September 19, 2003, www.miami.com/mld/miamiherald/news/opinion/6808600.htm [accessed March 2, 2004]. Only aliens legally resident in the United States, however, can be recruited into the military, although recruiters have crossed into Mexico looking for young people with U.S. residency papers.

8. Eric Schmitt, "Boom Times for U.S. Military Recruiters," *International Herald Tribune*, September 22, 2003, 8.

Chapter 3: Globalization and War

Epigraph quoted in W. B. Merewether and Sir Frederick Smith, *The Indian Corps in France* (London: John Murray, 1918), xi. The quote refers to the arrival of the Indian Corps in France in October 1914, two months after the beginning of World War I. Lord French was the commander of the British Expeditionary Force in France in 1914, and Lord Curzon was viceroy of India.

1. Letter 388 in David Omissi, *Indian Voices of the Great War: Soldiers' Letters, 1914–18* (London: Macmillan. 1999), 228.

2. This loyalty, and the hope it would lead to self-rule, was evident in a resolution passed in 1915 by the Indian National Congress stating: "This Congress rejoices to place on record the deep sense of gratitude and pride in the heroic conduct of the Indian troops whose deeds of valour and conspicuous

humanity and chivalry in the Great War are winning the respect of a civilized mankind for the Mother Country and resolves to send a message of hearty and affectionate greetings to them and their comrades in arms, with fervent prayers for their well-being and success." Quoted in Philip Mason, *A Matter of Honour: An Account of the Indian Army, Its Officers and Men* (London: Jonathan Cape, 1974), 447.

3. "English not good!"

4. Letter 374 in Omissi, *Indian Voices of the Great War*, 219.

5. Letter 260 in Omissi, *Indian Voices of the Great War*, 160.

6. Letter 269 in Omissi, *Indian Voices of the Great War*, 164.

7. Letter 448 in Omissi, *Indian Voices of the Great War*, 258.

8. Letter 448 in Omissi, *Indian Voices of the Great War*, 258.

9. Letter 654 in Omissi, *Indian Voices of the Great War*, 356.

10. Letter 171 in Omissi, *Indian Voices of the Great War*, 114.

11. Letter 592 in Omissi, *Indian Voices of the Great War*, 324.

12. For the most part this refers to British Indian army officers serving in India and other Europeans resident in India, not Indians *per se*.

13. OIOC L/PJ/12/655, Middle East Military Censorship Fortnightly Summary Covering Indian Troops [hereafter OIOC L/PJ/12/655], no. 156, September 8–21, 1943.

14. OIOC L/PJ/12/655, no. 156, September 8–21, 1943.

15. OIOC L/PJ/12/655, no. 176, June 14–27, 1943.

16. Ice and whiskey.

17. "Real" or "authentic."

Chapter 4: War and Culture in Global Context

1. See their website, www.unpo.org [accessed July 20, 2004].

2. The term British soldiers used for warriors among the indigenous peoples of the eastern Sudan.

3. "President Sworn-In to Second Term," available at whitehouse.gov/news/releases/2005/01/20050120-1.html.

4. Remarks by the president at the Twentieth Anniversary of the National Endowment for Democracy, November 6, 2003, www.whitehouse.gov/news/releases/2003/11/print/20031106-2.html [accessed November 8, 2003].

5. On the role of Vietnamese women in the wars of liberation, see Sandra C. Taylor, *Vietnamese Women at War: Fighting for Ho Chi Minh and the Revolution* (Lawrence: University Press of Kansas, 1999).

6. "President Bush discusses Freedom in Iraq and the Middle East," remarks by the president at the twentieth anniversary of the National Endowment for Democracy, November 6, 2003, www.whitehouse.gov/news/releases/2003/11/print/20031106-2.html [accessed November 8, 2003].

7. Quoted in Brian Knowlton, "U.S. to 'Stay the Course' in Iraq," *International Herald Tribune,* October 28, 2003, 1.

8. Knowlton, "U.S. to 'Stay the Course' in Iraq."

9. President's Radio Address, November 1, 2003, available at www.white house.gov/news/releases/2003/11/print/20031101.html [accessed November 3, 2003].

Chapter 5: "Terror" and the Politics of Global War

1. "Bin Laden's warning: full text," Sunday, October 7, 2001, news.bbc .co.uk/1/low/world/south_asia/1585636.stm [accessed 25 September 2003].

2. Carlos H. Conde, "Manila Struggles with Deadly Violence in the South," *International Herald Tribune,* February 15, 2005, 6.

3. Quoted in Carlos H. Conde, "On Mindanao, Jihad Looms If Peace Talks Fail," *International Herald Tribune,* October 12, 2004, 2.

4. "Al-Qa'ida Website, Back On-Line Publishes Book about Its War on the U.S. and Bombing in Saudi Arabia," Middle East Media Research Institute, Special Dispatch, Jihad and Terrorism Studies, no. 569.

5. Quoted in Conde, "On Mindanao, Jihad Looms If Peace Talks Fail," 2.

6. The Eastern Turkistan Islamic Movement. See the U.S. State Department report *Patterns of Global Terrorism 2003*, available on www.state.gov/s/ct/ rls/pgtrpt/2003/c12153.htm [accessed September 15, 2004].

7. "Al-Qa'ida Website."

8. Unlike Victor Hanson (2002), Huntington fails to draw the same conclusion from the quantitative evidence of Western violence in the twentieth century. The many millions of dead from the two world wars far exceed the dead from the conflicts along what Huntington sees as the perimeter of Islam. Presumably, Huntington does not conceive Nazi Germany, modernizing imperial Japan or the Soviet Union as "Western." For a counterargument, see John Gray, *Al Qaeda and What It Means to Be Modern:* "The twentieth century's grand experiments with revolutionary terror were not assaults on the West. They expressed ambitions that have been harboured only in the West" (117).

9. Quoted in Alain Gresh, "The War of a Thousand Years," *Le Monde Diplomatique,* September 2004, 5.

10. Osama bin Laden, "Resist the New Rome," *Guardian*, January 6, 2004, 23.

11. "Address to a Joint Session of Congress and the American People," September 20, 2001, www.whitehouse.gov/news/releases/2001/09/20010920-8 .html [accessed September 7, 2004].

12. Bin Laden, "Resist the New Rome," 23.

13. The large statues were destroyed by the Taliban at bin Laden's request in March 2000.

14. John Prados, "Notes on the CIA's Secret War in Afghanistan," www.history cooperative.org/journals/jah/89.2/prados.html, 4 [accessed August 12, 2003]. This is an online version of an article in *Journal of American History* 89, 2.

15. Quoted in Gresh, "The War of a Thousand Years," 5, and Brian Knowlton, "Comments on Islam Irk the White House," *International Herald Tribune,* October 20, 2003, 6.

16. "Address to a Joint Session of Congress and the American People."

17. "Address of the President to the Nation," September 7, 2003, www.white house.gov/news/releases/2003/09/print/20030907–1.html; "President Discusses the Future of Iraq," speech at the American Enterprise Institute, February 26, 2003, www.whitehouse.gove/news/releases/2003/02/print/200302.

18. See the U.S. State Department report *Patterns of Global Terrorism 2003,* xii, available on www.state.gov/s/ct/rls/pgtrpt/2003/c12153.htm [accessed September 15, 2004].

19. The irony of condemning Muslim violence via the papacy—which licensed the Crusades—does not seem to have occurred to Netanyahu.

20. Quoted in "The Time of Killing," *Harper's Magazine* 309, no. 1850 (July 2004), 23.

21. BBC News Online, "In Full: Al-Qa'ida statement," October 10, 2001, news.bbc.co.uk/1/low/world/middle_east/1590350.stm [accessed September 25, 2003].

22. Quoted in Nick Paton Walsh et al., "Putin's Warning as Terror Deaths Top 360," *Observer,* September 5, 2004, 3.

23. "President Condemns Terrorism in Russia," President's remarks to the Press Pool, Russian Embassy, Washington D.C., September 12, 2004, www .whitehouse.gov/news/releases/2004/09/20040912–1.html [accessed 21 September, 2004].

24. "Address of the President of Russia Vladimir Putin," September 4, 2004, press release with unofficial translation provided by Embassy of the Russian Federation, London, UK, www.great-britain.mid.ru/GreatBritain/pr_rel/pres 22-04.htm [accessed September 21, 2004].

25. Bridget Kendall, "Analysis: Putin's drastic measures," BBC News online, September 13, 2004, news.bbc.co.uk/1/hi/world/europe/3653084.stm [accessed September 21, 2004].

26. Associated Press, "Russia Plows New Funding into Fighting Terrorism," *International Herald Tribune,* September 15, 2004, 3.

27. "Address of the President of Russia Vladimir Putin."

28. C. J. Chivers and Steven Lee Myers, "Chechen Rebels More Nationalist than Islamist," *International Herald Tribune,* September 13, 2004, 2. Two of the thirty-three hostage takers were in fact Arabs, not ten as the Russian Federal Security Service claimed. See C. J. Chivers, "Chechen Lists Details of Attack on School," *International Herald Tribune,* September 18–19, 2004, 6.

29. For information on the wars in Chechnya and casualty estimates see American Committee for Peace in Chechnya, www.peaceinchechnya.org; Project Ploughshares, Armed Conflicts Report 2003, Russia (Chechnya), www .ploughshares.ca/content/ACR/ACR00/ACR00-Russia.html [accessed September 21, 2004]; and GlobalSecurity.org, www.globalsecurity.org/military/world/ war/chechnya.htm [accessed September 21, 2004]. The estimate of the number of dead children is from the International Children of Chechnya, a nonprofit group. See Khassan Baiev, "The Scenes at Beslan Weren't So Unfamiliar," *International Herald Tribune,* September 13, 2004, 8. As of fall 2003, of 385,000 children living in Chechnya, two thousand were orphans, twenty-five thousand had only one parent, and 5,500 were disabled. Seth Mydans, "In Chechnya, a Siege with No End," *International Herald Tribune,* October 4, 2004, 3.

30. C. J. Chivers, "Chechen Guerrilla's Winding Path to Terror," *International Herald Tribune,* September 16, 2004, 8.

31. Quoted in Mydans, "In Chechnya, a Siege with No End," 3.

32. See Chivers, "Chechen Lists Details of Attack on School," 6. He used a derogatory term for "Russia."

33. Quoted in Steven R. Weisman, "U.S. Responds Gingerly to Putin's Power Move," *International Herald Tribune,* September 15, 2004, 3.

34. Associated Press, "Sharon Asks for Global Alliance to Fight Terror," *International Herald Tribune,* September 6, 2004, 3.

35. Figures are from the Israeli Information Center for Human Rights in the Occupied Territories, available on the web at www.betselem.org.il/ [accessed September 21, 2004].

36. Steven Erlanger, "Faded Hopes Litter Intifada's 4-Year Legacy," *International Herald Tribune,* October 4, 2004, 5.

37. For estimates see www.iraqbodycount.net/; Carl Conetta, "The Wages of War: Iraqi Combatant and Noncombatant Fatalities in the 2003 Conflict," Project on Defense Alternatives Research Monograph 8; and Carl Conetta, "Disappearing the Dead: Iraq, Afghanistan, and the Idea of a 'New Warfare,'" Project on Defense Alternatives, Research Monograph 9. Both Project on Defense Alternatives monographs can be found on www.comw.org/pda/ [accessed September 21, 2004]. See also Norimitsu Onishi, "A Single Week's Tally of Death for the Iraqis," *International Herald Tribune,* October 20, 2004.

38. "Excerpts from 'Bin Laden' tape," *Guardian,* April 15, 2004, www.guardian .co.uk/print/0,3858,4902190–111026,00.html [accessed April 25, 2004].

39. Project for the New American Century, "Letter to President Bush on Israel, Arafat and the War on Terrorism," April 3, 2002, www.newamericancentury .org/Bushletter-040302.htm [accessed May 17, 2004].

40. "Memorandum of Agreement between the United States and the State of Israel Regarding Joint Political, Security and Economic Cooperation," JINSA Online, April 21, 1988, www.jinsa.org/articles/view.html?documentid = 182 [accessed May 17, 2004].

41. "U.S.-Israel Joint Statement on Strategic Cooperation," JINSA Online, April 30, 1996, www.jinsa.org/articles/view.html?documentid=184 [accessed May 17, 2004].

42. Jason Vest, "The Men from JINSA and CSP," *Nation*, September 2, 2002, www.thenation.com/doc/Print.mhtml?I=20020902&s=vest [accessed May 18, 2004].

43. Quoted in "Remarks by the President at the United States Air Force Academy Graduation Ceremony," June 2, 2004, www.whitehouse.gov/news/releases/2004/06/40040602.html [accessed June 3, 2004[.

44. "Remarks by the President at the United States Air Force Academy Graduation Ceremony."

45. "President Speaks to American Israel Public Affairs Committee," www.whitehouse.gov/news/releases/2004/05/20040518–1.html [accessed May 18, 2004].

46. The Gallup Organization, "Americans Show Increased Support for Israel following Terrorist Attacks," September 19, 2001, www.gallup.com/content/login.aspx?ci=4915 [accessed May 12, 2004].

47. Quoted in NewsMax.com Wires (UPI), "Hard-line Israeli Supporters Boo Wolfowitz," April 16, 2002, www.newsmax.com/archives/articles/2002/4/15/204626.shtml [accessed May 17, 2004].

48. Quoted in Barbara Slavin, "Don't Give Up 1967 Lands, Delay Tells Israel Lobby," *USA Today*, April 23, 2002, www.usatoday.com/news/world/2002/04/24/aipac.htm [accessed May 18, 2004].

49. Gideon Samet titled one of his columns in *Haaretz* "The Israelization of America," April 4, 2003, www.haaretzdaily.com/hasen/objects/pages/PrintArticleEn.jhtml?itemNo=280488 [accessed May 18, 2004].

50. "President Speaks to American Israel Public Affairs Committee." Brent Scowcroft, national security advisor to President H. W. Bush, comments that President G. W. Bush is "mesmerized" by Ariel Sharon: "Sharon just has him wrapped around his little finger. . . . When there is a suicide attack [followed by an Israeli reprisal] Sharon calls the president and says, 'I'm on the front line of terrorism,' and the president says, 'Yes you are.'" Quoted in Glenn Kessler, "Scowcroft Is Critical of Bush," *Washington Post*, October 16, 2004, A02.

51. Alan Travis, "We Like Americans, We Don't Like Bush," *Guardian*, October 15, 2004, 4.

52. "President Speaks to American Israel Public Affairs Committee."

53. "President Speaks to American Israel Public Affairs Committee."

54. "Remarks by the Vice President to the Heritage Foundation," October 10, 2003, new.heritage.org/Research/MiddleEast/h1800.cfm?renderforprint=1 [accessed October 13, 2003].

55. "President Condemns Terrorist Act," statement by the president, October 4, 2003, www.whitehouse.gov/news/releases/2003/10/20031004–1html [accessed May 17, 2004].

56. Quoted in Amir Oren, "Facing the Common Enemy," *Haaretz,* July 30, 2002, www.haaretzdaily.com/hasen/pages/ShArt.jhtml?itemNo = 192149& contrassID = 2&su bContrassID = 4&sbSubContrassID = 0&listSrc = Y [accessed May 17, 2004].

57. Seymour Hersh, "Moving Targets," *New Yorker,* December 8, 2003, www .newyorker.com/printable/?fact/031215fa_fact [accessed April 1, 2004].

58. Sean Rayment, "US Tactics Condemned by British Officers," *Daily Telegraph,* April 11, 2004.

59. Quoted in Hersh, "Moving Targets," 4.

60. Quoted in Rayment, "US Tactics Condemned by British Officers."

61. Quoted in Manfred Gerstenfeld, "The End of American Jewry's Golden Era: An Interview with Daniel Pipes," May 2, 2004, www.campus-watch.org/ article/id/1138 [accessed May 15, 2004].

62. Gerstenfeld, "The End of American Jewry's Golden Era."

63. Samet, "The Israelization of America." The Golani Infantry Brigade is an elite Israeli unit, and Tul Karm is a city and refugee camp on the West Bank. Karbala is a town in Iraq.

64. Thomas Friedman, "Jews, Israel and America," *International Herald Tribune,* October 25, 2004, 8.

REFERENCES

Allin, Dana H., and Steven Simon. 2003. "The Moral Psychology of US Support for Israel." *Survival* 45, no. 3.

Allison, Graham. 2004. *Nuclear Terrorism: The Ultimate Preventable Catastrophe*. New York: Times Books.

Anderson, Fred. 2001. *Crucible of War: The Seven Years' War and the Fate of Empire in British North America, 1754–1766*. New York: Vintage Books.

Anonymous. 2004. *Imperial Hubris: Why the West Is Losing the War on Terror*. Washington, D.C.: Brassey's.

Appadurai, Arjun. 1996. *Modernity at Large: Cultural Dimensions of Globalization*. Minneapolis: University of Minnesota Press.

Aron, Raymond. 1974. *The Imperial Republic: The United States and the World 1945–1973*. Englewood Cliffs, N.J.: Prentice Hall.

Barkawi, Tarak. 2004. "Peoples, Homelands, and Wars? Ethnicity, the Military, and Battle among British Imperial Forces in the War against Japan." *Comparative Studies in Society and History* 46, no. 1:134–63.

———. 1998. "Strategy as a Vocation: Weber, Morgenthau and Modern Strategic Studies." *Review of International Studies* 24, no. 2:159–84.

Barkawi, Tarak, and Mark Laffey. 2001. *Democracy, Liberalism and War: Rethinking the Democratic Peace Debate*. Boulder, Colo.: Lynne Rienner.

Bates, Milton. 1996. *The Wars We Took to Vietnam*. Berkeley: University of California Press.

Bender, Thomas, ed. 2002. *Rethinking American History in a Global Age*. Berkeley: University of California Press.

Bennison, Amira K. 2002. "Muslim Universalism and Western Globalization." In *Globalization in World History,* ed. A. G. Hopkins, 2002. London: Pimlico.

Biderman, Albert D. 1963. *March to Calumny: The Story of American POW's in the Korean War*. New York: Macmillan.

Black, Jeremy. 1998. *War and the World: Military Power and the Fate of Continents*. New Haven, Conn.: Yale University Press.

Bond, Brian. 1998 [1984]. *War and Society in Europe 1870–1970*. Stroud, U.K.: Sutton.

Boot, Max. 2002. *The Savage Wars of Peace: Small Wars and the Rise of American Power*. New York: Basic Books.

Bracken, Paul. 1983. *The Command and Control of Nuclear Forces*. New Haven, Conn.: Yale University Press.

Brands, H. W. 1993. *The Devil We Knew: Americans and the Cold War*. Oxford: Oxford University Press.

Brodie, Bernard. 1971. *Strategy and National Interests: Reflections for the Future*. Strategy Papers no. 7. New York: National Strategy Information Center.

Brysk, Alison. 2000. *From Tribal Village to Global Village: Indian Rights and International Relations in Latin America*. Palo Alto, Calif.: Stanford University Press.

Burke, Jason. 2003. *Al-Qaeda: Casting a Shadow of Terror*. London: I. B. Tauris.

Cain, P. J., and A. G. Hopkins. 2002. *British Imperialism, 1688–2000*. 2d ed. Harlow, U.K.: Longman.

Callwell, Col. C. E. 1996 [1906]. *Small Wars: Their Principles and Practice*. Lincoln: University of Nebraska Press.

Campbell, David. 1992. *Writing Security: United States Foreign Policy and the Politics of Identity*. Minneapolis: University of Minnesota Press.

Carr, Caleb. 1992. *The Devil Soldier: The Story of Frederick Townsend Ward*. New York: Random House.

Carr, E. H. 1946. *The Twenty Years' Crisis 1919–1939: An Introduction to the Study of International Relations*. London: Macmillan.

Carruthers, Susan L. 2000. *The Media at War: Communication and Conflict in the Twentieth Century*. London: Macmillan.

———. 1998. "'The Manchurian Candidate' (1962) and the Cold War Brainwashing Scare." *Historical Journal of Film, Radio and Television* 18, no. 1.

Castle, Timothy N. 1993. *At War in the Shadow of Vietnam: U.S. Military Aid to the Royal Lao Government 1955–1975*. New York: Columbia University Press.

Chandra, Bipan, Mridula Mukherjee, Aditya Mukherjee, K. N. Panikkar, and Sucheta Mahajan. 1989. *India's Struggle for Independence 1857–1947*. New Delhi: Penguin Books (India).

Clarke, Richard. 2004. *Against All Enemies: Inside America's War on Terror*. New York: Free Press.

Clausewitz, Carl von. 1976. *On War*. Princeton, N.J.: Princeton University Press. Trans. and ed. Michael Howard and Peter Paret. Princeton, N.J.: Princeton University Press, 1976.

Clayton, Anthony. 1988. *France, Soldiers and Africa*. London: Brassey's.

Clifford, James. 1997. *Routes: Travel and Translation in the Late Twentieth Century*. Cambridge, Mass.: Harvard University Press.

Cohen, Eliot A. 1985. *Citizens and Soldiers: The Dilemmas of Military Service*. Ithaca, N.Y.: Cornell University Press.

Cohen, Stephen P. 1971. *The Indian Army: Its Contribution to the Development of a Nation*. Berkeley: University of California Press.

Collins, Larry and Dominique Lapierre. 1997. *Freedom at Midnight: The Epic Drama of India's Struggle for Independence*. London: HarperCollins.

Comaroff, John. 1991. "Humanity, Ethnicity, Nationality." *Theory and Society* 20, no. 5.

Conboy, Kenneth, and James Morrison. *Feet to the Fire: CIA Covert Operations in Indonesia, 1957–1958*. Annapolis, Md.: Naval Institute Press.

Conetta, Carl. 2003. *The Wages of War: Iraqi Combatant and Noncombatant Fatalities in the 2003 Conflict*. Project on Defense Alternatives Research Monograph no. 8. Cambridge, Mass.: Commonwealth Institute, available at www.comw.org/pda/0310rm8.html.

Connell, John. 1959. *Auchinleck: A Critical Biography*. London: Cassell.

Cooper, Frederick, and Ann Laura Stoler. 1997. *Tensions of Empire: Colonial Cultures in a Bourgeois World*. Berkeley: University of California Press.

Creveld, Martin van. 1991. *The Transformation of War*. New York: Free Press.

Davis, Mike. 2001. *Late Victorian Holocausts: El Niño Famines and the Making of the Third World*. London: Verso.

Devji, Faisal. 2005. *Landscapes of the Jihad: Militancy, Morality and Modernity*. London: Hurst.

Dittmar, Linda, and Gene Michaud, eds. 1990. *From Hanoi to Hollywood: The Vietnam War in American Film*. New Brunswick, N.J.: Rutgers University Press.

Doty, Roxanne. 1996. *Imperial Encounters*. Minneapolis: University of Minnesota Press.

Doyle, Michael. 1983. "Kant, Liberal Legacies, and Foreign Affairs." *Philosophy and Public Affairs* 12, nos. 3 and 4.

Drake, Michael S. 2001. *Problematics of Military Power: Government, Discipline and the Subject of Violence*. London: Frank Cass.

Drayton, Richard. 2002. "The Collaboration of Labour: Slaves, Empires, and Globalizations in the Atlantic World, *c*. 1600–1850." In *Globalization in World History*, ed. A. G. Hopkins, 2002. London: Pimlico.

Duffield, Mark. 2002. "War as a Network Enterprise: The New Security Terrain and Its Implications." *Cultural Values* 6, nos. 1 and 2:153–65.

Du Picq, Ardant. 1921. *Battle Studies: Ancient and Modern Battle*. New York: Macmillan.

Echenberg, Myron. 1991. *Colonial Conscripts: The Tirailleurs Sénégalais in French West Africa, 1857–1960*. Portsmouth, U.K.: Heinemann.

Enloe, Cynthia. 1980. *Ethnic Soldiers: State Security in a Divided Society.* Harmondsworth, U.K.: Penguin Books.

Escobar, Arturo. 1995. *Encountering Development: The Making and Unmaking of the Third World.* Princeton, N.J.: Princeton University Press.

Evans, Humphrey. 1960. *Thimayya of India: A Soldier's Life.* New York: Harcourt, Brace.

Fanon, Frantz. 1967. *The Wretched of the Earth.* Harmondsworth, U.K.: Penguin Books.

Fay, Peter Ward. 1993. *The Forgotten Army: India's Armed Struggle for Independence 1942–1945.* Ann Arbor: University of Michigan Press.

Featherstone, Donald. 1992. *Victorian Colonial Warfare: India.* London: Blandford.

Freedman, Lawrence. 1989. *The Evolution of Nuclear Strategy.* 2d ed. London: Macmillan.

Fujitani, T., Geoffrey M. White, and Lisa Yoneyama. 2001. *Perilous Memories: The Asia-Pacific War(s).* Durham, N.C.: Duke University Press.

Fukuyama, Francis. 1992. *The End of History and the Last Man.* New York: Free Press.

Fussell, Paul. 2000 [1975]. *The Great War and Modern Memory.* Oxford: Oxford University Press.

Gaddis, John Lewis. 1982. *Strategies of Containment: A Critical Appraisal of Postwar American National Security Policy.* Oxford: Oxford University Press.

Ghosh, K. K. 1969. *The Indian National Army: Second Front of the Indian Independence Movement.* Meerut: Meenakshi Prakashan.

Gibson, James William. 1994. *Warrior Dreams.* New York: Hill and Wang.

Giddens, Anthony. 1985. *The Nation-State and Violence.* Cambridge, U.K.: Polity.

Goody, Jack. 2004. *Islam in Europe.* Cambridge, U.K.: Polity.

Gray, Jack. 2002. *Rebellions and Revolutions: China from the 1800s to 2000.* Oxford: Oxford University Press.

Gray, John. 2003. *Al Qaeda and What It Means to Be Modern.* London: Faber and Faber.

———. 2002. *False Dawn: The Delusions of Global Capitalism.* London: Granta Books.

Gregory, Derek. 2004. *The Colonial Present: Afghanistan, Palestine, Iraq.* Oxford, U.K.: Blackwell.

Gupta, Akhil, and James Ferguson. 1997. *Culture, Power, Place: Explorations in Critical Anthropology.* Durham, N.C.: Duke University Press.

Hall, Catherine. 2002. *Civilising Subjects: Metropole and Colony in the English Imagination 1830–1867.* Cambridge, U.K.: Polity.

Halper, Stefan, and Jonathan Clarke. 2004. *America Alone: The Neo-conservatives and the Global Order.* Cambridge: Cambridge University Press.

Hanson, Victor Davis. 2002. *Carnage and Culture: Landmark Battles in the Rise of Western Power.* New York: Anchor Books.

———. 1989. *The Western Way of War: Infantry Battle in Classical Greece.* Oxford: Oxford University Press.

Held, David, Anthony McGrew, David Goldblatt, and Jonathan Perraton. 1999. *Global Transformations: Politics, Economics, Culture.* Cambridge, U.K.: Polity.

Hernon, Ian. 2002. *Britain's Forgotten Wars: Colonial Campaigns of the 19th Century.* Stroud, U.K.: Sutton.

Hirst, Paul, and Grahame Thompson. 1999. *Globalization in Question: The International Economy and the Possibilities of Governance.* 2d ed. Cambridge, U.K.: Polity.

Hitchens, Christopher. 2002. *The Trial of Henry Kissinger.* London: Verso.

Hobson, John M. 2004. *The Eastern Origins of Western Civilization.* Cambridge: Cambridge University Press.

Hochschild, Adam. 2002. *King Leopold's Ghost: A Story of Greed, Terror and Heroism in Colonial Africa.* London: Pan Books.

Hollis, Rosemary. 2004. "The US Role: Helpful or Harmful?" In *Unfinished Business: Iran, Iraq and the Aftermath of War,* ed. Lawrence Potter and Gary Sick. New York: Palgrave.

Holsti, Kalevi J. 1996. *The State, War and the State of War.* Cambridge: Cambridge University Press.

Hoogvelt, Ankie. 2001. *Globalization and the Postcolonial World: The New Political Economy of Development.* 2d ed. Basingstoke, U.K.: Palgrave.

Hopkins, A. G., ed. 2002. *Globalization in World History.* London: Pimlico.

Howard, Michael. 1983. *Clausewitz.* Oxford: Oxford University Press.

———. 1978. *War and the Liberal Conscience.* Oxford: Oxford University Press.

———. 1976. *War in European History.* Oxford: Oxford University Press.

———. 1962. *The Franco-Prussian War: The German Invasion of France, 1870–1871.* London: Rupert Hart-Davis.

Hunt, Michael H. 1987. *Ideology and U.S. Foreign Policy.* New Haven, Conn.: Yale University Press.

Huntington, Samuel P. 1996. *The Clash of Civilizations and the Remaking of World Order.* New York: Touchstone.

———. 1993. "The Clash of Civilizations?" *Foreign Affairs* 72, no. 3 (Summer): 22–49.

Hynes, Samuel. 1998. *The Soldiers' Tale: Bearing Witness to Modern War.* London: Pimlico.

Jackson, Robert H. 1990. *Quasi-states: Sovereignty, International Relations and the Third World.* Cambridge: Cambridge University Press.

James, C. L. R. 1994 [1938]. *The Black Jacobins: Toussaint L'Ouverture and the San Domingo Revolution.* London: Alison and Busby.

Jeffords, Susan. 1994. *Hard Bodies*. New Brunswick, N.J.: Rutgers University Press.

———. 1989. *The Remasculinization of America*. Bloomington: Indiana University Press.

Joas, Hans. 2003. *War and Modernity*. Cambridge, U.K.: Polity.

Johnson, Chalmers. 2000. *Blowback: The Costs and Consequences of American Empire*. New York: Henry Holt.

Kagan, Robert. 2003. *Paradise and Power: America and Europe in the New World Order*. London: Atlantic Books.

Kahin, Audrey R., and George McT. Kahin. 1995. *Subversion as Foreign Policy: The Secret Eisenhower and Dulles Debacle in Indonesia*. New York: New Press.

Kaldor, Mary. 1999. *New and Old Wars: Organized Violence in a Global Era*. Cambridge, U.K.: Polity.

Kaplan, Lawrence F., and William Kristol. 2003. *The War over Iraq: Saddam's Tyranny and America's Mission*. San Francisco: Encounter Books.

Kaplan, Robert. 2000. *The Coming Anarchy*. New York: Random House.

Kant, Immanuel. 1992. *Kant's Political Writings*. Cambridge: Cambridge University Press.

Karnow, Stanley. 1984. *Vietnam*. London: Penguin.

Karp, Walter. 2003 [1979]. *The Politics of War: The Story of Two Wars Which Altered Forever the Political Life of the American Republic (1890–1920)*. New York: Franklin Square.

Kaul, Lt. Gen. B. M. 1967. *The Untold Story*. Bombay: Allied.

Keohane, Robert O., ed. 1986. *Neorealism and Its Critics*. New York: Columbia University Press.

Kiernan, V. G. 1998 [1982]. *Colonial Empires and Armies 1815–1960*. Stroud, U.K.: Sutton.

Klare, Michael. 1995. *Rogue States and Nuclear Outlaws: America's Search for a New Foreign Policy*. New York: Hill and Wang.

Klein, Naomi. 2000. *No Logo: Taking Aim at the Brand Bullies*. London: Flamingo.

Kolko, Gabriel. 2002. *Another Century of War?* New York: New Press.

———. 1988. *Confronting the Third World: United States Foreign Policy, 1945–1980*. New York: Pantheon Books.

———. 1985. *Anatomy of a War: Vietnam, the United States, and the Modern Historical Experience*. New York: Pantheon Books.

Lawrence, Sir Henry. 1859. *Essays on the Indian Army and Oude*. Serampore: Friend of India.

Lewis, Bernard. 1990. "The Roots of Muslim Rage: Why So Many Muslims Deeply Resent the West and Why Their Bitterness Will Not Be Easily Mollified." *Atlantic Monthly* 226, no. 3 (September 1990): 47–60.

Lewis, Martin W. and Kären E. Wigen. 1997. *The Myth of Continents: A Critique of Metageography*. Berkeley: University of California Press.

Lewy, Guenther. 1978. *America in Vietnam*. Oxford: Oxford University Press.

Lincoln, Bruce. 1989. *Discourse and the Construction of Society: Comparative Studies of Myth, Ritual, and Classification*. Oxford: Oxford University Press.

Mack, Andrew. 1975. "Why Big Nations Lose Small Wars: The Politics of Asymmetric Conflict." *World Politics* 27, no. 2:175–200.

Mackenzie, John M. 1986. *Propaganda and Empire: The Manipulation of British Public Opinion 1880–1960*. Manchester, U.K.: Manchester University Press.

Mamdani, Mahmood. 2004. *Good Muslim, Bad Muslim: America, the Cold War, and the Roots of Terror*. New York: Pantheon Books.

Mandelbaum, Michael. 2002. *The Ideas That Conquered the World: Peace, Democracy, and Free Markets in the Twenty-first Century*. Oxford, U.K.: PublicAffairs.

Mann, Michael. 1993. *The Sources of Social Power: The Rise of Classes and Nation-States, 1760–1914*. Cambridge: Cambridge University Press.

———. 1986. *The Sources of Social Power: A History of Power from the Beginning to A.D. 1760*. Cambridge: Cambridge University Press.

Marcus, Harold. 2002. *A History of Ethiopia*. Berkeley: University of California Press.

Marx, Karl, and Friedrich Engels. 1967 [1888]. *The Communist Manifesto*. London: Penguin Books.

Mason, Philip. 1974. *A Matter of Honour: An Account of the Indian Army, Its Officers and Men*. London: Jonathan Cape.

Masselos, Jim. 1991. *Indian Nationalism: An History*. New Delhi: Sterling.

Masters, Jack. 1961. *The Road Past Mandalay*. London: Michael Joseph.

McClintock, Michael. 1992. *Instruments of Statecraft: U.S. Guerrilla Warfare, Counter-insurgency, and Counter-terrorism, 1940–1990*. New York: Pantheon Books.

McNeill, William H. 1982. *The Pursuit of Power: Technology, Armed Force and Society since A.D. 1000*. Chicago: University of Chicago Press.

Merewether, Lt. Col. W. B., and Lt. Col. Sir Frederick Smith. 1918. *The Indian Corps in France*. London: John Murray.

Metcalf, Thomas R. 1995. *Ideologies of the Raj*. Cambridge: Cambridge University Press.

Mintz, Sidney W. 1985. *Sweetness and Power: The Place of Sugar in Modern History*. London: Penguin.

Mittelman, James H., ed. 1996. *Globalization: Critical Reflections*. Boulder, Colo.: Lynne Rienner.

Mockler, Anthony. 2003 [1984]. *Haile Selassie's War*. Oxford: Signal Books.

Moon, Penderel, ed. 1973. *Wavell: The Viceroy's Journal*. London: Oxford University Press.

Morris, Dick. 1997. *Behind the Oval Office*. New York: Random House.

Morris, Donald R. 1965. *The Washing of the Spears: The Rise and Fall of the Zulu Nation*. New York: Simon and Schuster.

Mosse, George L. 1990. *Fallen Soldiers: Reshaping the Memory of the World Wars*. Oxford: Oxford University Press.

Narayan, B. K. 1978. *General J. N. Chaudhuri: An Autobiography*. New Delhi: Vikas.

National Commission on Terrorist Attacks upon the United States. *The 9/11 Commission Report*. New York: W. W. Norton.

Netanyahu, Benjamin. 1995. *Fighting Terrorism: How Democracies Can Defeat Domestic and International Terrorists*. New York: Farrar, Straus, Giroux.

Neuman, Stephanie G. 1986. *Military Assistance in Recent Wars*. New York: Praeger.

Ohmae, Kenichi. 1995. *The End of the Nation State: The Rise of Regional Economies*. London: HarperCollins.

———. 1994. *The Borderless World: Power and Strategy in the Global Marketplace*. London: HarperCollins.

Omissi, David. 1999. *Indian Voices of the Great War: Soldiers' Letters, 1914–18*. London: Macmillan.

———. 1994. *The Sepoy and the Raj: The Indian Army 1860–1940*. London: Macmillan.

Ó Tuathail, Gearóid. 1996. *Critical Geopolitics*. Minneapolis: University of Minnesota Press.

Panitch, Leo. 1996. "Rethinking the Role of the State." In *Globalization: Critical Reflections*, ed. James H. Mittelman. 1996, 83–113. Boulder, Colo.: Lynne Rienner.

Parker, Geoffrey. 1988. *The Military Revolution: Military Innovation and the Rise of the West, 1500–1800*. Cambridge: Cambridge University Press.

Perle, Richard. 2000. "Iraq: Saddam Unbound." In *Present Dangers: Crisis and Opportunity in American Foreign and Defense Policy*, ed. Robert Kagan and William Kristol. San Francisco: Encounter Books.

Perry, F. W. 1988. *The Commonwealth Armies: Manpower and Organisation in Two World Wars*. Manchester, U.K.: Manchester University Press.

Polanyi, Karl. 1944. *The Great Transformation: The Political and Economic Origins of our Time*. Boston: Beacon.

Porch, Douglas. 2000. *Wars of Empire*. London: Cassell.

Powell, Colin. 1995. *My American Journey*. New York: Random House.

Prados, John. 1996. *President's Secret Wars: CIA and Pentagon Covert Operations from World War II through the Persian Gulf*. Chicago: Elephant.

Race, Jeffrey. 1972. *War Comes to Long An: Revolutionary Conflict in a Vietnamese Province*. Berkeley: University of California Press.

Ralston, David B. 1990. *Importing the European Army: The Introduction of Euro-*

pean Military Techniques into the Extra-European World, 1600–1914. Chicago: University of Chicago Press.

Ready, J. Lee. 1985. *Forgotten Allies.* 2 vols. [London:] McFarland.

Reich, Bernard. 1984. *The United States and Israel: Influence in the Special Relationship.* New York: Praeger.

Reno, William. 1998. *Warlord Politics and African States.* Boulder, Colo.: Lynne Rienner.

Roberts, Michael. 1956. *The Military Revolution 1560–1660.* Belfast: Belfast University Press.

Robertson, Roland. 1992. *Globalization: Social Theory and Global Culture.* London: Sage.

Robin, Ron. 2001. *The Making of the Cold War Enemy: Culture and Politics in the Military-Intellectual Complex.* Princeton, N.J.: Princeton University Press.

Robinson, Piers. 2002. *The CNN Effect: The Myth of News, Foreign Policy and Intervention.* London: Routledge.

Robinson, William I. 1996. *Promoting Polyarchy: Globalization, US Intervention, and Hegemony.* Cambridge: Cambridge University Press.

Rogers, C. J., ed. 1995. *The Military Revolution Debate: Readings on the Military Transformation of Early Modern Europe.* Boulder, Colo.: Westview.

Roy, Olivier. 2004. *Globalised Islam: The Search for a New Ummah.* London: Hurst.

Russett, Bruce. 1993. *Grasping the Democratic Peace: Principles for a Post–Cold War World.* Princeton, N.J.: Princeton University Press.

Said, Edward W. 1979. *Orientalism.* New York: Vintage Books.

Schmitt, Carl. 1996 [1932]. *The Concept of the Political.* Chicago: University of Chicago Press.

Sharma, Lt. Col. Gautam. 1996. *Nationalisation of the Indian Army (1885–1947).* New Delhi: Allied.

Shaw, Martin. 2000. *Theory of the Global State: Globality as an Unfinished Revolution.* Cambridge: Cambridge University Press.

———. 1988. *Dialectics of War: An Essay in the Social Theory of Total War and Peace.* London: Pluto.

Singer, Peter W. 2003. *Corporate Warriors: The Rise of the Privatized Military Industry.* Ithaca, N.Y.: Cornell University Press.

Small, Melvin, and J. David Singer. 1982. *Resort to Arms: International and Civil Wars, 1816–1980.* Beverly Hills, Calif.: Sage.

Smith, Adam. 1993 [1776]. *Wealth of Nations.* Oxford: Oxford University Press.

Steger, Manfred B. 2005. *Globalism: Market Ideology Meets Terrorism.* Lanham, Md.: Rowman & Littlefield.

———. 2002. *Globalism: The New Market Ideology.* Lanham, Md.: Rowman & Littlefield.

REFERENCES

Stein, George H. 1966. *The Waffen SS: Hitler's Elite Guard at War 1939–1945.* Ithaca, N.Y.: Cornell University Press.

Strange, Susan. 1996. *The Retreat of the State: The Diffusion of Power in the Contemporary World Economy.* Cambridge: Cambridge University Press.

Taylor, Sandra C. 1999. *Vietnamese Women at War: Fighting for Ho Chi Minh and the Revolution.* Lawrence: University Press of Kansas.

Thomson, Janice E. 1994. *Mercenaries, Pirates and Sovereigns: State-Building and Extraterritorial Violence in Early Modern Europe.* Princeton, N.J.: Princeton University Press.

Tilly, Charles. 1992. *Coercion, Capital, and European States, AD 990–1992.* Cambridge, U.K.: Blackwell.

Tomlinson, John. 1999. *Globalization and Culture.* Chicago: University of Chicago Press.

Trench, Charles. 1988. *The Indian Army and the King's Enemies 1900–1947.* London: Thames & Hudson.

Turner, Bryan S. 1994. *Orientalism, Postmodernism and Globalism.* London: Routledge.

Voigt, Johannes H. 1987. *India in the Second World War.* New Delhi: Arnold-Heinemann.

Walker, R. B. J. 1993. *Inside/Outside: International Relations as Political Theory.* Cambridge: Cambridge University Press.

Waltz, Kenneth H. 1979. *Theory of International Politics.* New York: McGraw-Hill.

Weart, Spencer R. 1998. *Never at War: Why Democracies Will Not Fight One Another.* New Haven, Conn.: Yale University Press.

Weber, Max. 1978. *Economy and Society: An Outline of Interpretive Sociology.* 2 vols. Berkeley: University of California Press.

Weldes, Jutta. 1999. *Constructing National Interests: The United States and the Cuban Missile Crisis.* Minneapolis: University of Minnesota Press.

Winter, Jay. 1995. *Sites of Memory, Sites of Mourning: The Great War in European Cultural History.* Cambridge: Cambridge University Press.

Wolf, Charles, and Katherine Watkins Webb, eds. 1987. *Developing Cooperative Forces in the Third World.* Lexington, Ky.: Lexington Books.

Wolf, Eric R. 1997. *Europe and the People without History.* Berkeley: University of California Press.

Woodward, Bob. 2004. *Plan of Attack.* New York: Simon and Schuster.

Woodward, Susan. 1995. *Balkan Tragedy: Chaos and Dissolution after the Cold War.* Washington, D.C.: Brookings Institution.

Young, Marilyn B. 2003. "In the Combat Zone." *Radical History Review,* no. 85:253–64.

INDEX

absolute war. *See* total war
agriculture, subsidization of, 7
Air America, 55
Alexander the Great, x
Allawi, Iyad, 120
American Israel Public Affairs Committee (AIPAC), 161, 162
Amritsar, massacre at, 67
Arafat, Yasser, 158
Arbenz, Jacobo, 54–55
Ardant du Picq, Charles-Jean-Jacques-Joseph, 39
Aron, Raymond, 54
auto insurance, 10–11

balance of power, military, 100, 131
Bali, 163
Ball, George, 159
Basayev, Shamil, 149–50
Basque Fatherland and Liberty (ETA), 130
Behind Enemy Lines (film), 118
Berg, Nicholas, 162
bin Laden, Osama, 130–31, 135–36, 138–43, 147, 151
Black, Jeremy, 51
The Black Jacobins (James), 16
Boer War, 100–101
Bonaparte, Napoleon, x, 17, 35–37

The Borderless World (Ohmae), 5
borders, strengthening of, 6–7
Bose, Subhas Chandra, 88–89
Bosnia, 111, 118
Boykin, William, 144, 164
brand-name manufacturing, 12–13
Bremer, L. Paul, 120
Britain: Enclosure Acts, 8; foreign soldiers used by, 44–46, 48–49 (*see also* Indian army); and India, 61–90; Indian army controlled by, 68–76; Indian army's significance for, 61–62, 65–66, 74–75; and Indian independence, 64–68; and Iraq war, 164; and Japanese in World War II, 123–24; and Middle East, 139; naval buildup by, 100; war and free trade, 20–24; Zulu battles of, 116–17. *See also* United Kingdom
British East India Company, 21–22, 44
British Indian army. *See* Indian army
Brodie, Bernard, 112
Brysk, Alison, 99
Burma, 123–24
Bush, George W.: on free trade and peace, 20; and Iraq war, 105–6, 120, 128, 156–57; on Islam, 165; and Israel, 158–59, 161–63, 179n50; neoconservatism and, 115, 156–57; on al-Qaeda, 138; on September 11, 2001 attacks,

144; tariffs imposed by, 6; on terrorism, 134, 144–45, 148, 152, 154, 160, 162

Cain, P. J., 22
Callwell, C. E., 70
Campbell, David, 96
Carr, E. H., 52–53, 106
caste system, ix–x
casualties of war: civilian, 145–51; Civil War, 39; Indian army, 81–82; in Vietnam War, 114; World War I, 40
Central Intelligence Agency (CIA): and Afghanistan conflict, 142; covert operations of, 48, 54–55, 136, 164; and Iran, 136; and Israel, 164
Chechnya, 147–50
Cheney, Dick, 150, 157, 162–63
China: anti-Japanese war of, 130; mercenary forces in, 45; opposition to Westerners in, 23; U.S. history affected by, 24; war and free trade, 20–24
Chomsky, Noam, 105
Christianity, 164–65
Churchill, Winston, ix, 86
Cimino, Michael, 116
Civil Air Transport, 54
civilian casualties of war, 145–51
Civil War, 39
civilizations: clash of, 137–45; persistence of, 133, 137, 142; terrorism versus, 145–51, 162–63. See also culture
Clarke, Jonathan, 156
Clarke, Richard, 156–57
clash of civilizations theory, 137–45
Clausewitz, Carl von, 29, 34–38, 128
Clinton, Bill, 111, 160
Cobden, Richard, 19, 24
Cold War: designation of enemy during, 152; indigenous forces used by U.S. in, 47–48; national identity construction during, 96, 112, 152; U.S. imperialism during, 54–56; U.S.–USSR conflicts during, 62
Comaroff, John, 143
The Coming Anarchy (Kaplan), 104

communications: globalization concept and, 11–18; nineteenth-century global, 14; al-Qaeda and, 141; resistance to globalization aided by, 13
Congress Party (India), 64, 74, 88
container cargo, 6, 7
Corn Laws (1843), 19
Correlates of War (CoW) project, 53–55
Cosmatos, George P., 118
Courage under Fire (film), 118
Crimean War (1854), 44
Crispi, Francesco, 108
Cronkite, Walter, 110
culture, 91–126; globalization and, 97–99; global North-South distinction, 101–7; interconnection through, 92, 94–95; Orientalism and war, 107–22; relativization of, 79–80, 98, 100; role of, 91–92; territory and, 94–95. See also civilizations
Curzon, Lord George Nathaniel, 59, 74, 76

The Deer Hunter (film), 116
de Gaulle, Charles, 49
DeLay, Tom, 162
democracy: free trade and, 19–20; globalization practices counter to, 4, 11; promotion of, as justification for war, 155–58. See also democratic peace theory
democratic peace theory, 52–57
divide-and-rule principle, 72–73, 135
Doty, Roxanne, 102
Dyer, Reginald, 67, 72
Dyncorp, 136

economics: artificiality of free markets, 7–9; brand-name manufacturing, 12–13; end-of-state argument and, 5–7; globalization concept and, 1–4; and global North-South distinction, 103–5; influences on, 7–8; international framework for, 9; of Iraq war, 105–6; neoliberalism and, 2–4; war and development of modern, 32–33; war and free trade, 18–25

Eisenhower, Dwight D., 47–48, 160
Enclosure Acts, 8
Endfield, Cy, 117
The End of the Nation State (Ohmae), 5
Ethiopia, 107–9
ethnicity, 98–99
Europe: United States versus, 165–66; war and free trade, 20–21
European Union, economic framework of, 9
Ever-Triumphant Army, 46
Ever-Victorious, 46
Executive Outcomes, 45
export processing zones (EPZs), 12
extra-territorial legislation, 7

failed states, 104
Falklands War, 53
Fanon, Frantz, 43
Ferguson, James, 94–96
Fighting Terrorism (Netanyahu), 153
Foot Locker, 13
Ford, Gerald, 159
Foreign Rifle Corps, 45–46
France, foreign soldiers used by, 45, 49
Frankenheimer, John, 112
free trade: artificiality of, 7–9; disruptive effects of, 23–24; peace and, 19–20, 23–24; protectionism and, 3, 6–7; war and, 18–25. *See also* economics; neoliberalism
French Revolution, 16, 36
From Tribal Village to Global Village (Brysk), 99
Fukuyama, Francis, xi, 19–20
Fulbright, J. William, 158–59
Fuqua, Antoine, 119
"Fuzzy-Wuzzy" (Kipling), 103

Gandhi, Mohandas K., 64, 67, 88
Germany, 49, 161
Gettysburg, Battle of (1863), 39
Giap, Vo Nguyen, 109–10
Gibson, Mel, 116
Gilroy, Paul, 144
globality, 98–99, 125

globalization: concept of, 1–4, 11–18; criticisms of, xi–xii; end-of-state argument and, 5–11; "global" character of, 18, 93–94, 97–99, 125; historical instances of, 14–17; inevitability of, 10, 20; interconnecting character of, 12, 17–18, 50–51; and North-South distinction, 101–7; paradoxes of, 3–4; resistance to, 11, 13; soldiers and, ix–x; war in relation to, ix–xiii, 92–93, 125–26, 171–72
global North versus South, 101–22; colonial war, 102–3; economics, 103–5; Iraq war, 105–6, 120–22; military Orientalism, 107–22
Goody, Jack, 140
Gordon, Charles "Chinese," 46
Government of India Act (1935), 67
Gray, John, 4, 141, 164, 165–66
The Green Berets (film), 117, 118–19
Gupta, Akhil, 94–96

Haiti, 16–17
Halper, Stefan, 156
Hamburger Hill (film), 113
Hanson, Victor Davis, 146
Helms-Burton Act, 7
Hitler, Adolf, 42, 128
Hollywood films, 112, 116–19
Hopkins, A. G., 22
House Un-American Activities Committee, 96
humanitarian intervention, 105–6, 127
Huntington, Samuel, 132, 137–39, 142
Hussein, Saddam, 156, 158
hyperglobalizers, 6

The Ideas That Conquered the World (Mandelbaum), 20
identity construction: Cold War and, 96, 112; Islamic, 142–44; states and, 96–97, 100–101, 108; United States and, 101, 109–22, 143–44, 152, 159, 163–65; war and, 96–97, 100–101, 142–43. *See also* nationalism
ideology: post–World War I, 41–42; ter-

rorism and, 130–32; total war and, 41–42, 128–29; of War on Terror, 154–55

imperialism: global North-South distinction and, 102–3; military and, 69–72, 83, 85–89; war and, 46–47, 54–56, 102–3, 107–8, 116–17

India: exposure to Western ideas, ix–x, 76–80; independence of, 64–68, 85, 88–89; significance for Britain of, 65; soldiers' comparisons of Europe to, 78–80. *See also* Indian army

Indian army, ix–x, 61–90; Bengal army, 70–71; British control of, 45–46, 68–76; cultural experience through war, 76–80; Indian officers in, 85–89; morale of, 84; significance for Britain of, 61–62, 65–66, 74–75; social divisions in, 71–73, 80–83; World War I, 64–66; World War II, 64

Indian National Army, 89

industrial society, war and, 28, 37

The Influence of Sea Power upon History (Mahan), 100

interchangeability in weapons, 37

interconnection: culture as medium of, 92, 94–95; globalization and, 12, 17–18; of states, 94–95; war and, xii–xiii, 50–51, 92–93, 123, 172; of West and Islam, 140

International Crisis Group, 136

International Monetary Fund (IMF), xi, 2, 4, 63

Invaders from Mars (film), 112

Invasion of the Body Snatchers (film), 112

Iran, 136

Iran and Libya Sanctions Act, 7

Iraq war (1990–1991), 111

Iraq war (2003), 20, 105–6, 115, 120–22, 156–57, 164–65

Irish Republican Army (IRA), 130, 145

Irvin, John, 113

Islam: and conflict, 137–38; fundamentalism, 140–42; and global resistance, 136–37; identity construction and, 142–44; war connecting United States and, xiii; West versus, 130–33, 137–45, 154–55, 165; as world religion, 133

Israel: terrorism as defined by, 150–56; United States and, 157–66

Italy, 107–9

Jackson, Robert, 104

James, C. L. R., 16

Japan, 123–24

Jardine, William, 22

Jeffords, Susan, 111

Jemaah Islamiya, 163

Joas, Hans, 104

Johnson, Lyndon, 83, 110–11

Jünger, Ernst, 76–78, 80

justifications of war: American idealistic, 113, 115, 120, 157; humanitarian intervention, 105–6, 127; "just war" tradition, 146; liberal, 19–20, 103, 127–28; preservation of civilization, 145–51; promotion of democracy, 155–58

"just war" tradition, 146

Kagan, Robert, 161

Kalahari bushmen, 95

Kant, Immanuel, 19

Kaplan, Lawrence F., 157

Kaplan, Robert, 104

Karzai, Hamid, 135–36

Keegan, John, 134

Kellog, Ray, 117

Khrushchev, Nikita, 112

Kipling, Rudyard, 102–3

Kissinger, Henry, 125

Klein, Naomi, 12–13

Klinghoffer, Leon, 162

Kotcheff, Ted, 118

Kristol, William, 157

Kuwait, 111

laissez-faire, 2

Leopold II (king of Belgium), 14, 46

Lewis, Bernard, 133

Lewis, Martin, 161

Lincoln, Bruce, 143
Lindh, John Walker, 144
Linlithgow, Lord Victor Alexander John, 67
Lynch, Jessica, 117

Mahan, A. T., 100
Mali, 7
The Manchurian Candidate (film), 112
Mandelbaum, Michael, 20
Mann, Michael, 60
Mao Zedong, 24
Marcos, Ferdinand, 136
Marcus, Harold, 108
Martel, Charles, 154
Marx, Karl, 28
Marxism-Leninism, 141
Mason, Philip, 62, 81
mass production, 37
McNamara, Robert, 112
McNeill, William, 33
Menelik (emperor of Ethiopia), 108
Menzies, William Cameron, 112
mercenaries, 44
Mercenaries, Pirates and Sovereigns (Thomson), 44
Middle East, Western influence in countries of, 135–36, 139. *See also* Israel; Palestinians
military: colonial, 69–72, 83, 85–89; comparative strength of state's, 100–101; Orientalism concerning, 107–22; recruitment for, 83; society in relation to, 80–90; training for, 33–34, 69–70. *See also* Indian army
Military Professional Resources, Inc., 45
Mindanao, Philippines, 133–37
Missing in Action (film), 118
modernity and modernization, 98, 99, 100, 103–4
Moore, John, 118
Moore, Michael, 105
Moro Islamic Liberation Front, 134
Moro National Liberation Front, 134
Muhammad, Omar Bakri, 147
Muslims. *See* Islam
Mussolini, Benito, 109

nationalism: in India, 65–67, 82–83; military buildup and, 100–101; total war and, 41–42
nation-state ontology of world politics, 34, 43–50, 52, 56, 94
nation-states. *See* states
NATO, 47
naval power, 100
neoconservatism, 115, 156–57, 165
neoliberalism: globalization concept and, 2–4; global problems stemming from, xi–xii; politics of, 3–4, 8–11; principles of, 2; war and free trade, 18–25
Netanyahu, Benjamin, 146, 153–58
New York World (newspaper), 97
Nike, 12–13
No Logo (Klein), 12
North, global. *See* global North versus South
North American Free Trade Agreement (NAFTA), 9, 10–11
nuclear weapons, 125

Ohmae, Kenichi, 5–7, 9, 29
On Perpetual Peace (Kant), 19
Ontario, Canada, 10–11
On War (Clausewitz), 35
opium, 21–23
Opium War (1839–1842), 22
Orientalism, 107–22; Iraq war and, 120–22; principles of, 107; Vietnam War and, 109–20
Orientalism (Said), 107
Ottoman Empire, 141

Palestinians, 145, 150–56, 158, 163
Palmerston, Prime Minister (Henry John Temple), 22
Panama Canal, 47
Panitch, Leo, 11
Paradise and Power (Kagan), 161
peace: democracy and, 52–57; free trade and, 19–20, 23–24
Pearl, Daniel, 162
Peres, Shimon, 160
Pettigrew, James J., 39

Philippines, 133–37, 163
Pickett, George E., 39
Pipes, Daniel, 165
pirates, 44
politics: centralization of state, 3–4; free trade and, 23; nationalism and, 42; neoliberalism and, 3–4; of terrorism, 129–30, 148, 150; war and, 35, 127–29, 131
Pol Pot, 141
poverty in global South, 103–5
Powell, Colin, 111
private military companies, 44–45
Project for a New American Century, 157
property, 8
protected markets, 3, 6–7
Punjab, India, 68
Putin, Vladimir, 148–50

al-Qaeda, 45, 135–37, 140–42, 144, 145, 156–59, 163
Qutb, Muhammad, 140
Qutb, Sayyid, 140–41

racism, Indian army and, 85–88
Rambo films, 101, 117
Rambo First Blood Part II (film), 118
Reagan, Ronald, 111, 160
realism, political, 128–29
Red Brigades, 130
Red Scare, 96
regime change, 54–56
Reid, Richard, 139, 144
relativization of culture, 79–80, 98, 100
Robertson, Roland, 18, 79, 93–94, 97–99, 102
rogue states, 104, 155
Rorke's Drift (1879), 116–17
Rostow, Eugene, 159–60, 163
Rowlatt Act (1919), 66–67
Rumsfeld, Donald, 156
Russett, Bruce, 55
Russia, 147–50. *See also* USSR

Said, Edward, 107–8
Saving Private Lynch (television movie), 117

Saving Private Ryan (film), 117
Sawyer, Diane, 117
Schmitt, Carl, 127, 131
School of the Americas, 47
Scowcroft, Brent, 179n50
September 11, 2001 attacks, 144
Serbia, 111
Sharon, Ariel, 125, 150, 162, 179n50
Shaw, Martin, 28–29, 94, 97, 172
shock therapy, global economics and, 3
Siegel, Don, 112
slavery, 15–17
Smith, Adam, 19, 24
social science, war as absent topic from, 28–29, 171–72
society. *See* civilizations; culture; war and society approach
Somme offensive (1916), 40
South, global. *See* global North versus South
Soviet Union. *See* USSR
Spielberg, Steven, 117
states: centralization of power in, 3–4; end of, 5–11; failed, 104; identity construction of, 96–97, 100–101, 108 (*see also* nationalism); instruments of interstate relations, 35; interconnection of, 94–95; international framework for, 9–10, 99–100; neoliberalism and power of, 3–4, 8–11; rise of modern, 31–34; rogue, 104; sovereignty of, 43–44; Third World, 46–47, 103–4; war and organization of, 40–41; war in relation to, 29–34, 43–50, 56, 94–101; war on terror as reinvigorating, 131. *See also* nation-state ontology of world politics
Steger, Manfred, 2
Storm of Steel (Jünger), 76
sugar, 15–16

Taiping Rebellion (1850–1864), 23
Taliban, 141
tariffs, 3, 6–7
Tears of the Sun (film), 119
technology: globalization concept and, 11–18; weapons, 37–40, 51

telegraph, 14

territory, culture and, 94–95

terrorism: Chechen, 147–50; and civilian deaths, 145–51; civilization versus, 145–51, 162–63; definition of, 145; designated as sole enemy, 152–53; European versus American perspective on, 166; global character of, 135–37; Islam-West conflict and, 132–33; Israeli perspective on, 151–56; politics of, 129–30, 148, 150; sources of, refusal to acknowledge, 152–53; state resurgence as result of, 131; unitary character of, alleged, 150, 154, 158, 162–63; weak versus strong in, 129–30, 134, 151, 155–56

Tet offensive, 109–10

Thatcher, Margaret, 4

Third World: and global North-South distinction, 101–7; military forces in, 46–48, 50; resistance movements in, 135; states in, 46–47, 103–4; U.S. relations with, 62–63

Thomson, Janice, 44–49

Tomlinson, John, 15

total war, 36–42; ideology and, 41–42; India and, 65–66; limited versus, 36–37, 128; state organization for supply of, 40–41; weapons technology and, 37–40

Toussaint L'Ouverture, 16–17

trade protection, 3, 6–7

The Transformation of War (Van Creveld), 104

Treaty of Nanking, 22

The Twenty Years' Crisis (Carr), 52

Uncommon Valor (film), 118

United Kingdom: global economy and, 3–4; and Iraq war, 105. *See also* Britain

United Nations: and humanitarianism, 125; peacekeeping missions of, 105

United States: Chinese role in history of, 24; and Cold War, 47–48, 62, 96, 112; Europe versus, 165–66; foreign soldiers used by, 46, 48; global economy

and, 3; global politics and, 4, 7; Hollywood representation of war involving, 112, 116–19; idealistic concept of war in, 113, 115, 120, 157; identity construction of, 101, 109–22, 143–44, 152, 159, 163–65; imperialism of, 54–56; and Iraq war, 20, 105–6, 115, 120–22, 156–57, 164–65; Israel and, 151, 157–66; and Middle East, 139; NATO and, 47; Philippines and, 133–37; and private military companies, 45; al-Qaeda and, 141–42; Vietnam War's significance for, 101, 109–20; war connecting Muslim world and, xiii

Unrepresented Nations and Peoples Organization, 99

U.S. Institute of Peace, 165

U.S.-Israel Counter-Terrorism Cooperation Accord, 160

USSR, 62, 161

Van Creveld, Martin, 104

Verdun, Battle of (1916), 40

Vietnam War: and American self-perception, 113–20; military Orientalism and, 109–13; opposition to, 83–84; U.S. and foreign soldiers in, 47, 48; and Vietnam syndrome, 111–20

Voltaire, 29

Wallace, Randall, 116

war: autonomous character of, 35–37; Clausewitz on, 34–38; democratic peace theory and, 52–57; Eurocentric bias of studies of, 29, 42–43, 49; foreign soldiers used in, 44–50; free trade and, 18–25; globalization in relation to, ix–xiii, 92–93, 125–26, 171–72; and global North-South distinction, 102–7; Hollywood representation of, 112, 116–19; humanity achieved in, 122–26; identity construction through, 96–97, 100–101, 142–43; imperialism and, 46–47, 54–56, 102–3, 107–8, 116–17; interconnecting character of, xii–xiii, 50–51, 92–93, 123, 172; liberal conception of, 19–20, 103, 127–28; limited versus total, 36–37, 128; manufacture of supplies for, 40–41; in national-international world, 94–101; national populace entering into, 36–38; Orientalism concerning, 107–22; political character of, 35, 127–29, 131; preservation of civilization as justification for, 145–51; and rise of modern state, 31–34; states in relation to, 29–34, 43–50, 56, 94–101; styles of, 134; total, 36–42, 128; weapons technology and, 37–40, 51. *See also* justifications of war; war and society approach

war and society approach: globalization of, 60–63; Indian army, 61–90; overview of, 28–30; rise of modern state, 31–34; West-Islam conflict and, 143–44

War on Terror, 150, 154–55. *See also* terrorism

Ward, Frederick Townsend, 46

Wayne, John, 117, 118–19

weapons, and nature of war, 37–40

weapons of mass destruction (WMD), 155

Weber, Max, 28, 43

Weinberger, Casper, 111

West: Chinese opposition to, 23; fundamentalist criticism of, 140–41; ideological representation of, 160–61, 165; Indian exposure to, ix–x, 76–80; Islam versus, 130–33, 137–45, 154–55, 165; Middle Eastern politics influenced by, 135–36, 139; al-Qaeda influenced by, 141

Westmoreland, William, 109

We Were Soldiers (film), 116

"The White Man's Burden" (Kipling), 102–3

Wigen, Karen, 161

Willis, Bruce, 119

Wilson, Woodrow, 41, 96–97

Wolf, Eric, 50–51

Wolfowitz, Paul, 156, 161–62

World Bank, 2

World Trade Organization (WTO), 2, 7, 9

worldviews. *See* civilizations; ideology

World War I, 40–41, 49, 64–65, 76–78, 82

World War II, 42, 49, 82, 84, 88, 109, 123–25, 130, 160–61

Writing Security (Campbell), 96

Yeltsin, Boris, 149

Young, Marilyn, 116

Zakaria, Fareed, 138

Zito, Joseph, 118

Zulu (film), 117

ABOUT THE AUTHOR

Tarak Barkawi earned his Ph.D. in political science at the University of Minnesota and is lecturer in international security at the Centre of International Studies, University of Cambridge. He specializes in the study of war, armed forces, and society in North-South relations.